1999

CAMBRIDGE STUDIES IN
ANGLO-SAXON ENGLAND
27

REPRESENTATIONS OF THE NATURAL
WORLD IN OLD ENGLISH POETRY

CAMBRIDGE STUDIES IN
ANGLO-SAXON ENGLAND

FOUNDING GENERAL EDITORS
MICHAEL LAPIDGE AND SIMON KEYNES
CURRENT GENERAL EDITORS
SIMON KEYNES AND ANDY ORCHARD

Volumes published

REPRESENTATIONS OF THE NATURAL WORLD IN OLD ENGLISH POETRY

JENNIFER NEVILLE

Royal Holloway, University of London

CAMBRIDGE
UNIVERSITY PRESS

PUBLISHED BY THE PRESS SYNDICATE OF THE UNIVERSITY OF CAMBRIDGE
The Pitt Building, Trumpington Street, Cambridge CB2 1RP, United Kingdom

CAMBRIDGE UNIVERSITY PRESS
The Edinburgh Building, Cambridge CB2 2RU, UK   http://www.cup.cam.ac.uk
40 West 20th Street, New York, NY 10011–4211, USA   http://www.cup.org
10 Stamford Road, Oakleigh, Melbourne 3166, Australia

First published 1999

Printed in the United Kingdom at the University Press, Cambridge

Typeset in Garamond 11/13pt   CE

A catalogue record for this book is available from the British Library

Library of Congress cataloguing in publication data
Neville, Jennifer, 1968–
Representations of the natural world in Old English poetry / Jennifer Neville.
p.   cm. – (Cambridge studies in Anglo-Saxon England; 27)
Includes bibliographical references and index.
ISBN 0 521 64036 9 (hardback)
1. English poetry – Old English, ca. 450–1100 – History and criticism.
2. Nature in literature.
I. Title. II. Series.
PR217.N49   1999
829'.1– dc21   98-7922 CIP

ISBN 0 521 64036 9 hardback

To my parents

Contents

Acknowledgements

I am grateful to the Commonwealth Scholarship Commission and the Social Sciences and Humanities Research Council of Canada for their support throughout the writing of this book. I would also like to convey my thanks to Christ's College, Cambridge; their contributions allowed me to attend conferences and courses that have proven invaluable to my research. I owe a great debt to many people, but especially to Professor Michael Lapidge, for his guidance and attention to detail, to Dr Andy Orchard, for his supportive interest and advice, to Dr Sean Miller, for his unfailing generosity, to Dr Parshia Lee-Stecum, for his painstaking commentary, and to Dr Carlos Pittol, for his support on so many levels.

Abbreviations

AN&Q	*American Notes & Queries*
ASE	*Anglo-Saxon England*
ASPR	The Anglo-Saxon Poetic Records, ed. G. P. Krapp and E. V. K. Dobbie, 6 vols. (New York, 1931–42)
Bosworth–Toller	*An Anglo-Saxon Dictionary*, ed. J. Bosworth and T. N. Toller (Oxford, 1898)
CCSL	Corpus Christianorum, Series Latina (Turnhout)
CSASE	Cambridge Studies in Anglo-Saxon England
De doctrina Christiana	*Sancti Aurelii Augustini de doctrina Christiana libri quattor*, ed. W. M. Green, Corpus Scriptorum Ecclesiasticorum Latinorum 80 (Vienna, 1963)
DOE	*The Dictionary of Old English*, ed. A. C. Amos *et al.* (Toronto, 1988–)
EETS os	Early English Text Society, original series
EETS ss	Early English Text Society, supplementary series
ELN	*English Language Notes*
ES	*English Studies*
Historia ecclesiastica	*Bede's Ecclesiastical History of the English People*, ed. and trans. B. Colgrave and R. A. B. Mynors, (Oxford, 1969)
JAF	*Journal of American Folklore*
JEGP	*Journal of English and Germanic Philology*
JIES	*Journal of Indo-European Studies*
LSE	*Leeds Studies in English*
MÆ	*Medium Ævum*

MGH AA	Monumenta Germaniae Historica, Auctores Antiquissimi
MLN	*Modern Language Notes*
MLR	*Modern Language Review*
MP	*Modern Philology*
MS	*Mediæval Studies*
Neophil	*Neophilologus*
NLH	*New Literary History*
NM	*Neuphilologische Mitteilungen*
N&Q	*Notes & Queries*
OED	*The Oxford English Dictionary*, ed. J. A. Simpson and E. S. C. Weiner, 2nd edn, 20 vols. (Oxford, 1989)
PL	Patrologia cursus completus, Series Latina, ed. J.-P. Migne, 221 vols. (Paris, 1844–64)
PMLA	*Publications of the Modern Language Association of America*
PQ	*Philological Quarterly*
RES	*Review of English Studies*
SM	*Studi medievali*
SMC	Studies in Medieval Culture
SN	*Studia Neophilologica*
SP	*Studies in Philology*
TRHS	*Transactions of the Royal Historical Society*

1

Introduction: defining the natural world

> what we observe is not nature in itself but nature exposed to our method of questioning.[1]

> Monge sindon   geond middangeard
> unrimu cynn,   þe we æþelu ne magon
> ryhte areccan   ne rim witan;
> þæs wide sind   geond world innan
> fugla ond deora   foldhrerendra
> wornas widsceope,   swa wæter bibugeð
> þisne beorhtan bosm,   brim grymetende,
> sealtyþa geswing ...   (*The Panther* 1–8a)[2]

Representations of the natural world in Old English poetry, like the creatures described in *The Panther*, are difficult *ryhte areccan* 'to declare rightly', for their 'method of questioning' is foreign to modern minds. We can begin to appreciate the difference between our own conception of the natural world and that represented in Old English poetry by noting that the Anglo-Saxons did not have a word to indicate 'the natural world' in their native language. They did have words for 'nature' in the sense of 'essence' or 'character': *cynd* means 'native constitution, natural qualities,

---

[1] Heisenberg, *Physics and Philosophy*, p. 46.

[2] 'There are many, countless races through the earth; their nature we cannot rightly declare, nor know their number, because the multitudes of birds and land-treading beasts are widely distributed through the world, as [widely as] the water, the roaring sea, the surge of salt-waves, surrounds this bright womb.' Unless otherwise noted, all quotations in Old English are taken from ASPR, except for quotations from *Beowulf*, which are taken from *Beowulf and the Fight at Finnsburg*, ed. Klaeber. Translations are my own.

race, social rank'[3]; *cynde* means 'natural, innate, inborn'[4]; *gecynd* means 'native constitution, innate disposition, established order of things, natural condition, manner, species, offspring, natural right'; *cyn* means 'race, class, species'; *æðelo* means 'nature' in addition to 'nobility, nobility of birth, birthright, noble race'.[5] The Anglo-Saxons also had words for the world as a whole: *sceaft* means 'creation, origin, what is created, a creature'; *gesceaft* means 'the creation, a created being or thing, creature, element'.[6]

We, too, might describe these concepts using the word 'nature' but not 'the natural world'. For those living in the twentieth century, the natural world includes animals, plants, the weather, bodies of water and land-scape, not the abstract idea of innate characteristics or the religious idea of the world as a creation of God. For people today the natural world specifically excludes and is defined by the exclusion of: (1) supernatural elements, and (2) human elements. Old English writers, however, have left behind no word or phrase to describe what now appears to be a straightforward and basic entity.

This gap in the Old English vocabulary is not an accident caused by the loss of manuscripts. It reflects the absence of the concept itself. Of course, the Anglo-Saxons did depict, for example, birds and storms in their poetry. However, in these texts it is not possible to separate natural from supernatural phenomena: devilish sea-monsters (*niceras*), whales, wolves, demons (*þyrsas*), deer, blood-thirsty, man-shaped creatures (the Grendelkin), birds – all inhabit the same landscapes and interact with human beings in parallel ways.[7] As a result, on a basic level the Anglo-Saxons did not have a word or expression for the modern conception of the natural world because they did not conceive of an entity defined by

---

[3] See *DOE*, s.v. *cynd*.   [4] See Bosworth–Toller, s.v. *cynde*.

[5] See *DOE*, s.v. *gecynd*, *cyn* and *æðelo*. The focus on characteristic properties present from birth in these Old English words accurately translates the meaning of the Latin *natura* as explained by Isidore: 'Natura dicta ab eo quod nasci aliquid faciat. Gignendi enim et faciendi potens est' 'Nature is said to be that which causes something to be born. It is the power of giving birth and making' (*Etymologiae* XI.i.1, ed. Lindsay). For the meaning of 'nature' inherited from Aristotle (nature as a principle of movement and existence), see Weisheipl, *Nature and Motion*, pp. 5–7.

[6] See Bosworth–Toller, s.v. *gesceaft*. For further discussion of the words in this paragraph, cf. also *A Thesaurus of Old English*, ed. Roberts, Kay and Grundy.

[7] These creatures appear in *Beowulf*, *The Whale*, *Maxims II* and *Guthlac* and will be discussed further below.

the exclusion of the supernatural.[8] On the other hand, the modern definition of the natural world as all that is external to humanity can be applied to Old English poetry, for the Anglo-Saxons did represent many entities defined as strange, frightening and alien to humanity – things that modern critics would collectively call 'the Other'. One could collect these members of 'the Other' and be more than half correct if one wanted to label them 'the Anglo-Saxon natural world'.[9] The problem cannot be solved merely by seeking a different label or more inclusive definition for 'the natural world', however, for the Anglo-Saxons did not have a word to designate 'the Other', either. They did not conceive of this group of entities as a specific, identifiable whole, and their representation of them maintains many irreconcilable elements.[10] As a result, although the present investigation will refer to representations of 'the natural world', it will include entities which would no longer be considered compatible with natural phenomena, and it will not create a convenient, anachronistic category for them. Instead, it will group together representations that share basic similarities and analyse their functions in their respective texts.

ACTUAL PHYSICAL CONDITIONS

Before analysing the texts in which these representations take place, however, it may be useful to examine the physical conditions actually experienced by the Anglo-Saxons. England has a northern but temperate climate, with an average temperature of about $9°C$.[11] Its heavy precipitation is legendary but not dangerous; such precipitation is, in fact, not exceptional in comparison with other European countries.[12] Although modern inhabitants of the island are unlikely to express pleasure with the

---

[8] Gurevich, *Categories of Medieval Culture*, pp. 6, 9; K. L. Jolly, 'Father God and Mother Earth: Nature-Mysticism in the Anglo-Saxon World', in *The Medieval World of Nature: A Book of Essays*, ed. J. E. Salisbury (New York, 1993), pp. 221–52, at 224. Cf. also J. P. Tripp, Jr, *Literary Essays on Language and Meaning in the Poem Called Beowulf: Beowulfiana Literaria* (Lampeter, 1992), pp. 25–6.

[9] Chapters 2, 3 and 4 examine these types of representations of 'the natural world'.

[10] Chapters 5 and 6 examine representations which exemplify the contradictory and disunited character of 'the natural world'.

[11] Schuurmans and Flohn, 'Climate Variability', pp. 65–117, at 75.

[12] *Ibid.*, p. 104.

climate, neither are they likely to see themselves threatened by it. The Anglo-Saxons, however, were less proficient at fortifying themselves against weather conditions: although modern inhabitants consider cold and wetness unpleasantly inconvenient, the same conditions could justifiably, even inevitably, be considered pernicious if, instead of insulated walls, central heating and sealed doors and windows, there were only drafty, one-room dwellings heated by single fires for protection from the elements.[13] There is also some evidence that the weather endured by the Anglo-Saxons was more severe than that experienced now. While the rise of the Roman Empire was accompanied by an amelioration in climate, its fall coincided with a deterioration in climatic conditions. In the centuries following, the Anglo-Saxons lived through colder, stormier weather, rougher seas and more snow than that experienced previously, and worse weather than that experienced now.[14] The weather did not break until near the end of the Anglo-Saxon period – (the beginning of the 'Medieval Warm Epoch' (900–1400 AD).[15]

It is tempting to view the correspondences between cultural events and climatic change as more than coincidence, to say that clement weather facilitated the rise of the Roman Empire, inclement weather helped determine its fall, and continuing harsh conditions maintained the 'dark' character of the Dark Ages, but other factors must be considered. Otherwise, having attributed the stifling of the Anglo-Saxons to oppressive weather, one would be unable to explain why the later, harsher conditions of the 'Little Ice Age' (1400–1800 AD) did not stifle the Renaissance, Reformation and Romantic eras.[16] It is possible that climate

[13] Cameron, *Anglo-Saxon Medicine*, p. 5. For a summary of some of the archaeological evidence for living quarters, see R. Cramp, 'The Hall in *Beowulf* and in Archaeology', in *Heroic Poetry in the Anglo-Saxon Period*, ed. Damico and Leyerle, pp. 331–46.

[14] During this period winters are documented, often for the first time; there were record snowfalls and unprecedented ice on rivers, even on so southerly rivers as the Nile. See H. H. Lamb, *Climate, History and the Modern World* (London, 1982), p. 157.

[15] H. H. Lamb, 'Climate in the Last Thousand Years: Natural Climatic Fluctuations and Change', in *The Climate of Europe*, ed. Flohn and Fantechi, pp. 25–44, at 35–8.

[16] It has been argued that the climactic conditions during this period did, in fact, have 'severe economic and demographic impacts upon many societies in preindustrial Europe'. See C. Pfister, 'The Little Ice Age: Thermal Wetness Indices for Central Europe', in *Climate and History: Studies in Interdisciplinary History*, ed. R. I. Rotberg and T. K. Rabb (Princeton, NJ, 1981), p. 116.

is only historically significant in frontier areas and that its effects are marginal when discussing change in history.[17]

However significant the climate was in political terms, the challenge posed by the weather had far-reaching consequences for most individuals. Exposure to cold and damp made the Anglo-Saxons prone to diseases of the joints and intensified the virulence of the infectious diseases that plagued them.[18] Unprotected by modern medical treatments like antibiotics, the Anglo-Saxons had every reason to fear a world that attacked them daily with mysterious weapons, leaving them crippled or dead.[19] Now we know that, although their diet was adequate to ward off starvation, many Anglo-Saxons suffered from vitamin and mineral deficiencies, and their resistance to disease was consequently low.[20] We also know that diseases are spread by mosquitoes,[21] that water bears harmful parasites (liver flukes, for example)[22] and that a lack of hygiene is dangerous. Although the Anglo-Saxons assumed correctly that some of their ailments travelled invisibly through the air,[23] for the most part they did not understand the sources of illness and consequently could do little to defend themselves from it.[24] The medical texts that remain from this period testify that the Anglo-Saxons fought back against the threats from this invisible component of

---

[17] J. L. Anderson, 'History and Climate: Some Economic Models', in *Climate and History: Studies in Past Climates and their Impact on Man*, ed. T. M. L. Wigley, M. J. Ingram and G. Farmer (Cambridge, 1981), pp. 337–55, at 351.

[18] Cameron, *Anglo-Saxon Medicine*, p. 5.

[19] '[Barbarian man's] views of the nature of disease remain disjointed but, since he knows well that he can sustain injury at his own hands or those of others, he commonly conceives that his symptoms are due to injuries inflicted by beings like himself, and that his sufferings are produced by weapons or agents comparable to those that he himself employs.' Grattan and Singer, *Anglo-Saxon Magic and Medicine*, p. 3.

[20] Cameron, *Anglo-Saxon Medicine*, pp. 6–9.

[21] Malaria was probably endemic in Anglo-Saxon England; this, coupled with dietary iron deficiencies, struck the female population especially hard (*ibid.*, pp. 10 and 17–18).

[22] *Ibid.*, p. 10.

[23] See, for example, the charm, *For a Sudden Stitch*. For discussion of this charm, see below, pp. 120–1.

[24] The Anglo-Saxon doctor or leech has been described as being 'concerned only with the day-to-day treatment of symptoms and hardly ever with principles drawn from the simplest theory. It would indeed be too much to say that the leech was interested in "disease", because that is an abstraction which he had not reached' (Grattan and Singer, *Anglo-Saxon Magic and Medicine*, p. 92).

their environment with a wide variety of strategies, both rational and mystical,[25] but gravesites indicate that it was a losing battle: Anglo-Saxon life expectancy was short.[26]

In contrast, the visible agents of the natural world – animals – posed less of a threat; Britain does not support many dangerous animals.[27] Although scorpions do exist in Britain, along with many species of wasps and bees, there are no native invertebrates that could cause the Anglo-Saxons to fear for their lives, as, for example, the North American black widow spider might. Reptiles are not especially prevalent in Europe and even less so in Britain; snakes, generally the most feared of reptiles, exist in only three species, of which none is over two metres in length and only one, the adder, is poisonous (its bite, moreover, is not lethal).[28] Birds are, as in most places, innocuous. Most mammals, too, are harmless, the majority being small rodents. At present the largest carnivores are foxes, but the Anglo-Saxons also shared their environment with the more formidable bear and wolf.[29] Both of these deserve healthy, health-preserving respect, but are unlikely to have been responsible for large numbers of deaths. Along with the wild boar, which was still common[30] and perhaps more dangerous because of its aggressiveness, they were the only animals likely to make the Anglo-Saxons feel threatened.

Like the weather, however, animals could attack indirectly; otherwise harmless shrews, mice, rats, hares and moles devoured the crops that formed the staples of the human diet, small predators like foxes harassed poultry, and wolves took their toll on sheep. Even the vegetable world contributed its share of resistance, not only through plants that armed themselves, like thistles and nettles,[31] but also in the form of crop-

---

[25] Cameron, *Anglo-Saxon Medicine*, chapters 12 and 13, pp. 117–58.

[26] *Ibid.*, p. 5.

[27] See *Kingfisher Natural History*, ed. Chinery.

[28] *Ibid.*, pp. 272–4.

[29] And also presumably the wild cat. Domestic cats are present in Anglo-Saxon England from the eighth century, but there are no certain descriptions of wild cats in Old English, although there are references to their lairs in place names. See Jordan, *Die altenglischen Säugertiernamen*, pp. 34–5. Jordan also argues that lynx must have been present as well (*ibid.*, p. 37). For discussion of the demise of wild cats and other, now extinct predators, see A. Dent, *Lost Beasts of Britain* (London, 1974) and Freethy, *Man and Beast*, pp. 243–5 and 252–3.

[30] Freethy, *Man and Beast*, pp. 250–2.

[31] See Aldhelm's *Enigma XLVI: Urtica* (Nettle).

choking weeds. The task of cultivation in itself was a battle[32] in which the Anglo-Saxons struggled to extract what they needed from the land, without the bulwarks provided by later advances in knowledge and technology:

The most advanced systems of crop-rotation known to the age required that every year half or a third of the cultivated soil should lie fallow. Often indeed, fallow and crops followed each other in irregular alternation, which allowed more time for the growth of weeds than for that of the cultivated produce; the fields, in such cases, represented hardly more than a provisional and short-lived conquest of the waste land, and even in the heart of the agricultural regions nature tended constantly to regain the upper hand. Beyond them, enveloping them, thrusting into them, spread forests, scrub and dunes.[33]

Under such circumstances, a fearful defensiveness with respect to natural phenomena may appear inevitable: wind and precipitation battered against flimsy structures erected as defence, disease struck with its invisible weapons, the vegetable world opposed human beings in their need to eat, small animals leached away that which was wrestled from the land and wolves haunted the wilderness.

SELECTIVITY

This apparently inevitable fearfulness before the power of the natural world should not be accepted unquestioned. However much damage shrews, mice, rats, moles, hares and foxes did, they have no place in Old English poetry.[34]

---

[32] Exeter Book *Riddle 34* describes one weapon – the rake – used in this battle against nature.

[33] M. Bloch, *Feudal Society*, volume 1: *The Growth of Ties of Dependence*, trans. L. A. Manyon, 2nd ed. (London, 1962), p. 61.

[34] Most are mentioned only in glossaries; see Jordan, *Die altenglischen Säugertiernamen*, pp. 66–8, 75–8, 80–3 and 85–91. One might note also that Anglo-Latin poets describe animals not mentioned in Old English: in his *Enigmata* Aldhelm describes the silkworm, antlion, locust, midge, water strider, hornet, clam, crab, leech, elephant, minotaur and unicorn, and the later poet Eusebius adds the scorpion (*Aenigma LI: De Scorpione*). For further discussion of these texts, particularly Aldhelm's *Enigmata*, see below, pp. 192–5. Although one might explain the exclusion of many of these creatures on the basis of their not being native to Anglo-Saxon England, Old English poets were not averse to describing alien creatures – see, for example, the translation of Lactantius's *The Phoenix*.

Yet spiders,[35] bees,[36] boars,[37] stags,[38] dragons,[39] hawks, swans, whales,[40] birds,[41] wolves,[42] fish and bears[43] do. However unpleasant the climate and conditions, the natural environment was less hostile than the human environment.[44] Yet it is represented as a power more terrifying than human threats.[45] One might suppose that the representation of wild beasts and the wind reflects a misapprehension of the most significant

[35] There appears to be a spider in the charm, *Against a Dwarf*, but it only exists by textual emendation – the manuscript itself reads *spiden wiht*, not *spiderwiht* (9b). It has also been suggested that the spider is actually a dwarf; see Skemp, 'The Old English Charms', p. 294. There does appear to have been a connection between dwarves and spiders; see Grimm, *Teutonic Mythology*, pp. 471 and 1497 and Jamborn, 'Peri Didaxeon', pp. 149–53. For further discussion of this charm, see below, pp. 103–4 and 117.

[36] Bees appear briefly in Exeter Book *Riddle 27*, and possibly in Exeter Book *Riddle 57* (other solutions include swallows, starlings, hailstones, raindrops, swifts, jackdaws, musical notes and demons – see Muir, *The Exeter Anthology*, p. 623). Bees are also addressed in *The Bee Charm*. For explanation of some elements of the charm on the practical grounds of bee-keeping, see Spamer, 'The Old English Bee Charm'. See also E. P. Hamp, 'Notes on the Old English Bee Charm', *JIES* 9 (1981), 338–40. Bees also figure prominently in Aldhelm's prose *De virginitate* 14–19 and *Enigma XX: Apis*.

[37] The boar appears in *Maxims II* 19b–20a. The boars mentioned in *Beowulf* tend to be images on armour and treasure (303b, 1111–12a, 1286b, 1453a); they are once used in a metaphor for human fierceness (1328a).

[38] The stag appears in *Beowulf* 1368–72a and in Exeter Book *Riddles 88* and *93*.

[39] Dragons appear in *Beowulf* and *Maxims II* 26b–7a.

[40] The hawk, swan and whale all appear in *Beowulf*; for a discussion of their role in the poem, see Metcalf, 'Ten Natural Animals'. The hawk is also mentioned in *The Battle of Maldon* (7–8). The swan appears in Exeter Book *Riddle 7*. The whale is examined in detail in *The Whale*.

[41] References to birds other than swans and hawks (and the eagles and ravens that help to make up the 'Beasts of Battle') occur in *Guthlac* 733b–8 and 916–19a, *The Phoenix* (other than the phoenix itself, at 158b–67 and 335b–41a), *The Wanderer* 47 and 81, *The Seafarer* 19b–22 and 53–5a, *Maxims II* 38b–9a, and Aldhelm's *Enigmata XXII: Acalantida, XXVI: Gallus, XXXI: Ciconia, XXXV: Nycticorax, XLII: Strutio, XLVII: Hirundo, LVII: Aquila, LXIII: Corbus*, and *LXIV: Columba* (Goldfinch, Cock, Stork, Night owl, Ostrich, Swallow, Eagle, Raven and Dove).

[42] Excluding appearances as one of the 'Beasts of Battle', the wolf appears in *Maxims II* 18b–19a, *Fortunes of Men* 12b–13a, and *Maxims I* 146–51.

[43] Fish are described in *Maxims II* 27b–8a and 39b–40a, bears in *Maxims II* 29b–30a.

[44] For further discussion of the dangerously unsettled character of Anglo-Saxon society, see below, pp. 84–8.

[45] For further discussion of natural as opposed to human threats, see below, pp. 38–40.

source of danger on the part of a primitive society,[46] and cite as evidence the selective silences regarding rodents and other, apparently innocuous wildlife: the Anglo-Saxons could afford to ignore much of what they experienced daily and instead represented creatures that they experienced relatively infrequently, such as dragons. One might note also the complete lack of concern for local wildlife in the popular *Liber monstrorum*, which does not contain a single animal that the Anglo-Saxons could ever have met in England.[47] That is, while it may be true that the Anglo-Saxons drew upon more than fear and paranoia when representing natural phenomena in their poetry,[48] it is equally true that they drew upon less than their complete experience of the physical environment. The physical reality of 'the natural world' could play a very small role in determining what of it was represented and how it was represented.

Understanding representations of 'the natural world' in Old English poetry thus demands more than knowledge of the physical reality experienced by the Anglo-Saxons. It requires an examination of each act of representation in its context, for, while the selectivity of the list of animals represented in Old English poetry is obvious, the criteria under-lying its selection are not. For example, one need not query too closely the omission of small, insignificant creatures like moles; the heroic tone of most Old English poems renders their inclusion inappropriate. On the other hand, the deer, which undoubtedly figured largely in Anglo-Saxon heroic life as quarry for the noble pastime of hunting, as well as a common source of food for feasts,[49] appears only as the source of material

---

[46] For example, the animals that probably did the most harm to the Anglo-Saxons were not fierce, powerful beasts like wolves and boars but parasite-carrying sheep and mosquitoes (Cameron, *Anglo-Saxon Medicine*, pp. 10–11), neither of which, as far as can be discerned from the surviving texts, inspired any fear. We would not, of course, expect a people without the benefit of microscopes to consider a sheep or mosquito dangerous. Cf. the view that 'a reputation for heroism is not made by killing creatures that are believed to be harmless or beneficent – sheep for instance' (K. Sisam, *The Structure of Beowulf* (Oxford, 1965), p. 25).

[47] For further discussion of the *Liber monstrorum*, see below, pp. 31–3.

[48] They also drew upon earlier texts, for example. For further discussion of the Anglo-Saxons' use of inherited sources, see below, pp. 38–40.

[49] The large number of deer bones found in Anglo-Saxon sites indicates that venison was an important part of the Anglo-Saxon diet. See C. J. Arnold, *An Archaeology of the Early Anglo-Saxon Kingdoms* (London, 1988), p. 118. For discussion of the importance of feasting in Old English poetry, see Magennis, *Images of Community*, pp. 60–75.

for inkpots (Exeter Book *Riddles* 88 and 93) and as part of an anecdote designed to emphasise traits of a landscape – Grendel's mere (*Beowulf* 1368–72). In fact not many animals, whether literary or native, appear regularly in poetry; being noticeable, useful, or even dangerous, does not guarantee a place in an Old English poem. The main exceptions, the 'Beasts of Battle',[50] are a literary technique particular to Old English poetry, used to introduce a climax in human relations, a battle. This rhetorical technique offers a useful starting point, for I shall argue that the representation of 'the natural world' in Old English poetry generally is a literary technique characteristic of Old English poetry, though not always so easily identified and defined as the 'Beasts of Battle'.

REPRESENTATION AND VALUE STRUCTURES

A representation is an act of assimilation and interpretation: to represent an object is to place it within a structure that assigns value and meaning to it. Representation thus necessarily involves politics – in the sense of principles, aims and policies – even if the agenda is merely to create a recognisable depiction of the natural world. For example, in early modern England writers represent animals so as to emphasise their sharp differentiation from the human race, and thus for such writers 'the natural world' comprises traits inferior to those of human nature.[51] The depiction of such traits does not merely provide facts about creatures; it reveals how the human race views itself, what it prizes and despises, through its assimilation of otherwise neutral data to value-laden patterns. To insult

[50] The 'Beasts of Battle' type-scene has been summarised as follows: 'in the wake of an army, the dark raven, the dewy plumaged eagle and the wolf of the forest, eager for slaughter and carrion/food, give voice to their joy'. See Griffith, 'Convention and Originality', p. 184. For examples, see *Elene* 27b–30a and 110b–13a, *Beowulf* 3024b–7, *Genesis* 1983b–5a, 2087b–9a and 2159b–61, *The Battle of Brunanburh* 60–5a, *Exodus* 162–7, and *Judith* 205b–12a. For further discussion, see A. Renoir, 'Crist Ihesu's Beasts of Battle: A Note on Oral-Formulaic Theme Survival', *Neophil* 60 (1976), 455–9; F. P. Magoun, Jr, 'The Theme of the Beasts of Battle in Anglo-Saxon Poetry', *NM* 56 (1955), 81–90; F. C. Robinson, 'Notes on the Old English *Exodus*', *Anglia* 80 (1962), 363–78 at 365–8; J. R. Hall, '*Exodus* 166b, *cwyldrof*: 162–7, the Beasts of Battle', *Neophil* 74 (1990), 112–21; A. Bonjour, '*Beowulf* and the Beasts of Battle', *PMLA* 72 (1957), 563–73.

[51] Thomas, *Man in the Natural World*, p. 40.

someone, for example, Shakespeare assigns animal characteristics to the offending human party through labels such as 'ingrateful fox' or 'detested kite'.[52] The representation of animals may also serve more traditionally political ends, such as the early modern interpretation of the bee-hive as a model state, with a 'king' served obediently by workers committed to the good of the community[53] – that is, writers can interpret the natural world, and thus represent it, as a justification of the established, hierarchical order. However realistic or objective a representation appears, it inevitably depends upon such choices and judgements.[54]

The reliance of representation upon value structures – whether personal, social, political or religious – renders evaluation on the basis of right or wrong impossible. The modern inclination to reject 'inaccurate' views of the natural world (that is, views that do not award primacy to the evidence of the senses or technological extensions of the senses)[55] involves its own bias, for value structures determine every representation of the natural world,[56] including the present ones proposed and supported by modern science, despite the common belief that 'Science is neither bad nor good but only false or true'.[57] Although it is difficult for those living after the Scientific Revolution[58] to recognise the value judgement in this statement, or to regard science as anything other than the most accurate

---

[52] See *King Lear*, ed. K. Muir, 8th ed. (London, 1952), III.vii.28 and I.iv.272.

[53] Thomas, *Man in the Natural World*, pp. 62–6.

[54] Cf. Koestler, *The Sleepwalkers*, p. 103.

[55] Clair, *Unnatural History*, p. 14.

[56] Koestler, *The Sleepwalkers*, p. 15; S. L. Jaki, 'Introduction', in P. Duhem, *To Save the Phenomena: An Essay on the Idea of Physical Theory from Plato to Galileo*, trans. E. Doland and C. Maschler (Chicago, 1969), p. xxv; F. Capra, *The Tao of Physics: An Exploration of the Parallels between Modern Physics and Eastern Mysticism*, 3rd ed. (London, 1992), p. 317.

[57] C. Sherrington, *Man on his Nature*, 2nd ed. (Cambridge, 1951), p. 260. Cf. also Cassiodorus's opinion in *An Introduction to Divine and Human Readings by Cassiodorus Senator*, trans. L. W. Jones, Records of Civilization: Sources and Studies 40 (New York, 1946), p. 179.

[58] 'Since [the Scientific Revolution of the sixteenth and seventeenth centuries] changed the character of men's habitual mental operations even in the conduct of the non-material sciences, while transforming the whole diagram of the physical universe and the very texture of human life itself ... it looms ... as the real origin both of the modern world and of the modern mentality.' H. Butterfield, *The Origins of Modern Science 1300–1800*, 2nd ed. (London, 1957), pp. vii–viii.

and useful way to approach the natural world,[59] it is not difficult to observe that the Anglo-Saxons applied different principles and pursued different aims. However difficult it is to scrutinise the value structures determining present representations, neglecting the choices and judgements involved in representation can only misrepresent representations of 'the natural world' in Old English poetry.

Some of the value structures contributing to these representations can easily be identified. For example, one can isolate aims which are as straightforwardly didactic as those identified in early modern representations. Often these aims are related to morality and appear misguided and misleading by the standards controlling modern representations of the natural world.[60] The Old English poem *The Panther*, a translation from the Latin *Physiologus*,[61] for example, provides an abundance of descriptive information: the creature is friendly to all but the dragon, beautiful, multicoloured, unique and loveable; it rests three days after eating and then emits a pleasant sound and odour from its mouth which attract man and beast alike (15–54). These traits would be unlikely to allow one to identify a panther (or leopard).[62] It is more important, however, to observe that the poem's representation of the panther maintains aims different from those of a modern field guide than to point out that the writer had never observed a panther. The intention of the description is to illuminate the characteristics and actions of Christ; like the panther created by the poem's representation,

> Swa is dryhten god, dreama rædend,
> eallum eaðmede oþrum gesceaftum,
> duguða gehwylcre, butan dracan anum,
> attres ordfruman. Þæt is se ealda feond,

---

[59] F. Durham and R. D. Purrington, *Frame of the Universe: A History of Physical Csomology* (New York, 1983), p. viii.

[60] Among the many critics who voice this view are Crombie, *Augustine to Galileo*, p. 35; J. D. North, *Stars, Minds, and Fate: Essays in Ancient and Medieval Cosmology* (London, 1989), p. x; Clair, *Unnatural History*, p. 12; Whewell, *History of the Inductive Sciences*, I, 216; Kimble, *Geography in the Middle Ages*, pp. 1–2; Leclercq, *The Love of Learning*, p. 164; Dreyer, *A History of Astronomy*, pp. 207–8.

[61] For discussion of the Old English *The Physiologus* and its sources, see below, p. 186, n. 42 and pp. 190–2.

[62] For the identification of the panther as a leopard, see George and Yapp, *Naming of the Beasts*, p. 53.

þone he gesælde   in susla grund,
ond gefetrade   fyrnum teagum,
biþeahte þreanydum,   ond þy þriddan dæge
of digle aras,   þæs þe he deað fore us
þreo niht þolade,   þeoden engla,
sigora sellend.   Þæt wæs swete stenc,
wlitig ond wynsum   geond woruld ealle.
Siþþan to þam swicce   soðfæste men
on healfa gehwone   heapum þrungon
geond ealne ymbhwyrft   eorþan sceata.

(The Panther 55–68)[63]

The poem presents traits – however fictional – chosen to promote its point about the nature of Christ rather than to identify the creature itself. Its representation thus blatantly displays the 'interplay' between its 'method of questioning'[64] and the natural world.

MISREPRESENTATION AND MODERN VALUE STRUCTURES

It is in this context that critics' responses to representations of the natural world in Old English poetry should be seen, for too often the understanding of the natural world in the 'Dark Ages' has been unfavourably compared to that in earlier and later ages, as either a vestige of Greek science[65] or a hiatus before the reawakening of later periods.[66] Many

---

[63] 'So the lord God, the ruler of joys, is gracious to all other creatures, to each man, except for the dragon alone, the source of venom. That is the old enemy, whom he delivered into the abyss of misery, and fettered with fiery cords, [and] covered with afflictions, and on the third day [he] arose from the grave, after he, the prince of angels and giver of victories, endured death for us for three nights. That was a sweet fragrance, beautiful and delightful through all the world. Afterwards men firm in truth thronged to the fragrance in crowds from every side, through the whole extent of the corners of the earth.'

[64] Heisenberg, *Physics and Philosophy*, p. 69.

[65] This is almost a commonplace, but see, for example, E. Grant, *Physical Science in the Middle Ages* (New York, 1971), pp. 8 and 12; W. Singer, *From Magic to Science: Essays on the Scientific Twilight* (New York, 1958), p. xx; W. H. Stahl, *Roman Science: Origins, Development, and Influence to the Later Middle Ages* (Westport, CT, 1962), p. 249; Whewell, *History of the Inductive Sciences*, I, 185; M. Cary and E. H. Warmington, *The Ancient Explorers* (London, 1929), p. 190; Wright, *Geographical Lore*, p. 57.

[66] This, too, is a commonplace. See, for example, R. C. Dales, *The Intellectual Life of Western Europe in the Middle Ages* (Washington, DC, 1980), p. 59; Gatch, *Loyalties and*

critics, especially historians of science, perceive no progress in (and questionable maintenance of) thought itself at this time, and propose that only after the inhabitants of Western Europe rediscovered Greek science in the twelfth century did they interact significantly with the natural world. When such critics mention the 'Dark Ages', they allot to it a few pages at most, often blaming the stifling effect of patristic dogma for its lack of curiosity and intellectual vigour,[67] and beginning with a formulaic statement such as, 'In the Dark Ages, there was no progress in _____.'[68] Some critics vault from the discoveries made by the Greeks to their rediscovery in Arabic texts without any indication of the intervening distance, centuries and transformations.[69]

Such accounts imply that *no* representations of the natural world occurred in the 'Dark Ages' – or, at least, nothing except degenerate, sterile and disfigured misconceptions. Of course, the stated intention of many of these accounts – to outline the development of specifically scientific concepts – may explain their dismissive omissions and attendant over-simplifications: if the ideas which are privileged by modern, scientifically oriented societies play little part in the Anglo-Saxons' representations, studying such representations may be seen to offer little of value or interest. Yet later, more 'observant' and 'intellectually gifted' times necessarily develop from an awareness of their past and, if nothing else, construct their own representation of the natural world as a corrective to and contradiction of the 'degeneracy' of the 'Dark Ages'; the early Middle Ages thus contribute, however negatively and indirectly, to the developments of the High Middle Ages. In fact, the contribution must be more significant, for Old English poetry presents not one, derivative representation but multiple, contradictory and often lively representations of 'the natural world'.

Yet these representations have often received little attention for themselves. Critics of the High Middle Ages, for example, characterise

---

Traditions, pp. 19–20; S. Sambursky, *The Physical World of Late Antiquity* (London, 1962), p. xii; C. D. Hellman, *The Comet of 1577: Its Place in the History of Astronomy*, Columbia University Studies in History, Economics, and Public Law 510 (New York, 1944), p. 65; G. Abetti, *The History of Astronomy*, trans. B. B. Abetti (London, 1954), p. 44.

[67] See, for example, Abrams, 'The Development of Medieval Astronomy', p. 194.

[68] See, for example, Doig, *Concise History of Astronomy*, p. 44.

[69] See, for example, C. H. Cotter, *A History of Nautical Astronomy* (London, 1968).

the developments of their period in opposition to the 'Dark Ages', stressing that the High Middle Ages initiated a new (everywhere the emphasis is on 'new')[70] or 'increased interest in the natural world'.[71] Although this approach to the High Middle Ages has illuminated enough of the 'Dark Ages' to render the comparison meaningful, and although questions such as, 'What has been lost?' and 'What is not yet there?' are valid and productive questions, the information revealed through this approach can only be negative and thus possesses a limited ability to elucidate what *is* there. This limited, negative approach may have affected the portrayal of the High Middle Ages, for one can learn only a limited amount from observing that the High Middle Ages marked new developments from the 'Dark Ages' and that the 'Dark Ages' lacked the developments of the High Middle Ages. Such a circular process of defining one period in opposition to another only defined in terms of the first may have resulted in an imperfect understanding of the High Middle Ages. More important for the present discussion, a tangential or negative approach defines the representations carried out in Old English poetry hardly at all and can misrepresent the complexities involved in its representations of 'the natural world'.

Other critics, especially those writing late in the nineteenth or early in the twentieth century, have sought in Old English poetry the origin of a kind of poetry best exemplified in the Romantic poetry of Wordsworth and Shelley.[72] That is, they seek to find the 'germs' of an English poetic tradition of nature poetry.[73] In Old English poetry they see either an unaffected, fresh and intense feeling for nature,[74] such as was sought by

---

[70] P. Brown, *Society and the Holy in Late Antiquity* (London, 1982), p. 325; T. Gregory, *Anima mundi: la filosofia di Guglielmo di Conches e la scuola di Chartres*, Pubblicazioni dell'Istituto di Filosofia dell'Università di Roma 3 (Florence, 1955), 176. Cf. also M. Lapidge, 'Ideas of Natural Order in Early Medieval Latin Poetry' (unpubl. PhD dissertation, Univ. of Toronto, 1971), p. 234.

[71] R. Southern, quoted by N. F. Cantor in *Inventing the Middle Ages: The Lives, Works, and Ideas of the Great Medievalists of the Twentieth Century* (New York, 1991), p. 356.

[72] See, for example, Pons, *Le thème et le sentiment de la nature*, p. 116.

[73] E. D. Hanscom, 'The Feeling for Nature in Old English Poetry', *JEGP* 5 (1903–5), 439–63.

[74] See, for example, G. L. Swigget, 'Old English Poetry', *MLN* 8 (1893), 159; F. W. Moorman, *The Interpretation of Nature in English Poetry from Beowulf to Shakespeare*, Quellen und Forschungen zur Sprach- und Kulturgeschichte der germanischen Völker 95 (Strassburg, 1905), p. 33. Cf. also the similar conception of a 'spontaneous overflow

modern poets like Robert Graves, or a limited, underdeveloped sensitivity to nature's beauty.[75] It is clear that these critics analyse Old English poetry on the basis of the poetic conventions of their time; in looking for the origins of poetry contemporary with themselves, they either find what they are looking for or see little of interest.

Judged from the perspective of modern science, classical Greek philosophy, Renaissance cosmology or Romantic poetry, the representation of 'the natural world' in Old English poetry can appear disappointing, limited, erroneous, stagnant, even unimaginative. This judgement, however, derives from inappropriate comparisons. These representations of 'the natural world' are not hampered by unscientific, closed-minded approaches to the natural world, by insufficient technology or by a failure of sensibility; they are not depictions of the natural world at all – not in the senses accepted by later literary critics and those examining the natural world with the scientific method and its tools.[76] Although 'the natural world' in Old English poetry does contain elements that are included in a modern definition of the natural world – winds, seas and animals, for example – it is not a category in contrast with the supernatural. It is not really a self-sufficient, externally defined entity at all. It is instead a reflection of human constructions. With this focus on intangible concepts, it is unsurprising that the representation of 'the natural world' is not inevitably tied to physical reality.

TANGLED TRADITIONS

One of the human constructions served by representations of 'the natural world' in Anglo-Saxon texts was religion; through the allegorical description of *The Panther* the Old English poet, like his or her source, conveyed Christian truths. Representations of 'the natural world' in Old English poetry are not, however, characterised and controlled by a consistent assimilation of data to the cause of morality, just as they are not, as in some modern representations, ruled by the desire for ever more precise

of emotion' in early Celtic nature poetry; see Jackson, *Studies in Early Celtic Nature Poetry*, pp. 81–2 and 104.

[75] See, for example, R. Burton, 'Nature in Old English Poetry', *Atlantic Monthly* 73 (1894), 476–87, at 487.

[76] Gurevich, *Categories of Medieval Culture*, pp. 4–5.

measurements of cause and effect. Some texts do reveal a concern with determining and limiting meaning (allegorical and otherwise),[77] and it is evident that the Anglo-Saxons did attempt to assimilate 'the natural world' through the process of interpretation as well as through physical means (hunting, domestication, etc.).[78] However, 'the natural world' that they represented in their poetry does not conform to any scheme that they might have inherited from Christian patristic writers or classical models. Nor can one attribute deviations from these authorities to the vestiges of pagan Germanic mythology that survived the Anglo-Saxons' conversion to Christianity. The physical conditions endured by the Anglo-Saxons, classical philosophy and science, Christian dogma and Germanic tradition can all be seen to have contributed to the representation of 'the natural world' in Old English poetry, but no dominant tradition or amalgamation of traditions emerges from this mixture. This is perhaps unsurprising, since Anglo-Saxon literature spans or, at least, draws upon a period of five centuries; one could not expect there to be a single view throughout the whole corpus. One could, however, expect there to be a gradual incorporation of Christian ideology into originally pagan forms of expression (oral-formulaic, heroic poetry, for example), followed by an infusion of the classical theories that accompanied the arrival of literacy and scholarship. Unfortunately, no trace of any progression can be found. The Anglo-Saxons appear not to have been concerned to develop a consistent cosmological scheme or approach to the 'natural world', and they used isolated elements from all of their sources without any apparent awareness of inconsistency.

Examining the representation of 'the natural world' in Old English poetry, therefore, cannot reveal what apparently did not exist: a single, particularly Anglo-Saxon cosmological scheme or world view, an Anglo-Saxon 'natural world'. Although this lack is interesting in itself and raises the question of why the Anglo-Saxons did not attempt to reconcile and integrate the elements and traditions available to them, the question is probably unanswerable; a combination of many factors – such as a paucity of texts relevant to ideas of cosmology, limited understanding of the texts that were available, an unsettled political climate, the continuing vitality

---

[77] See below, pp. 190–6.

[78] B. Guillemain, 'Avant-Propos', in *Le monde animal et ses représentations au moyen-âge (XIᵉ–XVᵉ siècles)* (Toulouse, 1985), pp. 7–8, at 7.

of contradictory, co-existing traditions, and even racial personality[79] – may be considered but cannot ultimately be proven critical. What remains instead is to examine the structures in which the representation of 'the natural world'[80] *did* participate, since it did not participate in a single theory of the universe. What emerges is that the representation of the 'natural world' is never an end in itself and is always ancillary to other issues. It acts as a literary device, used to define what were apparently more important issues: the state of humanity and its position in the universe, the establishment and maintenance of society, the power of extraordinary individuals, the proximity of the deity to creation and the ability of writing to control and limit information.

[79] Cf. Pons, *Le thème et le sentiment de la nature*, p. 149.

[80] Although it is important to remember the differences between modern and Anglo-Saxon conceptions, 'the natural world' will not appear in quotation marks throughout the rest of this book.

2

Defining and confining humanity

Hu sculon wit nu libban   oððe on þys lande wesan,
gif her wind cymð,   westan oððe eastan,
suðan oððe norðan?   Gesweorc up færeð,
cymeð hægles scur   hefone getenge,
færeð forst on gemang,   se byð fyrnum ceald.
Hwilum of heofnum   hate scineð,
blicð þeos beorhte sunne,   and wit her baru standað,
unwered wædo.   Nys unc wuht beforan
to scursceade,   ne sceattes wiht
to mete gemearcod,   ac unc is mihtig god,
waldend wraðmod.   To hwon sculon wit weorðan nu?

(Genesis 805–15)[1]

The Old English Adam's dramatic lament echoes the elegiac complaints in *The Wanderer*, *The Seafarer* and *The Wife's Lament* and probably should not be read without reference to such poems: as the first 'Anglo-Saxon' exile, Adam is the model for all following generations[2] and suffers the

---

[1] 'How shall we two live now or exist in this land if the wind comes here from west or east, from south or north? A dark cloud will rise up, a shower of hail touching the sky; frost will advance in its midst, which is intensely cold. Sometimes the bright sun will shine hot from the heavens and dazzle, and we two stand here naked, unprotected by any clothing. There is nothing before us [to act as] a shield against showers, nor any chattel marked out as food, but mighty God, the ruler, is angry with us. What must become of the two of us now?'

[2] This creation of models or examples that recur again and again throughout the poem is typical of the Old English *Genesis A*; all the events of the poem can be seen to follow one of the two patterns (loyalty or disloyalty) established in the brief account of the fall of the angels. See L. N. McKill, 'The Artistry of the Noah Episode in *Genesis A*', *English Studies in Canada* 13 (1987), 121–35, at 134. Cf. also P. J. Lucas, 'Loyalty and

19

archetypal miseries of exile – deprivation and exposure to the forces of the natural world.[3] Positioned where it is, however, between the commission of the original sin and God's sentencing, Adam's lament does more than establish an archetype; it sets out the human race's new place in the universe.

In fact, Adam answers his own question, *To hwon sculon wit weorðan nu?* 'What must become of us now?' or, more literally, 'What must we become now?' In the space of twenty-five lines Adam describes the complete reversal that the human race has incurred as a result of his and Eve's action: once the favoured new creation granted power over the marvellous new world, the replacement for those relegated to the torments of hell after forfeiting their rights to heaven, the human race is now characterised by its lack of access to heaven, its frightening proximity to hell (which Adam can see and hear from where he stands (792b–4a)) and its subjection to the power of the natural world. Although God has yet to announce the new life of hardship that awaits (927–38), Adam reveals that he is already well aware of the change in humanity's status as a consequence of losing God's favour. In the long run the most important aspects of this new status are those mentioned first: the proximity of hell and inaccessibility of heaven. In the present, however, Adam defines his existence by describing the threat of the natural world.[4]

The use of the natural world in the context of the myth of the Fall can, of course, be found elsewhere: Milton's Adam similarly finds the evidence

---

Obedience in the Old English *Genesis* and the Interpolation of *Genesis B* into *Genesis A*', *Neophil* 76 (1992), 121–35 and Doane, *The Saxon Genesis*, p. 125.

[3] For the traditional expression of these miseries, see Greenfield, 'The Formulaic Expression of the Theme of "Exile"', pp. 200–6 and Irving, 'Image and Meaning', pp. 153–66.

[4] Cf. also Ælfric's description of the result of the Fall:

> þa þa he agylt hæfde, and Godes bebod tobræc,
> þa forleas he þa gesælþa, and on geswincum leofode,
> swa þæt hine biton lys bealdlice and flean,
> þone þe ær ne dorste se draca furþon hreppan.

> (*De falsis Diis*, in *Homilies of Ælfric: A Supplementary Collection*, ed. J. C. Pope, EETS os 259 and 60 (London, 1967–8), II, 679, 45–8)

'When [Adam] had sinned and broken God's command, he lost his prosperity and lived in hardship, so that lice and fleas boldly bit him, whom previously even the dragon dared not touch.'

of the Fall reflected everywhere in the natural world around him.[5] The Old English version of the story, however, uses the representation of the natural world in a more direct and less multivalent way. Its aim is not to consider the character of the natural world either before or after the Fall, nor to increase the sense of tragedy by making the Fall a cosmic catastrophe. Instead, the looming power of the natural world is represented specifically in contrast with Adam's (and all of humanity's) powerlessness; the depiction of nature's power, in fact, *is* the depiction of humanity's powerlessness. Adam does not state that he and Eve are incapable of withstanding the onslaught of wind, hail, frost, sun and rain, or that they will suffer, since merely describing what they must face without the benefit of outside help makes that clear enough. The natural world stands as a negative mirror for human capability, its power reflecting the unstated but apparent lack of human power. Describing the natural world at this particular place in the narrative thus serves to define the human condition.

This narrowly directed use of the natural world is as typical of Old English poetry as the elegiac lament of the exile: the natural world is always invoked for a discernible purpose, and the point of interest is the power with which it opposes human concerns. Throughout this book I shall argue that this purpose and interest are truly 'typical' of Old English poetry – that the representation of the natural world is not merely a descriptive element incidental to some poems but rather one of the Old English poets' traditional techniques for defining human issues. In this regard the specific target of the natural world's force (human concerns) is worth noting, for this specificity is not inevitable. For example, a roughly contemporary Irish poem describes how winter's cold afflicts various animals but is unable to touch human beings, who have quilts and featherbeds.[6] A later Old Norse poem designates the wind as the *selju...gandr* 'wolf [enemy] of the willow'.[7] Old English poetry, on the other hand, betrays little concern for or even consciousness of other creatures suffering from winter's afflictions; the Seafarer who laments his cold feet does not pity the sea birds with their icy feathers (*The Seafarer* 8b–10a and 24a).[8]

[5] *Paradise Lost* X.650–741.

[6] See poem 31 in *Golden Treasury of Irish Poetry*, ed. Greene and O'Connor, pp. 134–6.

[7] Turville-Petre, *Scaldic Poetry*, p. 23.

[8] Cf. the twelfth-century Irish poem in *Golden Treasury of Irish Poetry*, ed. Greene and O'Connor, number 37, pp. 154–6.

Although – or perhaps because – the Anglo-Saxons had access to many conflicting scientific and cosmological concepts in the classical writing that they inherited,[9] the representation of the natural world in Old English poetry does not take place in accordance with any over-riding, abstract ideas that they inherited regarding the natural world,[10] but rather in accordance with poetic tradition. I do not claim that Old English poets represented the natural world without regard to their authorities, or that they interpreted it in a uniquely creative way. However, their representation of the natural world is part of a poetic tradition that reflects and participates in their definition of themselves and is a response to issues of particular concern to themselves. In this chapter I will examine a group of texts in which the issue at hand is, as in Adam's lament, defining humanity – describing the human condition.

PLACING HUMANITY

It is not immediately obvious that representations of the natural world should be relevant to a description of humanity; one would expect homiletic and gnomic literature to offer more direct contemplation of the human condition. To a great extent this expectation is justified. The Vercelli Book Homilies, for example, often inform their audiences of their sinful nature, as well as the wretchedness of the human condition compared to the heavenly and the blessedness of the human condition compared to the hellbound,[11] while 'catalogue poems' like *Maxims I* inform us of 'the diversity of human experience within God's order'[12] and appear to 'epitomise ... the Anglo-Saxons' understanding of themselves and of their world'.[13] The representation of the natural world is not irrelevant to this defining of the human condition, for observations like

---

[9] See, for example, Lapidge, 'Stoic Cosmology'; Brehaut, *Encyclopedist of the Dark Ages*, pp. 15–16; Crombie, *Augustine to Galileo*, pp. 30–2; Wright, *Geographical Lore*, p. 43.

[10] See below, pp. 146–7.

[11] See, for example, Vercelli homily IX, in *The Vercelli Homilies*, ed. Scragg, pp. 158–84; for translations, see *The Vercelli Book Homilies: Translations from the Anglo-Saxon*, ed. L. E. Nicholson (Lanham, MD, 1991).

[12] Howe, *Old English Catalogue Poems*, p. 203. For further discussion of *Maxims I* and other catalogue poems, see below, pp. 186–90.

[13] *The Old English Rune Poem*, ed. Halsall, p. 40. See also Williams, *Gnomic Poetry in Anglo-Saxon*, p. 12.

forst sceal freosan, fyr wudu meltan, / *eorþe growan, is brycgian* 'frost must freeze, fire melt wood, the earth grow, ice make a bridge' (*Maxims I* 71–72) 'function as a kind of touchstone by which the truth of other maxims about human behaviour and society can be measured'.[14] Yet the representation of the natural world outside of gnomic literature can be equally informative, for in Anglo-Saxon terms the human condition is determined by its position in the universe, the fact of its existence in the midst of various powers. Humanity is first of all situated both morally and spatially between heaven and hell and is thus subject to forces from both.[15] The consequences of this position determine both human nature (partly divine and partly mortal) and the human condition (partly blessed and partly cursed). At the same time, humanity is situated in the natural world. Humanity's physical place, its literal context, renders it subject to forces additional to the mythological forces of Christianity, and the consequences of this are equally determinant of humanity's nature and condition.

This determination of consequences is, however, actually the reverse, a mirror image, of the process taking place, for what is under discussion here is not a literal but a literary place. The physical world must have determined much of Anglo-Saxon life, but the representation of that world in their poetry does not display an accurate or consistent relationship with what is known of actual physical conditions.[16] Rather, just as Anglo-Saxon writers (like many Christian writers) apparently observed that people were a mixture of good and evil and so constructed an image of them as being torn between heaven and hell,[17] so they represented the natural world, their immediate context, in response to observations about themselves. As they have left little direct self-speculation behind, the

---

[14] Larrington, *A Store of Common Sense*, p. 125. See also J. Mann, 'Proverbial Wisdom in the *Ysengrimus*', *NLH* 16 (1984), 93–109, at 93.

[15] Lee, *The Guest-Hall of Eden*, pp. 13–14; see also D. L. Jeffrey, 'The Self and the Book: Reference and Recognition in Medieval Thought', in *By Things Seen*, ed. Jeffrey, pp. 1–17, at 1.

[16] See the summary of physical conditions above, pp. 3–7.

[17] For the compounding of ideological and physical violence (from their Christian and Germanic heritages respectively) that characterises the Anglo-Saxon vision of this position, see J. P. Hermann, *Allegories of War: Language and Violence in Old English Poetry* (Ann Arbor, MI, 1989).

natural world's reflective and contrasting function has much to offer to an understanding of how the Anglo-Saxons viewed themselves.

An exception to the general paucity of 'life is like this' statements in Anglo-Saxon writing is Bede's famous account of the conversion of Edwin in his *Historia ecclesiastica*. The king's counsellor recommends the adoption of Christianity because it might be able to counteract the prevailing insecure state of humanity in this world. Conveniently enough, this definition of the human condition is made by locating the human being in its physical place, surrounded by the forces of the natural world:

'Talis' inquiens 'mihi uidetur, rex, uita hominum praesens in terris, ad conparationem eius quod nobis incertum est temporis, quale cum te residente ad caenam cum ducibus ac ministris tuis tempore brumali, accenso quidem foco in medio et calido effecto cenaculo, furentibus autem foris per omnia turbinibus hiemalium pluuiarum uel niuium, adueniens unus passerum domum citissime peruolauerit; qui cum per unum ostium ingrediens mox per aliud exierit, ipso quidem tempore quo intus est hiemis tempestate non tangitur, sed tamen paruissimo spatio serenitatis ad momentum excurso, mox de hieme in hiemem regrediens tuis oculis elabitur. Ita haec uita hominum ad modicum apparet; quid autem sequatur, quidue praecesserit, prorsus ignoramus.'

(*Historia ecclesiastica* II.xii (pp. 182–4))[18]

The counsellor's ultimate concern is what lies beyond the *uita hominum praesens in terris*, the present human condition; he uses the natural world as a simile to represent the vast unknown that lies outside of that present. The literal level of his speech, however, simultaneously provides an idea of the physical conditions experienced by the Anglo-Saxons[19] and a vivid

---

[18] '"Such", he said, "the present life of men on earth seems to me, king, in comparison with that time which is unknown to us: as if, while you were sitting at dinner with your leaders and ministers in the winter time, with the fire lit in the centre and the upper room filled with heat, with the raging storms of winter rains or snow everywhere outside, a sparrow were to arrive and fly swiftly through the house. As it enters through one door and soon exits through another, during the time when it is inside it is not touched by the winter storm, but nevertheless, after the briefest space of calm, when it has hastened forth, turning from winter and soon back into winter, it escapes your eyes. Thus this life of men appears for a moment; what follows, or what came before, we absolutely do not know."'

[19] From it, for example, one may speculate about the type of architectural structure that would allow a sparrow to fly through it, how comfortable and warm it would be and to what kinds of ailments the Anglo-Saxons would thence be prone. See Cameron, *Anglo-Saxon Medicine*, p. 6.

image of how an Anglo-Saxon viewed those conditions: from his perspective, the human race lives precariously, with only brief moments of respite in places of refuge like the hall, which is surrounded on all sides – besieged even – by the forces of the natural world, by rain, storm and snow. The natural world inescapably and overwhelmingly overshadows the human race with its vast power. In opposition to this, Edwin's counsellor suggests, one can only hope for the better state promised by Christianity.

What the counsellor primarily desires is knowledge of the unknown metaphorically represented by nature, but the new religion he advocates also addresses the problem raised by the literal surface of his simile: the helplessness of the human race in the face of nature's onslaught. The Christian God in Old English poetry not only promises a safer and more pleasant heaven for the future,[20] but is represented as a protective king in the present whose power surpasses that of the kings of the world, the *middangeard*; he is described again and again as a potent *mundbora* or *helm*[21] for his thegns.[22] Both literally and figuratively the counsellor's representation of the natural world makes a good case for the need for the Christian God: the unacceptable powerlessness and ignorance highlighted by nature's vast and unknowable power demands recourse to a superior source of power and knowledge.[23]

---

[20] Heaven is imagined as a place where *Nis þær hungor ne þurst, / slæp ne swar leger, ne sunnan bryne, / ne cyle ne cearo* 'there is no hunger or thirst, sleep or painful illness, no burning of the sun, no chill or sorrow' (*Christ* 1660b–2a); see also *The Wanderer* 114b–15.

[21] This word, like *eodor* 'enclosure' and *hleo* 'shelter', is used in poetry almost exclusively in a metaphorical way, to refer to kings as protectors of social groups. See P. Clemoes, '"Symbolic" Language in Old English Poetry', in *Modes of Interpretation*, ed. Brown, Crampton and Robinson, pp. 3–14, at 8.

[22] See, for example, *Guthlac* 788, *Juliana* 156, *Andreas* 277, *Christ* 566, *Genesis* 2422, among many others. In *Genesis* particularly, God is juxtaposed with human rulers who bear the same titles (for example, Pharaoh (1858) and the King of Sodom (2146)) but fall short of his protective power. For discussion of how the struggle to create and maintain architectural and social structures within the natural world serves to define kings in contrast with the creative and protective power of God, see below, pp. 62–9.

[23] For discussion of the relationship between knowledge, power and representing the natural world, see below, pp. 178–201.

THE AMORAL NATURAL WORLD

While the context and point of this passage, as of Adam's lament in *Genesis*, is specifically Christian, it is important to note that the natural world is not assigned any inherent moral status. It is physical and material even when it is symbolic. This is generally true of Old English poetry, contrary to what one might expect from texts created within a medieval Christian institution[24] – texts apparently created and reproduced to further a moral as well as intellectual education. Nature appears negative in Adam's lament and the counsellor's simile, as it does in *The Wanderer* and many other poems, but it is not evil like *Juliana*'s demonic assailant; likewise, although the sun is described as *godes condel beorht* 'God's bright candle' (*Battle of Brunanburh* 15) and the water of Noah's flood is called *wuldorcyninges / yða* 'the glory-king's waves' (*Genesis* 1384b–5a), nature is not divinely good like Guthlac's angelic defender.

This omission is surprising because the natural world could easily have been included in the struggle between God and the devil, on either side. There were authoritative if contradictory precedents for inscribing nature into a moral framework, whether as a setting or an actor in the narrative of the human race's journey from Creation to the Last Judgement.[25] For example, Augustine's approach could have provided a framework for representations of the natural world.[26] In this regard it is important to

[24] It has been argued that nature is only morally symbolic in such texts. See, for example, Leclercq, *The Love of Learning*, p. 165 and Clair, *Unnatural History*, p. 12.

[25] Or an individual from birth to death, or even the Church from its inception to the Second Coming – the natural world could be a potent referent on any of the many levels of medieval allegory. For a summary of the four levels of interpretation (*littera, allegoria, moralia, anagogia*), see N. Hinton, 'Anagogue and Archetype: The Phenomenology of Medieval Literature', *Annuale Mediaevale* 7 (1966), 57–73, at 59–60.

[26] It has been claimed that Augustinian ideology dominated Anglo-Saxon poetry (see, for example, Huppé, *Doctrine and Poetry*); although this view is probably too extreme, the Anglo-Saxons certainly were familiar with Augustine's works, as many manuscripts of his writings survive from the period (see Gneuss, 'Preliminary List', pp. 1–60), and writers like Bede and Aldhelm quote him often. For the texts known to Bede, see the list in M. L. W. Laistner, 'The Library of the Venerable Bede', in *Bede: His Life, Times and Writings: Essays in Commemoration of the Twelfth Centenary of His Death*, ed. A. H. Thompson (Oxford, 1935), pp. 237–66, at 263–6. For the texts known to Aldhelm, see the notes to his works in *Aldhelm: The Prose Works*, trans. Lapidge and Herren. Cf. also M. W. Bloomfield, 'Patristics and Old English Literature: Notes on Some Poems', in *Studies in Old English Literature in Honor of Arthur G. Brodeur*, ed. S. B. Greenfield

distinguish, however, between the natural world and the *natura* to which Augustine devotes much more of his attention, especially in his writings against the Pelagians. By *natura* Augustine designates a Platonic idea, an essential character; he uses the term most often to refer to the human race, not the natural world. In the course of his lifetime of writing Augustine places *natura* first on one side, to stress the goodness of God's creation,[27] and then on the other, in argument against Pelagius's declaration of the power of human will in its own salvation.[28] This inconsistency lies at the centre of the controversy that arose in the ninth century with Gottschalk of Orbais,[29] but, even if the Anglo-Saxons did concur that human *natura* was inescapably flawed,[30] such a view does not necessarily dictate a correspondingly negative approach to the natural world. Instead, the Anglo-Saxons could have seen in the natural world a more positive example of God's creation than that offered by human nature, as Augustine suggests in *De civitate Dei*:

Hanc tamen causam, id est ad bona creanda bonitatem Dei, hanc, inquam, causam tam iustam adque idoneam, quae diligenter considerata et pie cogitata omnes controuersias quaerentium mundi originem terminat, quidam haeretici non uiderunt, quia egenam carnis huius fragilemque mortalitatem iam de iusto supplicio uenientem, dum ei non conueniunt, plurima offendunt, sicut ignis aut frigus aut fera bestia aut quid eius modi; nec adtendunt, quam uel in suis locis

---

(Eugene, OR, 1963), pp. 36–43; P. B. Rollinson, 'The Influence of Christian Doctrine and Exegesis on Old English Poetry: An Estimate of the Current State of Scholarship', *ASE* 2 (1973), 271–84; M. P. Hamilton, 'The Religious Principle in *Beowulf*', *PMLA* 61 (1946), 309–30, at 311–12.

[27] See, for example, *De civitate Dei* XI.xxiii (in *Sancti Aurelii Augustini*, ed. Welldon), where he rejects Origen's assertion that the creation is evil by nature and states that sinful wills violate their own initially good *natura*, and *De civitate Dei* XII.v: *Naturae igitur omnes, quoniam sunt et ideo habent modum suum, speciem suam et quandam secum pacem suam, profecto bonae sunt* 'therefore all natures, since they are and thus have their own measure, their own kind, and their own kind of peace within them, assuredly are good'.

[28] For example, see *The Anti-Pelagian Works of Saint Augustine, Bishop of Hippo*, trans. P. Holmes and R. E. Wallis, vol. 3, The Works of Aurelius Augustine Bishop of Hippo 15 (Edinburgh, 1876), 332–5.

[29] Doane, *Saxon Genesis*, pp. 102–3. This debate was also known in Anglo-Saxon England; see Lapidge, 'Three Latin Poems from Æthelwold's School', pp. 244–5.

[30] Bede declares that Britain was cleansed of the *uirgulta Pelagianae pestis* 'thicket of Pelagian pestilence' even before the Anglo-Saxons were converted to Christianity (*Historia ecclesiastica* summary of contents I.xxii, p. 10).

naturisque uigeant pulchroque ordine disponantur, quantumque uniuersitati rerum pro sui portione decoris tamquam in communem rem publicam conferant uel nobis ipsis, si eis congruenter adque scienter utamur, commoditatis adtribuant, ita ut uenena ipsa, quae per inconuenientiam perniciosa sunt, conuenienter adhibita in salubria medicamenta uertantur; quamque a contrario etiam haec, quibus delectantur, sicut cibus et potus et ista lux, inmoderato et inopportuno usu noxia sentiantur. Unde nos admonet diuina prouidentia non res insipienter uituperare, sed utilitatem rerum diligenter inquirere, et ubi nostrum ingenium uel infirmitas deficit, ita credere occultam, sicut erant quaedam, quae uix potuimus inuenire; quia et ipsa utilitatis occultatio aut humilitatis exercitatio est aut elationis adtritio; cum omnino natura nulla sit malum nomenque hoc non sit nisi priuationis boni.   (*De civitate Dei* XI.xxii)[31]

Augustine argues here not only for the essential goodness of the creation which God made, but for its usefulness to humanity – not only in a physical sense, but also in a spiritual one, since the puzzle of how harmful creatures like wild beasts suit humanity's best interests reduces intellectual pride.[32] Such an approach to the natural world, like the exhortation in *De doctrina Christiana* to wring spiritual edification out of every representation of the natural world in divine texts,[33] allows for a flexible

---

[31] 'Nevertheless, certain heretics do not see this cause for good things being created, that is, the goodness of God – this cause, I say, so just and fitting, which, once it has been diligently considered and piously thought through, terminates all the controversies of those questioning the origin of the world. [They do not see this] because many things, since they do not suit the poor and fragile mortality of this flesh, coming already from a just punishment, [rather] strike against it, such as fire or cold or wild beasts or whatever of this sort. They do not consider how they flourish in their own places and natures [*naturis*] and in what beautiful order they are disposed, and how much grace they bring to the universe of things according to their own lot, as if to a common republic, or [how much] advantage they bestow on us ourselves, if we use them suitably and wisely. Thus even poisons, which are dangerous [when used in] unsuitable [ways], are turned into medicine administered for health [when used] suitably. In the same way, on the other hand, even those things in which [people] are delighted, like food and drink and light itself, are experienced as injurious when used in an immoderate and unsuitable [way]. Whence divine providence admonishes us not to vituperate things foolishly, but to inquire diligently about the utility of things, and, where our abilities or infirmity fail, [it admonishes us] to believe in a secret [utility], just as there were other things which we could hardly discover. This hiding of utility is either an exercise of humility or an impairment of pride, since no nature [*natura*] is entirely evil, and this [i.e. evil] is a name for nothing except the deprivation of good.'

[32] For discussion of the natural world as an intellectual challenge, see below, pp. 192–201.

[33] See *De doctrina Christiana* II.xxxix.

and positive curiosity about the natural world and moral justification for its representation and interpretation.

The study of the natural world advocated by Augustine appears to have been embraced by the Anglo-Saxons, along with texts by other authors who provided both 'raw data' regarding the natural world and interpretation of it. Thus Aldhelm's *Enigmata* reflect the Isidorian belief in the importance of the names of things[34] and in the value in contemplating and puzzling over objects in the natural world.[35] The *Liber monstrorum*, the *Wonders of the East* and *Letter of Alexander to Aristotle* not only use but emulate Pliny's gathering of the world's interesting facts and oddities.[36] Bede's *De natura rerum*, *De temporibus* and *De temporum ratione* assert the value in knowing about the physical world, even if that value tends to derive from the pragmatic use of astronomical knowledge for the determination of the date of Easter.[37] This view stands, however, in stark

---

[34] N. Howe, 'Aldhelm's *Enigmata* and Isidorian Etymology', *ASE* 14 (1985), 37–59, at 58.

[35] *Aldhelm: The Poetic Works*, trans. Lapidge and Rosier, p. 62. The Isidorian approach may, however, actually direct attention away from the natural world, for Isidore completely subordinates his encyclopedic material to the analytic methods of 'grammaticus'; his view of the world derives not from objects but from the etymology of their names; see J. Fontaine, *Tradition et actualité chez Isidore de Séville* (London, 1988), pp. 531–2. In this sense, Isidore contributes not so much a belief in the interest and value of the natural world but rather a strategy for understanding and controlling it – a strategy that was apparently attractive to Old English poets: 'whether we like it or not, such etymologies were an undeniable aspect of the medieval verbal imagination' (Frank, 'Some Uses of Paronomasia', p. 209). Cf. also below, pp. 193–5.

[36] Both Isidore and Pliny were available to the Anglo-Saxons, at least to Aldhelm and Bede; see the detailed notes provided by R. Ehwald (MGH AA 15) and C.W. Jones (CCSL 123A) respectively. For example, Aldhelm's *Enigmata LXIII: Corbus* and *XCI: Palma* echo Isidore's *Etymologiae* XII.vii.43 and XII.vii.1 respectively, and Bede's *De natura rerum* (*De varia altitudine caeli*) derives from Pliny's *Naturalis historia* II.lxxi.177. (see *C. Plini secundi naturalis historia libri XXXVII*, 6 vols., ed. C. Mayhoff and L. Ian (Stuttgart, 1967)). For the sources and analogues of the *Liber monstrorum*, see Orchard, *Pride and Prodigies*, pp. 318–19. Note especially the numerous references to Augustine, Pliny and Isidore.

[37] Bede's *De temporum ratione*, for example, describes at length (over 100 pages in the printed edition) the minute methods of calculating times and seasons based on celestial observations and computational manuals; his text ends with a discussion of the date of Easter. The shorter *De temporibus liber* likewise culminates in a discussion of Easter's date. See *Bedae opera de temporibus*, ed. C. W. Jones, The Medieval Adademy of America Publication 41 (Cambridge, MA, 1943).

contrast to many representations of the natural world in Old English poetry. It conflicts, for example, with the apparently fundamental view of the natural world expressed in the Old English metrical account of Creation (*Genesis* 92 to its incomplete ending at 168).[38] There the world is *idel ond unnyt* 'empty and useless' (106a) until divided, established and eventually adorned and bound;[39] that is, the organised, tamed and artificial (in the sense of 'artful', not the modern pejorative sense) have value, while the natural has at best an unrealised potential for value, at worst a hostile uselessness. An originally *idel ond unnyt* natural world can become valuable only by divine or human effort; it is meaningless, even horrible,[40] without reference to or contact with humanity. Thus the land or a horse is valuable because it *can* be cultivated or adorned, and receives full attention from a poet only once it has been so transformed[41] – once the empty *weste* 'wasteland' (*Genesis* 110a) has been transformed into Paradise (*Genesis* 206–34), and once the horse has been decorated with gold and exalted with an ornamented saddle (*Beowulf* 1035–41a).[42] In contrast, *Beowulf*'s *niceras* are never clearly defined or described;[43] even Grendel is left as a vague figure[44] and, in an ironic understatement, rejected as having no value: Beowulf *ne his lifdagas leoda ænigum / nytte tealde* 'did not account his life-days useful to any of the people' (793–4a). Although Grendel receives a great deal of attention within the poem, that attention is different from the intellectual curiosity and exploration

[38] For further discussion of this passage, see below, pp. 58–62 and 146–7.

[39] *Gesundrode* / *(a)dælde* (126a, 141a, 162b; 146b and 150b), *geseted* (100b, 166b), *gefrætwod* (215a), *gefetero{de}* (168a).

[40] Schrader, 'Sacred Groves', p. 81. Although I would not argue that such depictions of the natural world are allegorical, cf. also D. W. Robertson, Jr, 'The Doctrine of Charity in Mediaeval Literary Gardens: A Topical Approach Through Symbolism and Allegory', *Speculum* 26 (1951), 24–49.

[41] C. T. Carr, *Nominal Compounds in Germanic*, St. Andrews University 41 (London, 1939), 446. See also Robinson, *'Beowulf' and the Appositive Style*, pp. 70–4.

[42] For discussion of ornamentation, see Bessinger, 'Homage to Caedmon', pp. 98–102. In contrast with the detail regarding the horses' trappings, the poet provides little information about the horses themselves – no indication of breed or colour, for example (but cf. 1265a, where presumably the same horses are described as *æppel-fealuwe*).

[43] What the *niceras* are, in fact, is a test for Beowulf, and they are described fully enough for that purpose; see below, pp. 131–2.

[44] For discussion of the suspenseful effect of Grendel's vagueness, see below, p. 73 n. 74.

taught by Pliny or Isidore.[45] Similarly, the poet's representation of Grendel allows the multiplicity of interpretation described by Augustine[46] but does not demand it.

THE NATURAL WORLD IN CONTEMPORARY TEXTS

Although the Old English poems considered thus far do not share the view that the natural world is morally or intellectually useful, they do share their uses of the natural world with Anglo-Latin and Old English prose texts. That is, the defining function assigned to the natural world in Old English poetry is not a technique restricted to Old English poetry alone. As a result, although the present investigation is primarily concerned with Old English poetry, it will also refer to other texts, like the Latin and prose texts mentioned here, in order to clarify the characteristics of Old English poetic representation of the natural world. For example, even texts apparently inspired by authors like Pliny, which appear to list and describe wondrous creatures for their intrinsic interest, can be seen to reveal the Anglo-Saxons defining themselves against the natural world. The *Liber monstrorum* presents a wide variety of 'monsters', most of which are dangerous or deadly to human beings. The interest in

---

[45] On the other hand, it has been argued that *Beowulf* belongs to the same genre of encyclopedic compendia as the *Letter of Alexander* and *Wonders of the East* with which it is bound in its manuscript, and that the compiler of the manuscript, at least, did not find their approaches incompatible. See, for example, Brynteson, '*Beowulf*, Monsters, and Manuscripts', pp. 41–57; R. L. Reynolds, 'Note on *Beowulf*'s Date and Economic–Social History', in *Studi in Onore di Armando Sapori* (Milan, 1957), pp. 175–8. It has also been argued that the themes of exotic creatures and pagan pride unite the texts; see Orchard, *Pride and Prodigies*, pp. 169–71.

[46] For example, Hrothgar's framing of Grendel within a narrative of human peace, pride and reversal (1700–84) suggests that Grendel could be interpreted as punishment for pride. The poet's mention of Grendel's origins (100b–14) suggests that Grendel can be interpreted within a biblical context. Modern critics have, of course, fully exploited Grendel's interpretability. For interpretation of Grendel as the devil, an allegory of intemperance, a representative of a matrilineal tribe, and as an East Anglian *Shuck* (i.e. a marsh-haunting, spectral dog), see, for example, B. S Cox, *Cruces of Beowulf*, Studies in English Literature 60 (The Hague, 1971), 94–101; Lee, *Guest-Hall*, pp. 182–8; Fajardo-Acosta, 'Intemperance, Fratricide, and the Elusiveness of Grendel', pp. 205–10; F. Battaglia, 'The Germanic Earth Goddess in *Beowulf*?' *The Mankind Quarterly* 31 (1991), 415–46, at 430; Newton, *The Origins of 'Beowulf'*, pp. 142–4. For further interpretations of Grendel, see also below, pp. 70–81.

giant horned serpents and hippopotami appears quite distinct from the apparent indifference of the *Beowulf*-poet to *niceras*, but in fact these wondrous beasts are not substantially different. The *Beowulf*-poet's description of *niceras* focuses on their dangerous ferocity: these *hronfixas* (540b) and *meredeor* (558a) are *lað* 'hateful' (550a), *fah* 'hostile' (554a), *grim* 'fierce' (555a) and *mihtig* 'powerful' (558a). In the same way, the *cerastes* of the *Liber monstrorum* are horned serpents who,

non tam cornibus quam ore nocent et linguis, quae nimiam atrocitatem habere dicuntur,   (*Liber monstrorum* 3.15)[47]

and the hippopotami

quondam .CC. homines una hora in rapaces gurgitum uortices traxisse et crudelem in modum deuorasse narrantur.   (*Liber monstrorum* 2.9)[48]

While the *Liber monstrorum* often provides additional information (for example, size and colour), it, too, focuses on *ferocitas* 'fierceness'.[49] Its beasts are a similarly formidable range of foes in the natural world – only this time, luckily enough, safely distant in exotic locations. The author protests that many of these creatures are fictional,[50] but even as a fiction the text represents the natural world as hostile, and, most importantly, as capable of destroying human beings. The monsters' power to kill (and often eat) human beings is, in fact, the main source of interest in them;[51] the author states in the Prologue that he or she was asked for a description

---

[47] 'harm not only with their horns but also with their mouths and tongues, and are said to be exceedingly fierce'. Text is taken from Orchard, *Pride and Prodigies*; further references to this edition will be cited by section only.

[48] 'are said once to have dragged 200 men in one hour into violent whirlpools and devoured them fiercely'.

[49] E.g. *Lynces* II.v; common adjectives include *rapax* 'violent', *horribilis* 'horrible', *horrendus* 'fearful', *terribilis* 'terrible' and *dirissimus* 'very dreadful'.

[50]   'Quaedam tantum in ipsis mirabilibus uera esse creduntur, et sunt innumera-
        bilia quae si quis ad exploranda pennis uolare potuisset, et ita rumoroso
        sermone tamen ficta probaret, ubi nunc urbs aurea et gemmis aspersa litora
        dicuntur, ibi lapideam aut nullam urbem et scopulosa cerneret' (*Prologus*)
    'only some things among these wonders are believed to be true, and there are
    innumerable things which, if someone could fly with wings to investigate them, he
    would prove that, although they are invented by hearsay, where now there is said to be
    a golden city and shores strewn with gems, there he would perceive a stone city – or
    no city and rocky [shores]'.

[51] Orchard, *Pride and Prodigies*, p. 111.

of the creatures most terrifying to humanity.[52] The text as a whole thus not only demonstrates an interest in monsters and the wonderful variety of the world, but also, in its focus on the hostile and dangerous, depicts the human race as surrounded and often over-powered.

In the same way, illustrations accompanying some of the texts of the *Wonders of the East* make human 'weakness or defencelessness in contacts with these monstrous races' even more evident, as the usually over-sized monsters dominate the human figures accompanying them and protrude out of the frames meant to contain them.[53] The adventures of Alexander described in *The Letter of Alexander to Aristotle* also reinforce the impression of danger; Alexander must almost always kill the animals he meets in order to proceed with his journey. His battle against two- and three-headed serpents is only one episode in a particularly long night:

Eodon þa wyrmas and scluncon wundorlice, wæron him þa breost upgewende and on ðæm hricge eodon, and a swa hie hit geforan gelice mid þæm scillum gelice mid ðe muþe ða eorþan sliton and tæron. Hæfdon hie þa wyrmas þrie slite tungan, and þonne hie eðedon þonne eode him of þy muðe mid þy oroþe swylce byrnende þecelle. Wæs þæra wyrma oroð and eþung swiðe deadberende and æterne, and for hiora þæm wolbeorendan oroðe monige men swulton. Wið þissum wyrmum we fuhton leng þonne ane tide þære nihte, and hie þa wyrmas acwealdon .XXX.tig monna þære fyrde and minra agenra þegna .XX.

(*Letter of Alexander to Aristotle* §18)[54]

---

[52] 'De occulto orbis terrarum situ interrogasti et si tanta monstrorum essent genera credenda quanta in abditis mundi partibus per deserta et Oceani insulas et in ultimorum montium latebris nutrita monstrantur, et praecipue de his tribus orbis terrae generibus respondere petebas quae maximum formidinis terrorem humano generi incutiunt, ut de monstruosis hominum partibus describerem et de ferarum horribilibus innumerosisque bestiarum formis et draconum dirissimis serpentiumque ac uiperarum generibus.' (*Prologus*)

'You inquired about the secret location of the lands of the globe, and if so many races of monsters are to be believed, which are exhibited in the concealed territories of the world through the deserts and islands of the ocean and nourished in the recesses of the highest mountains; and you were seeking principally that it be answered concerning the three races of the land of the earth which strike the greatest terror of a horror in the human race, so that I should describe the monstrous births of men, and the horrible and numerous forms of wild beasts, and the most dreadful races of dragons and serpents and vipers'.

[53] Friedman, 'The Marvels-of-the-East Tradition', p. 334.

[54] 'Then the serpents came slinking strangely. Their bellies were upward and they moved on their backs, and they always rent and tore the earth before them with their scales

33

Although Alexander always triumphs over the natural world, he needs an army to do it, and many individuals lose their lives in the process. It is only when acting collectively, within the structures of society, that the human race can hope to stand against the natural world.

This idea of forming and living in societies, although in no way original to Anglo-Saxon thinkers, is an important issue for defining humanity.[55] In the *Wonders of the East*,[56] for example, there are several human-like creatures. The author carefully distinguishes many of them from humanity by ascribing to them animal heads or limbs[57] or radically non-human features;[58] unusual colour,[59] hairiness,[60] fiery breath[61] and large size[62] also serve to divide the monstrous races from the human. The concluding proofs of strangeness, of distinction from humanity, however, are often statements about their 'social' practices. While hostility is human enough, cannibalism is obviously an antisocial type of behaviour,

and with their mouths. The serpents had triple-split tongues, and when they breathed the breath came out of their mouths like a burning torch. The serpents' breath and breathing were very deadly and poisonous, and many men died because of their pernicious breath. We fought with these serpents for longer than an hour that night, and the serpents killed thirty men from the army and twenty of my own thegns.' Text is taken from Orchard, *Pride and Prodigies*, p. 236. I have expanded abbreviations for the word 'and'.

[55] The representation of the natural world also contributes to the defining of human society; see below, pp. 53–88.

[56] Text is taken from Orchard, *Pride and Prodigies*, pp. 184–202; references will be cited by section number only.

[57] E.g. *hi habbað olfenda fet and eoferes teð* 'they have camel's feet and boar's teeth' (§27), or *longe sceancan swa fugelas* 'long legs like birds' (§17), or *horses manan and eoferes tucxas and hunda heafda* 'horse's manes and boar's tusks and dog's heads' (§7).

[58] E.g. *tu neb on anum heafde* 'two noses on one head' (§11), or *earan swa fann* 'ears like fans' (§21), or *butan heafdum, ... on heora breostum heora eagan and muð* 'without heads, their eyes and mouths on their chests' (§15).

[59] E.g. the *sigelwara* 'Ethiopians', who are *sweartes hiwes on ansyne* 'dark-coloured on their faces' (§32); others' bodies have *marmorstanes hwitnysse* 'the whiteness of marble' (§27); some are even *on preosellices hiwes* 'tri-coloured' (§12).

[60] E.g. some have *beardas oþ cneow side and feax oð helan* 'beards down to their knees and hair to their heels' (§8).

[61] E.g. the breath of the Cynocephali *byð swylce fyres lig* 'is like a fiery flame' (§7).

[62] E.g. the *Hostes* have *fet and sceancan twelf fota lange, sidan mid breostum seofon fota lange* 'feet and legs that are twelve feet long, sides and chests that are seven feet long' (§13).

and one commonly attributed to the monstrous races;[63] eating raw fish or flesh is also noted,[64] as is giving away women[65] and fleeing from human contact.[66] In illustrations, they are often depicted nude. One could conclude, then, that for the Anglo-Saxons (and their sources) evidence of humanity resided in physical congruence to their own appearance, diet, diplomatic relations and clothing.[67] It would be interesting to pursue these 'signs' of humanity further, but for the present investigation it is more important to note that clear distinctions between the human and non-human were sought and asserted, even though the very existence of the monstrous races raised the question of intermediaries between them. The monstrous races rarely mix with humans; they tend either to eat them or flee. The careful distinction is not unusual; in fact, it is a characteristic found in much later literature.[68] In Anglo-Saxon literature, however, the distinction between humanity and the natural world involved not so much the assertion of human superiority (as in Elizabethan writing),[69] but rather the recognition of human inferiority to nature's power. Even when the monstrous races flee, they are larger and faster than human beings, and the ones that do not flee can be extremely dangerous.[70]

---

[63] E.g. *swa hwylcne mann swa hi gefoð, þonne fretað hi hine* 'whichever man they capture, they devour' (§13).

[64] E.g. *be hreawan fisceon {Homodubii} libbað and þa etaþ* 'the Doubtfully-Men live on and eat raw fish' (§8); others *be hreawan flæsce and be hunige lifigeað* 'live on raw flesh and honey' (§28).

[65] *Gyf hwylc mann to him cymeð þonne gyfað hi him wif ær hi hine onweg lætan* 'if anyone comes to them, they give him a woman before they let him go away' (§30).

[66] E.g. *gif hi hwylcne man on ðam landum ongitað oððe geseoþ oððe him hwylc folligende bið, þonne feorriað hi and fleoð, and blode þæt hi swætað* 'if they perceive or see anyone on the land or if someone is following them, they flee far away and sweat blood' (§12).

[67] Friedman, 'The Marvels-of-the-East Tradition', p. 322.

[68] Thomas, *Man in the Natural World*, pp. 30–6.

[69] *Ibid.*, pp. 28–9; see discussion above, pp. 10–11.

[70] The careful distinctions between human and non-human that are displayed in the depiction of the monstrous races may offer a useful perspective for the vexed question of whether or not Grendel is human. For further discussion of what Grendel is, see below, pp. 73–80, but note here that the basis of distinction is evidently not the species to which a creature or person belongs; the human characteristics ascribed to Grendel and the monstrous races may indicate that they are *homo sapiens*, but these in themselves do not grant human status.

NEGATION AND POWER

The division between the human and the non-human defines humanity; it characterises human nature through negation. In Old English poetry this defining negativity is characteristic not only of quasi-humans but of the natural world in general. For example, the Seafarer contrasts the sound of the ocean and the song of the sea birds with what he would have preferred, the pleasure, mead-drinking, laughter and company of men in the hall:[71]

> Þær ic ne gehyrde   butan hlimman sæ,
> iscaldne wæg.   Hwilum ylfete song
> dyde ic me to gomene,   ganetes hleoþor
> ond huilpan sweg   fore hleahtor wera,
> mæw singende   fore medodrince.
> Stormas þær stanclifu beotan, þær him stearn oncwæð
> isigfeþera;   ful oft þæt earn bigeal,
> urigfeþra;   ne ænig hleomæga
> feasceaftig ferð   frefran meahte.   (*The Seafarer* 18–26)[72]

Any suspicion that the Seafarer finds the beauty of the natural landscape an inspiring replacement for human company[73] is eliminated by the last line, which specifies that he is 'miserable' and missing 'protecting kin'.

---

[71] Cf. G. Morgan, 'Essential Loss: Christianity and Alienation in the Anglo-Saxon Elegies', *In Geardagum* 11 (1990), 15–33; Magennis, *Images of Community*, pp. 96–7.

[72] 'There I heard nothing but the roaring sea, the ice-cold wave. Sometimes I took the swan's song as mirth, the gannet's laughter and the curlew's voice for men's laughter, the gull's singing for mead-drinking. There storms beat the stone-cliffs; there the tern, icy-feathered, protested to himself; often the dewy-feathered eagle screeched; no protecting kin could comfort the miserable heart.'

[73] It has been argued – wrongly, in my view – that he seeks the sea because he delights in it, because communing with wild, untamed nature puts him in touch with God. See C. A. Ireland, 'Some Analogues of the O.E. *Seafarer* from Hiberno-Latin Sources', *NM* 92 (1991), 1–14, at 7–8. The Seafarer, however, is never said to feel as Guthlac does about the birds that visit and sing to him:

> Swa þæt milde mod   wið moncynnes
> dreamum gedælde,   dryhtne þeowde,
> genom him to wildeorum wynne,   siþþan he þas woruld forhogde.
>
> (*Guthlac* 739–41)

'Thus that gentle mind separated himself from the joys of mankind, served the lord, took the wild beasts as a joy for himself, since he despised this world.' For further discussion of *Guthlac*, see below, pp. 124–8.

This reaction is in strong contrast with that of an Irish poet contemplating the sea.[74] Where the Old English poet is reminded by the cries of sea birds of the human society that he lacks, the Irish poet revels in 'the voice of wondrous birds'. Where the Old English poet sees threatening ocean storms beating against cliffs, the Irish poet sees a 'smooth strand of clear headlands, / no gloomy thing'. Even whales, which are dangerous monsters in Old English poems,[75] are seen by the Irish poet as the 'greatest of wonders'. Although both Old English and Irish poets can describe a self-imposed exile for the sake of being closer to God, their use of the natural world serves different ends. For the Old English poet, the representation of the natural world helps to create the context of helplessness and alienation that motivates the seeking of God. For the Irish poet, the representation of the natural world creates the context of wonder and joy that surrounds the seeking of God. Although one might be tempted to ascribe the differences to national temperament, it would be an oversimplification to reduce the Seafarer's description to nothing more than a characteristically gloomy outburst from one born of a gloomy race: Old English poets do know how to express joy.[76] They do not, however, use the representation of the natural world to do it.

This Old English poet's approach to the natural world may also be usefully contrasted[77] with that of a much later seafarer:

> Where rose the mountains, there to him were friends;
> Where roll'd the ocean, thereon was his home;
> Where a blue sky, and glowing clime, extends,
> He has the passion and the power to roam;
> The desert, forest, cavern, breaker's foam,
> Were unto him companionship; they spake
> A mutual language, clearer than the tome

---

[74] See poem VI in Jackson, *Early Celtic Nature Poetry*, p. 9.

[75] For further discussion of whales, see below, pp. 131 and 191–2.

[76] Joy is normally associated with hall life; even heavenly joy tends to be expressed in terms of the hall (see, for example, *Genesis* 78–81 and *The Dream of the Rood* 139b–41). For discussion of the joy associated with feasting in the hall, see Magennis, *Images of Community*, pp. 42–8 and 62–73.

[77] Cf., however, the comparison of *The Seafarer* and *Childe Harold* in Pons, *Le thème et le sentiment de la nature*, where it is argued that Byron merely develops the ideas expressed in the Old English poem (p. 110).

Of his land's tongue, which he would oft forsake
For Nature's pages glass'd by sunbeams on the lake.

(Byron, *Childe Harold*, III.xiii)

For Old English poets, mountains, ocean, forests and caves do not connote the delightful escape that they do for Byron, but rather fear and emptiness;[78] the overwhelming presence of the natural world represents an appalling human absence.[79] Thus mountains appear dark and oppressive,[80] the ocean inspires fear not exhilaration,[81] forests are empty of joy[82] and caves are full of weeping not contemplation.[83] Although for Byron, too, nature and humanity were often antithetical to each other, in Old English poetry it is the human side which is positive. In the same way, the negative terms used in *Beowulf* to describe Grendel suggest opposition to and negation of human expectation or hope: the race of Cain to which he belongs is not a positive, fruitful line (*tudor*) but *untydras* 'evil progeny' (111a); his eyes are like an *unfæger* 'un-fair' (727b) light; his nails are *unheoru* 'not gentle' (987a); he murders *unwearnum* 'without hindrance' (741b) and *unmurnlice* 'unmourningly' (449b); and he himself is a creature of *unhælo* 'unsoundness' (120b).[84] What Grendel is not defines what the human is or should be.

The Anglo-Saxons inherited authoritative sources, however, that did

---

[78] This was true of most pre-Romantic writers. See M. H. Nicolson, *Mountain Gloom and Mountain Glory* (Ithaca, NY, 1959), p. 17; H. White, 'The Forms of Wildness: Archaeology of an Idea', in *The Wild Man Within: An Image in Western Thought from the Renaissance to Romanticism*, ed. E. Dudley and M. E. Novak (Pittsburgh, 1972), pp. 3–38, at 6–7. For more specific discussion, see Friedman, *Monstrous Races*, pp. 148–53.

[79] The Seafarer sees the vision of the storm striking against the cliff, for example, as representing the central truth of human life – that it is 'a precarious clinging to the edge of the abyss of extinction'; 'such a vision is both desired because it is true and feared because it is unbearable'. Irving, 'Image and Meaning', p. 158.

[80] See, for example, *The Wife's Lament* 30 and *Beowulf* 1356b–7 and 1409–11. For further discussion of these passages, see below, pp. 87 and 44. Note also that *The Phoenix* (21–5, quoted below, pp. 61–2) praises the earthly paradise for being devoid of mountains and cliffs of any kind (the poem emphasises its absolute exclusion by using seven different terms for such elevations).

[81] See, for example, *The Rune Poem*: *sæypa swyþe bregaþ* 'sea-waves terrify exceedingly' (65).

[82] See, for example, the *wynleas wudu* in *Beowulf* (1416a).

[83] See *The Wife's Lament* 27–41. Cf., however, Magennis's discussion of the forest as retreat in *Images of Community*, pp. 130–1, n. 66.

[84] Cf. Irving, *A Reading of 'Beowulf'*, p. 15.

not confirm this pessimistic view of humanity's relation to the natural world. Virgil's *Georgics*,[85] for example, might have supplied a different conceptual framework for approaching the natural world, one consistent with the physically challenging conditions that the Anglo-Saxons experienced and with the biblical account of the human race's relation to the natural world. In the Old English metrical *Genesis* God tells Adam:

> þu winnan scealt
> and on eorðan þe   þine andlifne
> selfa geræcan,   wegan swatig hleor,
> þinne hlaf etan,   þenden þu her leofast.   *(Genesis 932b–5)*[86]

Following the Fall, the human race must struggle continually against nature to survive. In the *Georgics* this necessity leads the poet to exhort man to subdue nature, to force it to yield its fruits: *exercetque frequens tellurem atque imperat aruis* '(the farmer) constantly disciplines the earth and commands the fields' *(Georgics* I.99). While disasters and set-backs are anticipated, human labour will prevail and nature will be conquered – the only uncertainty lies in the disruptions caused by human conflicts.[87] Presumably the same indomitable will was required of Anglo-Saxon agriculture in order to ensure a continuing food supply, but it does not penetrate the representation of the natural world in the clerically and heroically dominated poems that survive; the focus remains on the power of the natural world, not the power of humanity to resist or overcome it. Even Latin writers like Aldhelm, the Anglo-Saxon who knew Virgil best, add to the patristic sources of his *De virginitate* an 'unmistakably Anglo-

---

[85] Bede, Wulfstan of Winchester and Aldhelm, at least, were well-read in Virgil. For Bede, see M. L. W. Laistner, 'Bede as Classical and Patristic Scholar', *Transactions of the Royal Historical Society* 4th ser. 16 (1933), 69–94; for Wulfstan, see M. Lapidge, 'Æthelwold as Scholar and Teacher', in his *Anglo-Latin Literature*, pp. 183–223, at 206; for Aldhelm, see the detailed notes by Ehwald in MGH AA 15. Aldhelm quotes specifically from the *Georgics* in his riddle on the swallow (*XLVII: Hirundo*).

[86] 'You must struggle and gain your sustenance on the earth [for] yourself, bear a sweaty face [in order to] eat your bread, for as long as you live here.'

[87] Book II, at least, offers this positive view; the poem as a whole can be seen to offer a very ambiguous if not pessimistic view of the world. See A. J. Boyle, '*In Medio Caesar*: Paradox and Politics in Virgil's *Georgics*', in *Virgil's Ascraean Song: Ramus Essays on the Georgics*, ed. A. J. Boyle (Berwick, Australia, 1979), pp. 65–86; M. C. J. Putnam, *Virgil's Poem of the Earth: Studies in the Georgics* (Princeton, NJ, 1979), pp. 82–164.

Saxon' sense of the confrontation between human beings and the physical, monstrous power of the natural world.[88] In the same way, the awe-inspiring storm in Exeter Book *Riddle 3*[89] and the fens and cliffs described in *Beowulf* do not appear as stubborn but manageable obstacles to human domination of the landscape; they are not susceptible to human power at all. If the *Georgics* voices – however doubtfully – the Augustan ideal of control and order, most Old English poems contain something very different: a perception of human powerlessness.

One can also examine the depiction of human powerlessness in the Anglo-Saxon representation of the natural world in terms of the dominant ideology, Christianity. The attitude toward the physical discomfort endured by the Seafarer, for example, may be related to the idea that this world is wholly evil,[90] a tool of the devil that tests the faithful and must be endured and never trusted, even, or especially, when it appears pleasant:

> Bearwas blosmum nimað,   byrig fægriað,
> wongas wlitigiað,   woruld onetteð;
> ealle þa gemoniað   modes fusne

---

[88] Clemoes, *Interactions of Thought and Language*, pp. 20–2. Note *Georgics* III, however, where the natural world – a place full of snakes and ghastly diseases – appears similarly monstrous.

[89] This riddle is probably part of one large riddle composed of those designated in ASPR as Exeter Book *Riddles 1, 2* and *3*. For discussion of the divisions of these poems, see *Old English Riddles*, ed. Williamson, pp. 127–33; J. J. Campbell, 'A Certain Power', *Neophil* 59 (1975), 128–38; and Lapidge, 'Stoic Cosmology', p. 25. For convenience I retain the numbering of ASPR. For discussion of this riddle, see below, pp. 129–30, 133, 168–9 and 176.

[90] The idea of the world being evil was probably inherited ultimately from gnostic theories that the world was created not by God but by the fallen angels. Augustine accuses Origen of holding such beliefs (*De civitate Dei* XI.xxiii, in *Sancti Aurelii Augustini*, ed. Welldon); J. Le Goff indicates that medieval writers absorbed gnostic influence through their reading of the Apocrypha (*The Medieval Imagination*, trans. A. Goldhammer (Chicago, 1988), p. 43). For a summary of some gnostic tenets and a discussion of the 'Soul Journey', in which the soul faces an obstacle course of hostile entities trying to prevent its escape from the prison of the world, see M. W. Bloomfield, *The Seven Deadly Sins: An Introduction to the History of a Religious Concept, with Special Reference to Medieval English Literature* (East Lansing, MI, 1952), pp. 11 and 16. See also R. M. Grant, *Gnosticism and Early Christianity* (New York, 1959), pp. 15–40; H. Jonas, *The Gnostic Religion: The Message of the Alien God and the Beginnings of Christianity*, 2nd ed. (London, 1992).

sefan to siþe, þam þe swa þenceð
on flodwegas feor gewitan.
Swylce geac monað geomran reorde,
singeð sumeres weard, sorge beodeð
bitter in breosthord. Þæt se beorn ne wat,
esteadig secg, hwæt þa sume dreogað
þe þa wræclastas widost lecgað.   *(The Seafarer* 48–57)[91]

Again, although this description of summer shares similarities with both Irish and Welsh poems, the purpose of the description in *The Seafarer* is different from that in both Irish and Welsh. In Irish poems a landscape teeming with life tends to inspire a poet to praise and linger over its beauty.[92] Some Welsh poems echo this joy that the season brings to human beings,[93] but others contrast the growth and life in the natural world with the speaker's gloomy mood, much as the Seafarer does.[94] In fact, at least one Welsh poem, *Kintevin*, appears remarkably close to *The Seafarer* in its imagery, tone and even its sequence of ideas[95] as it moves from the beauty of May, to the song of the cuckoo, to the speaker's sadness over the loss of kinsmen, to travel over land and sea, to exile for God's sake, to facing God's throne.

Yet even this poem seems different from the Old English poem in its employment of the natural world. The situations of the speakers are identical, their solutions to the problem of lost kinsmen are identical, but where the Welsh poet explains that the grief apparently summoned by the cuckoo's song actually derives from the death of kinsmen, the Old English poet provides no explanation for the sorrow that his description of the natural world inspires.[96] Nevertheless, it is this landscape, whether

---

[91] 'The groves take bloom, the town grows fair, the fields brighten, the world hastens; all this exhorts the eager thought of the mind to the journey, of him who thinks to travel far on the waterways. Likewise the cuckoo, summer's guardian, exhorts [him], sings with a sad voice, proclaims bitter sorrow in the heart. The wealth-blessed man does not know what some endure who journey the paths of exile most widely.'

[92] See, for example, *Early Irish Lyrics Eighth to Twelfth Century*, ed. G. Murphy (Oxford, 1956), poems 43 and 52, at pp. 112–13 and 156–9; *Golden Treasury*, ed. Greene and O'Connor, poem 32, pp. 137–9.

[93] See, for example, *Early Celtic Nature Poetry*, ed. Jackson, pp. 73–4.

[94] *Ibid.*, pp. 53–6, for example.

[95] Cf. Henry, *Early English and Celtic Lyric*, pp. 67–9.

[96] Various critics have attempted to explain this sorrow by drawing attention to similar imagery in homilies on the Apocalypse. See J. E. Cross, 'On the Allegory in *The*

uncharacteristically amenable or characteristically fleeting like all worldly goods, that drives the Seafarer to pursue the harsh *mereflod* 'sea' (59b) in his mind. This vision of spring or summer[97] must be interpreted in the context of the harsh, wintry weather which dominates the beginning of the poem, especially since the Seafarer explicitly chooses the latter. The man for whom *on foldan fægrost limpeð* 'things happen most pleasantly on the earth' (13) is ignorant; he emphatically *ne wat* 'does not know' (12b and 55b), for a pleasant natural world does not accurately represent the higher reality in which the Seafarer believes; it may even obstruct knowledge of that reality.[98]

The Welsh poem does not contain these two contrasting visions of the natural world. More important, it does not use the natural world to reflect the condition of the human speaker.[99] Although the song of the cuckoo triggers the memory of lost kin, the activity of the natural world is shown to be almost irrelevant to the speaker's state; at best it provides a failed consolation, a beauty and joy far inferior to that gained from God.[100] *The Seafarer*, on the other hand, not only explicitly rejects such fair weather as irrelevant but also provides a representation of the natural world that accurately reflects the human condition: the state of humanity is represented by the miserable endurance of hostile weather, churning seas and indifferent wildlife described in the beginning of the poem (1–26). The Old English poet makes the connection between the speaker's

---

Seafarer – Illustrative Notes', *MÆ* 28 (1959), 104–5; G. V. Smithers, 'The Meaning of *The Seafarer* and *The Wanderer* (cont.)', *MÆ* 28 (1959), 1–22, at 7; R. F. Leslie, 'The Meaning and Structure of *The Seafarer*', in *The Old English Elegies: New Essays in Criticism and Research*, ed. M. Green (Rutherford, NJ, 1983), p. 106; N. F. Blake, '"The Seafarer", lines 48–49', *N&Q* 207 (1962), 163–4.

[97] For discussion of the Anglo-Saxons' division of the seasons, see E. R. Anderson, 'Seasons of the Year in Old English Language and in Old English Literature', *ASE* 26 (1997), 231–63. Cf. also my discussion in 'The Seasons in Old English Poetry', in *La ronde des saisons: les saisons dans la littérature et la société anglaises au moyen âge*, ed. L. Carruthers, Cultures et civilisations médiévales XVI (Paris, 1998), 37–49.

[98] Irving, 'Image and Meaning', p. 158.

[99] Note also that the Icelander Egill Stallagrímsson's *Sonatorrek* explores the feelings of one who has lost his kin, but it does not describe the natural world as an oppressive, isolating force – even though the sea is primarily responsible for his loss. See Turville-Petre, *Scaldic Poetry*, pp. 31–9.

[100] Egill's *Sonatorrek* provides another contrast in this regard, as the consolation found by the speaker comes from poetry, not from God or the natural world. See *ibid.*, p. 40.

physical state and his spiritual reality explicit; because he has *wræclastas widost lecgað* 'most widely travelled the paths of exile' (57) and suffered (*dreogan* (56a)) the attacks of the natural world, he knows

> þæt bið eorla gehwam   æftercweþendra
> lof lifgendra   lastworda betst,
> þæt he gewyrce,   ær he on weg scyle,
> fremum on foldan   wið feonda niþ,
> deorum dædum   deofle togeanes.   (*The Seafarer* 72–6)[101]

Through the depiction of the natural world, the state of the human race on earth reveals itself to be a state of perpetual siege. Passive endurance against the natural world is thus transformed into, and interpreted as, active performance of heroism against the devil.

'DEMONIC' ANTAGONISM

This interpretation seems to suggest an equivalence between the natural world and the devil – or, at least, that the natural world serves under his power.[102] Yet *The Seafarer* never states that the world is evil,[103] never hints that the wind, hail, sea and birds harbour a particular intent to harm the subject of the poem. Nor does it mention demonic forces in connection with any aspect of the natural world; the moral concept of the devil appears in its own 'environment', punctuated and separated from the description of the natural world by gnomic utterances (66b–71)[104] and followed inevitably by death, the Last Judgement and heaven. Other

---

[101] 'Therefore the best of last words for every man is the praise of the living saying afterwards that he gained advantage on the earth against the hostility of his enemies before he had to go away, [performed] brave deeds against the devil'.

[102] Satan traditionally claims power over the world; see *Christ and Satan*, for example, where he offers Christ power over *folc and foldan* 'people and lands' (685a).

[103] Likewise, although many critics have discussed *Beowulf* in terms of conflict between good and evil, 'No such categorical master terms...are used in the poem, but a varied range of epithets that we cannot simply boil down to ethical essences.' Duncan, 'Epitaphs for Æglæcan', p. 112.

[104] Gnomic declarations constitute one of the techniques used in Old English poems to frame individual sections or 'movements'. See Pasternack, *Textuality of Old English Poetry*, p. 37, n. 15. Cf. also C. B. Hieatt, 'On Envelope Patterns (Ancient and – Relatively – Modern) and Nonce Formulas', in *Comparative Research on Oral Traditions: A Memorial for Milman Parry*, ed. J. M. Foley (Columbus, OH, 1987), pp. 245–58.

Old English poems also fail to make the connection between a hostile natural world and the devil, even in the places where one might expect it[105] – in Guthlac's trials, for example, where the swirling attacks of the demons (390–3, for example) could easily have been accompanied by descriptions of natural phenomena like hail, wind and wolves, especially as the ordeals take place in the context of the fens, a place that, as *Beowulf* testifies, can contain terrors ranging from *wynleas wudu* 'joyless woods' (1416a) to wolves (presumably in the *wulfhleoþu* 'wolf-hills' (1358a)) to Grendel and his mother.[106] Guthlac, however, does not appear to suffer from his physical environment. When the demons come to see *hwæþre him þæs wonges wyn sweðrade* 'whether the joy of that place had dwindled for him' (*Guthlac* 352) after their assaults, they find that *wæs him botles neod* 'his home was a pleasure to him' (329a), rather like the forests and coastlands that often inspired Irish poets.[107] If Guthlac had been comemorated by an Irish poet, it appears likely that the poem would have contained the kind of detailed praise of birds and plants expressed in 'Manchán's Wish'.[108] *Guthlac*, however, contains almost no description of the land, water, vegetation and animal life that help to make the saint's home so pleasant for him.[109] Old English poets appear not to have been inspired to use the representation of the natural world in the same way as Irish poets, even when describing similar circumstances of comfort and joy. Instead, Old English poets reserve the representation of the natural world for use as a force to oppose and test their saints' resolve and powers of resistance.

Thus in *Andreas* the saint's suffering includes both demonic (or demonic-inspired) and environmental torments – the same misery of cold and hail depicted in *The Seafarer*, in fact:[110]

---

[105] There may be a connection between the natural world and the devil in *Solomon and Saturn II* 302–11. As there is a break in the manuscript at this point, however, the kind of connection posited is difficult to determine.

[106] *Maxims II* also suggests that a fen is a place one would naturally expect monsters (42b–3a).

[107] See, for example, *Early Irish Lyrics*, ed. Murphy, poems 2, 44 and 46, at pp. 4, 112–17 and 122–37.

[108] *Ibid.*, poem 12, at pp. 28–31.

[109] For further discussion of *Guthlac*, see below, pp. 124–8.

[110] The similarities between this and other descriptions of winter have led some critics to describe them as traditional 'set pieces' – that is, as decorative rather than functional.

Snaw eorðan band
wintergeworpum.   Weder coledon
heardum hægelscurum,   swylce hrim ond forst,
hare hildstapan,   hæleða eðel
lucon, leoda gesetu.   Land wæron freorig
cealdum cylegicelum,   clang wæteres þrym
ofer eastreamas,   is brycgade
blæce brimrade.   Bliðheort wunode
eorl unforcuð,   elnes gemyndig,
þrist ond þrohtheard   in þreanedum
wintercealdan niht.   (*Andreas* 1255b–65a)[111]

Soon afterwards the devil adds his taunts to the onslaughts of the weather
and human torturers to complete his assault of Andreas. The saint's
resolute resistance to all the devil's efforts, including the Mermedonian
torments that come at the devil's instigation, fulfils the general genre
requirement that a saint's life provide a moral example, but even in this
context the hardship of the weather is not ascribed to the devil, and it
does not display any evil will; it is merely part of the catalogue of
heroically endured trials. The hostility ascribed to the natural world in
Old English poetry cannot be explained by reference to the Christian
framework of the struggle against the devil.

The ideas and images in these texts can, however, be seen to operate in
the same way as the representations of the natural world in Adam's
lament do: they provide the context that defines the human race. The
verbs used to describe the weather in the passage from *Andreas*, for
example, emphasise the power of nature to immobilise, to bind (1255b)
and lock (1259a) not only the river's motion but also human settlements
(1259a).[112] That is, they reflect the human race's inability to move and

---

See R. E. Diamond, 'Theme as Ornament in Anglo-Saxon Poetry', *PMLA* 76 (1961),
461–8, and Martin, 'Aspects of Winter', pp. 377–8.

[111] 'Snow bound the earth with blizzards. The storm grew cold with fierce showers of
hail; also rime and frost, hoary warriors, locked up the land of men, the people's
dwelling. The lands were frozen with cold icicles, the water's torrent diminished
throughout the rivers, [and] ice bridged the dark sea-road. The brave warrior waited,
blithe at heart, mindful of courage, bold and firmly enduring in affliction during the
winter-cold night.'

[112] For discussion of this and other instances of binding by winter, as well as Latin
sources for this 'stock means of amplifying the topic of winter', see Martin, 'Aspects
of Winter', pp. 378–85. Although Old English poets may have copied motifs from

act against the natural world. This is a serious issue in a literature that describes the heroic ideal (as well as dangerous opposing powers) as moving quickly.[113] Against the natural world the human race falls far short of its ideals; as in *The Seafarer*, the nearest equivalent of heroic action is passive endurance.[114] This depiction of human helplessness in the natural world is, of course, an extension of the depiction of Andreas's confinement, and Andreas fulfils the 'ideal' of heroic endurance to its fullest extent, remaining cheerfully steadfast despite nature's cold grip and his other bonds and wounds. His ability to endure, however, is presented as exceptional, not characteristic of human nature. The narrator exclaims:

> Hwæt, ic hwile nu   haliges lare,
> leoðgiddinga,   lof þæs þe worhte
> wordum wemde,   wyrd undyrne
> ofer min gemet.   Mycel is to secganne,
> langsum leornung,   þæt he in life adreag,
> eall æfter orde.   Þæt scell æglæwra
> mann on moldan   þonne ic me tælige
> findan on ferðe,   þæt fram fruman cunne
> eall þa earfeðo   þe he mid elne adreah,
> grimra guða.   (*Andreas* 1478–87a)[115]

The narrator's 'modesty' in this passage is a familiar rhetorical gesture,[116] but the subject chosen to exemplify the difficulty of his task is revealing:

Latin poets, their descriptions of winter conform to traditional uses of representations of the natural world in Old English poetry.

[113] For example, in *Beowulf* speed is associated with Grendel (724b and 740a), Grendel's mother (1294a, 1541a and 2117b), men obeying their lords (991a, 1914a and 1975a), warriors in battle (2968b and 2983a) and, of course, Beowulf himself (224b, 748b, 963a, 1310a and 1576b).

[114] Cf. also the agony endured by the Cross in *The Dream of the Rood*: 'he must now endure the hardest fate a hero can suffer: to be blocked completely from taking any action. Action is the natural mode of the hero's being and his essential definition.' Irving, 'Crucifixion Witnessed', p. 106.

[115] 'Listen, for a while now I have announced with words the story [and] songs of the holy one, whose praise I have performed, a deed clearly beyond my ability. It is much to say all that he endured in his life after its beginning, a long study. It must be a man on the earth wiser in mind than I account myself who knows from the beginning all the hardship of the grim battles that he suffered with courage.'

[116] See, for example, the poet's self-deprecation in Tibullus III.vii.1–17 (*Tibullus: Elegies,*

it is not the miracles but the endurance that is specifically identified as remarkable. Andreas's stalwart if passive resistance to both demonic and natural forces serves to identify him as a saint, much as Beowulf's exceptional feats in the natural world identify him as a hero;[117] both prevail, they say, because their *ellen deah* 'courage was good' (*Beowulf* 573b, *Andreas* 460b).[118] Likewise, just as Andreas's ability to endure is exceptional, his escape from confinement is due to exceptional circumstances: divine intervention overturns the reality of Andreas' human state, demonstrating divine power by reversing all the natural effects of Andreas's recent experience. This effectively frees him from the grip of nature as well as from that of the Mermedonians, and the miraculous nature of this act is emphasised by the flourish of the row of flowering trees that spring up from the saint's shed blood (1448–9).

EROSION

Elsewhere the human race characteristically suffers not only confinement but diminishment and destruction from the natural world. As in Adam's lament, the point is not what the natural world is like but what the human race is like in the face of the power of the natural world. Often the representation of the natural world echoes Adam's helpless despair, as it characterises the human race as doomed to a ceaseless but inevitably futile struggle against the encroachments of the natural world. When it lapses in its efforts, when *feormynd swefað, / þa ðe beadogriman bywan sceoldon* 'the polishers who should adorn the battle-mask sleep' (*Beowulf* 2256b–7), deterioration begins and the earth reclaims what had been wrestled from it, whether a *dryncfæt deore* 'precious drinking vessel' (*Beowulf* 2254a), cultivated land or a magnificent city:

> Wrætlic is þes wealstan, wyrde gebræcon;
> burgstede burston, brosnað enta geweorc.
> Hrofas sind gehrorene, hreorge torras,
> hrungeat berofen, hrim on lime,

ed. G. Lee, 3rd ed. (Leeds, 1990), p.86). Cf. also Whitman, 'Medieval Riddling', p. 183.

[117] See below, pp. 129–38.

[118] For discussion of the different meanings behind these almost identical phrases (*gif his ellen deah* in *Andreas* 460b and *þonne his ellen deah* in *Beowulf* 573b), see P. Cavill, '*Beowulf* and *Andreas*: Two Maxims', *Neophil* 77 (1993), 479–87.

> scearde scurbeorge   scorene, gedrorene,
> ældo undereotone.   Eorðgrap hafað
> waldend wyrhtan   forweorone, geleorene,
> heardgripe hrusan,   oð hund cnea
> werþeoda gewitan.   Oft þæs wag gebad
> ræghar ond readfah   rice æfter oþrum,
> ofstonden under stormum;   steap geap gedreas . . .
> wurdon hyra wigsteal   westen staþolas,
> brosnade burgsteall.   Betend crungon
> hergas to hrusan.   Forþon þas hofu dreorgiað,
> ond þæs teaforgeapa   tigelum sceadeð
> hrostbeages hrof.   (*The Ruin* 1–11 and 27–31a)[119]

Such contemplation of the human race's powerlessness often leads to an exhortation to follow the Christian God. After a description of the world in which the human race attempts to maintain itself and the things that it values, the speaker in *The Wanderer*, like Edwin's counsellor, concludes by turning to something beyond the present, embattled existence – the *frofor* 'comfort' and *fæstnung* 'security' (115) in heaven:

> þas stanhleoþu   stormas cnyssað,
> hrið hreosende   hrusan bindeð,
> wintres woma,   þonne won cymeð,
> nipeð nihtscua,   norþan onsendeð
> hreo hæglfare   hæleþum on andan.
> Eall is earfoðlic   eorþan rice,
> onwendeð wyrda gesceaft   weoruld under heofonum.
> Her bið feoh læne,   her bið freond læne,
> her bið mon læne,   her bið mæg læne,
> eal þis eorþan gesteal   idel weorþeð!
> Swa cwæð snottor on mode,   gesæt him sundor æt rune.

---

[119] 'This wall-stone is ornamented, broken down by fate; the city fell to pieces, the work of giants crumbles. The roofs have fallen in, the towers are in ruins, robbed of their gates; [there is] frost on the mortar, the protection against rain [the roof] is gashed, cleft, fallen in, eaten away underneath with age. The earth's grasp holds the governing creators, [who have] rotted, vanished, with the hard grip of the earth, while a hundred generations of people have gone. Often this wall, grey with lichen and red-stained, endured one kingdom after another, stood against the storms; [though] tall and broad, it fell . . . Their fortification became waste places, the city crumbled. The restorers, the troops, fell dead to the earth. Therefore these dwellings are dreary, and this wide, red, wooden-beamed roof sheds its tiles.'

48

Til biþ se þe his treowe gehealdeþ,   ne sceal næfre his torn to rycene
beorn of his breostum acyþan,   nemþe he ær þa bote cunne,
eorl mid elne gefremman.   Wel bið þam þe him are seceð,
frofre to fæder on heofonum,   þær us eal seo fæstnung stondeð.

(*The Wanderer* 101–15)[120]

This passage has often been interpreted as 'pathetic fallacy', with the natural environment responding to the Wanderer's gloomy state of mind.[121] To some extent it is worth considering and maintaining this possibility, for one cannot prove conclusively which came first in the poet's mind, the Wanderer's mood or the grim environment. As the analysis thus far has shown, however, the natural world in Old English poetry is rarely described as being in 'sympathy' with human interests, as it can be in Old Norse poetry;[122] here again it is probably more accurate to say that it is represented as standing in opposition to human interests – that it is at best indifferent to human suffering and at worst actively hostile. Thus, while lines 112–14a offer gnomic advice for *acting* according to the heroic ideal (*mid elne gefremman*), the representation of the natural world preceding them suggests that the human race is not equal to the task. The natural world strikes, binds, sends missiles; the human race does not act in response but merely is, and not for long either, since everything human is *læne* 'loaned', and the world hastens to return to its primeval emptiness, to *idel weorþan* (110b).

The idea of progressive deterioration – *þes middangeard* / *ealra dogra*

---

[120] 'The storms strike against the rocky cliffs, the attacking snowstorm binds the earth, the howling of winter. Then the darkness comes; the night-shade grows dark [and] sends a fierce hailstorm from the north in enmity against men. All is full of hardship in the kingdom of the earth; the decree of fate changes the world for the worse under the heavens. Here wealth is [only] loaned, here the friend is loaned, here the man is loaned, here the kinsman is loaned. This place of the earth will become completely empty! Thus spoke the one wise in his mind, sat apart at the council. Good is he who keeps his promise; nor shall a man ever reveal the suffering from his heart too quickly, unless he knows a remedy first, [and knows how to] perform it with courage. It will be well for him who seeks favour and comfort for himself from the father in heaven, where for us all security stands.'

[121] For discussion of 'pathetic fallacy', see Curtius, *European Literature*, pp. 92–4.

[122] See, for example, the brief lament that Hallsteinn Þengilsson made for his father, in which the land droops at hearing the news of the death, and Sigvatr Þórðarson's description of the cliff's change in mood following the death of St Ólafr (Turville-Petre, *Scaldic Poetry*, pp. 42 and 86).

gehwam dreoseð and fealleþ 'every day this world fails and decays' (62b–3) – can be related to Christian beliefs in the Ages of Man[123] and the moral degradation continuing since the Original Sin. Wulfstan refers to this belief in explanation of the Vikings' successful attacks on the English people:

Leofan men, gecnawað þæt soð is: ðeos worold is on ofste, and hit nealæcð þam ende, and þy hit is on worolde aa swa leng swa wyrse; and swa hit sceal nyde for folces synnan ær Antecristes tocyme yfelian swyþe, and huru hit wyrþ þænne egeslic and grimlic wide on worolde. Understandað eac georne þæt deofol þas þeode nu fela geara dwelode to swyþe, and þæt lytle getreowþa wæran mid mannum, þeah hy wel spæcan, and unrihta to fela ricsode on lande. And næs a fela manna þe smeade ymbe þa bote swa georne swa man scolde, ac dæghwamlice man ihte yfel æfter oðrum and unriht rærde and unlaga manege ealles to wide gynd ealle þas þeode. And we eac for þam habbað fela byrsta and bysmara gebiden. *(Sermo Lupi ad Anglos* 1–18)[124]

Although both Wulfstan and the poet of *The Wanderer* describe a world growing inevitably worse, the differences between their depictions of that world are striking. Wulfstan ascribes the present suffering to the unrighteous acts of the people. He and his audience can thus expect that an improvement in morality will lead to an improvement in their plight; as Wulfstan says, the people must genuinely earn that *hit sceal heonanforð godiende weorðan* 'it shall henceforth turn for the better' (*Sermo Lupi* 22–3). There is no mention of the natural world. In *The Wanderer*, where the

---

[123] For discussion of the implications of the idea of the Seven Ages of Man on medieval thought, see R. A. Peck, 'Number as Cosmic Language', in *By Things Seen*, ed. Jeffrey, pp. 47–80, at 66–75; for discussion of the subject more generally, see J. A. Burrow, *The Ages of Man: A Study in Medieval Writing and Thought* (Oxford, 1988).

[124] 'Beloved men, know what is true: this world is in haste, and it approaches its end, and things in this world always are the worse the longer [they last], and it must necessarily grow much worse before the coming of the Antichrist because of the people's sins, and indeed it will then be terrible and grim widely in the world. Understand thoroughly also that the devil has now for many years led this people astray too much, and that there has been little truth among men, though they spoke well, and injustice has ruled too many in the land. And there were not always many men who thought about a remedy as thoroughly as one should, and daily one has heaped up one evil after another and raised up injustice and many bad laws entirely too widely throughout the people. And we have also for that reason experienced many injuries and insults.' Text is taken from *The Homilies of Wulfstan*, ed. D. Bethurum (Oxford, 1957), p. 267.

representation of the natural world helps to define the human condition, there is no suggestion that human action can change the current deterioration. The poem is no more pessimistic about the state of Anglo-Saxon morality than the homily – in fact, the last part of the poem seems very optimistic in comparison with Wulfstan's diatribe against *mannslagan, mægslagan, mæsserbanan, myltestran, wiccan* and *wælcyrian* 'man-slayers, kinsmen-slayers, priest-slayers, harlots, wizards and witches' (*Sermo lupi* 160–6) and the endless population of intolerable sinners. The focus in the two passages is different, however: despite *The Wanderer*'s exhortation to turn to God, the poem reveals humanity's physical powerlessness rather than its moral weakness. It is not sinfulness but the threat to survival in the hostile physical environment that motivates the seeking of God, of divine *frofor* and *fæstnung*, in the end. The different focus of each text is reflected by the choice of representing the natural world in the one and not in the other. Representing the natural world signals a preoccupation with power and human powerlessness, whatever the particular context.

Even in the moral context of hell, a comparison with the natural world serves to emphasise not sinfulness but humanity's subjection to outside powers:

Forþan gif hwylc man bið on helle ane niht, þonne bið him leofre, gif he þanon mot, þæt he hangie siofon þusend wintra on þam lengestan treowe ufeweardum þe ofer sæ standeð on þam hyhstan sæclife and syn þa fet gebundene to ðam hehstan telgan and þæt heafod hangige ofdunrihte and þa fet uprihte, and him sige þæt blod ut þurh þone muð, and hine þonne gesece ælc þæra yfela þe æfre on helle sy, and hine ælc yð gesece mid þam hehstan þe seo sæ forðbringð, and þeah hine ælc tor gesece þe on eallum clyfum syndon, þonne wile he eall þis þrowian wið ðan þe he næfre eft helle ne gesece.

(Vercelli homily IX 122–30)[125]

---

[125] 'Therefore if any man should be in hell for one night, then he would rather, if he might [depart] from there, that he hang for seven thousand winters at the top of the tallest tree which stands over the sea on the highest seacliff, and that his feet be bound to the highest branch and that his head hang downwards and his feet upwards, and that it appear to him that blood [go] out through his mouth, and that each of the evils which are in hell afflict him then, and that each wave afflict him with the highest which the sea brings forth, and though all the rocks which are on all the cliffs afflict him, he will then endure all this so long as he never seek hell again.' Text is taken from *Vercelli Homilies*, ed. Scragg, p. 170. I have expanded abbreviations.

Although the use of prose in this text might have led to a different approach to the natural world, this description demonstrates once again that being helplessly exposed to the power of the natural world is the worst of torments – worthy of comparison to hell.[126] The representation of the natural world here is, of course, incidental; the homily does not attempt to assign any particular meaning to the natural world. Yet this brief prose passage sums up the issues directing the poetic representation of the natural world discussed in this chapter. First, this description does not attempt to reflect the real physical conditions experienced by the Anglo-Saxons. Second, it does not draw upon any discernible cosmological scheme or inherited philosophy of the natural world. Third, even in a discussion of hell, it does not ascribe any moral status to the waves and rocks that torment the human victim. Instead, in this and all the passages discussed thus far, the representation of the natural world reveals the human condition to be a state of subjection to forces beyond its control and endurance. The depiction of nature's power – however accurate, complex, original, traditional or derivative it might be – serves to reflect and point to humanity's powerlessness; nowhere is this more evident, perhaps, than in the comparison of hell's torments with exposure to the elements. Literal accuracy and fidelity to previous authorities do play a role in some of these representations of the natural world, but such issues are subordinated to the purpose of locating the human race in its place amidst external powers, of confining and thus defining humanity.

[126] Similar in effect is Blickling homily XVI, whose description of the sorrows of hell includes many of the features of Grendel's mere. For discussion of the relationship between the two homilies, the *Visio sancti Pauli* and *Beowulf*, see below, p. 60, n. 27.

3

Constructing society: outside and inside, powerlessness and control

While the representation of the natural world can be seen to reflect the Anglo-Saxons' pessimistic view of the human condition generally, the use of negative or reverse traits in the depiction of monstrous races points toward the more specific and antagonistic roles that the natural world can play in Old English poetry: creatures like Grendel are not merely mirror images but negative forces, not merely different but destructive. The threat posed by the natural world thus appears to demand defensive postures and actions, to necessitate the forming of groups and structures within which humanity can live comparatively safely. However, as discussed earlier, what appears as the cause is more accurately understood as the effect: the Anglo-Saxons' conception of human society and its fragility leads to the representation of the natural world as a threat. By examining the representation of the natural world, we can observe Old English poets defining the purpose, creation and maintenance of their society.[1]

Historians and archaeologists as well as literary critics have already gathered a great deal of information about Anglo-Saxon society – for example, about the heroic lord-thegn relationship that ideally formed the basis of society (according to literature, at least),[2] about the rise and fall of

[1] Cf. Niles, *'Beowulf': The Poem*, p. 226. This chapter was unfortunately completed before the publication of Magennis's *Images of Community*, which addresses the issue of defining society from another angle. I have incorporated references to this work as much as possible, especially where our different approaches have overlapped.

[2] See, for example, P. Wormald, 'Anglo-Saxon Society and its Literature', in *The Cambridge Companion to Old English Literature*, ed. Godden and Lapidge, pp. 1–22; K. O'Brien O'Keeffe, 'Heroic Values and Christian Ethics', in *The Cambridge Companion to Old English Literature*, ed. Godden and Lapidge, pp. 107–25; and Harris, 'Love and Death in the *Männerbund*'.

dynasties,[3] about settlement patterns,[4] about the emergence of a concept of the English nation,[5] about law codes and the developments in government caused by the technology of writing,[6] about the roles of the church[7] and about trade and the economy.[8] The representation of the natural world in Old English poetry does not contribute any new, concrete details to this evidence, but does offer another perspective from which to view what is known and what has been reconstructed. For example, the writer of *Maxims I* compares raging and calm seas with political interactions between peoples:

> Storm oft holm gebringeþ,
> geofen in grimmum sælum; onginnað grome fundian
> fealwe on feorran to londe, hwæþer he fæste stonde.
> Weallas him wiþre healdað, him biþ wind gemæne.
> Swa biþ sæ smilte,
> þonne hy wind ne weceð;
> swa beoþ þeoda geþwære, þonne hy geþingad habbað,
> gesittað him on gesundum þingum, ond þonne mid gesiþum healdaþ
> cene men gecynde rice.
>
> (*Maxims I* 50b–8a)[9]

---

[3] See, for example, F. M. Stenton, *Anglo-Saxon England*, 3rd ed. (Oxford, 1971), pp. 32–94, 202–75 and 320–93.

[4] See, for example, D. Hill, *An Atlas of Anglo-Saxon England* (Oxford, 1981) and J. Tait, *The Medieval English Borough: Studies on its Origins and Constitutional History* (Manchester, 1936).

[5] S. Fanning, 'Bede, Imperium, and the Bretwaldas', *Speculum* 66 (1991), 1–26; Wormald, 'Bede, the *Bretwaldas* and the Origins of the *Gens Anglorum*', pp. 100–5; E. John, '"Orbis Britanniae" and the Anglo-Saxon Kings', in his *Orbis Britanniae and Other Studies*, Studies in Early English History 4 (Leicester, 1966), 1–63, at 11–14; H. R. Loyn, *The Governance of Anglo-Saxon England, 500–1087*, The Governance of England 1 (London, 1984), 23–9 and 130.

[6] See, for example, Clanchy, *From Memory to Written Record*; Kelly, 'Anglo-Saxon Lay Society'; S. Keynes, 'Royal Government and the Written Word in Late Anglo-Saxon England', in *Uses of Literacy in Early Medieval Europe*, ed. McKitterick, pp. 226–57; P. Wormald, 'The Uses of Literacy in Anglo-Saxon England and its Neighbours', *Transactions of the Royal Historical Society* 5th ser. 27 (1977), 95–114.

[7] For the role that the church may have played in weakening the institution of slavery, for example, see D. A. E. Pelteret, *Slavery in Early Mediaeval England from the Reign of Alfred until the Twelfth Century*, Studies in Anglo-Saxon History 7 (Woodbridge, 1995), 255–6.

[8] See R. Hodges, *The Anglo-Saxon Achievement: Archaeology and the Beginnings of English Society* (Ithaca, NY, 1989).

[9] 'A storm often brings the sea, the ocean, into grim conditions; the grim, dark ones

Against waves whipped up by the wind stand walls; against the chaos of conflict stand treaties and sound (i.e. traditional or 'natural') governing. In both cases safety is the result of defensive structures. The depiction of social structures as bulwarks against destructive forces neither corroborates nor contradicts historical records of treaties like the Anglo-Danish treaty of 878, but it does supplement the facts still extant by providing an emotional context – that is, the passage in *Maxims I* suggests how agreements and rulers could be seen as a comforting and necessary defence against a political uncertainty as frightening and devastating as the ocean.[10] The natural world symbolises the forces – here human conflict – capable of destroying society.

The impression of impending chaos is not restricted to *Maxims I*: the crumbling walls in *The Ruin* and *The Wanderer* also bear witness to the need for structures that will stand firm in humanity's defence. The use of the natural world as a symbol in *Maxims I*, however, is not a constant or even common feature of Old English poetry;[11] unlike later medieval literature,[12] it does not favour allegories, does not construct visionary landscapes in which the images of the natural world possess specific referents.[13] In addition, while the natural world is represented always with reference to some human concern, it is unusual to see humanity or human society symbolised by the natural world, except, as in this case, when the aspect described is negative. Compare, for example, the description of fierce warriors as wolves in *The Battle of Maldon* (*wælwulfas* 'slaughter-wolves' (96a)) and the Old English *Genesis* (*hildewulfas* 'battle-

begin to hasten from afar toward the land, [to see] whether it will stand firm. The walls hold against them; on them the wind is subdued. Just as the sea is mild when the wind does not arouse it, so are the people harmonious when they have reconciled [themselves], [when they] rest themselves in safe circumstances, and when bold men hold the native realm with their companions.'

[10] This poetic image of risk and uncertainty is confirmed by the evidence of law codes – see J. Campbell, 'Early Anglo-Saxon Society According to Written Sources', in his *Essays in Anglo-Saxon History* (London, 1986), pp. 131–8; see also Campbell's discussion of the instability resulting from feuding and the struggle for power among *reges*, *subreguli*, *principes* and *duces*, in 'Bede's *Reges and Principes*', pp. 92–3.

[11] In fact the use of natural imagery in *Maxims I* has been seen as more characteristic of Welsh nature poetry. See Henry, *Early English and Celtic Lyric*, p. 132.

[12] See, for example, Alan of Lille's *De planctu naturae*. For further discussion of this text, see below, p. 204.

[13] P. Piehler, *The Visionary Landscape: A Study in Medieval Allegory* (London, 1971), p. 10.

wolves' (2051a)). *The Battle of Maldon* unambiguously assigns the negative, frightening traits associated with the natural world[14] to the Vikings, both reducing the attackers to a level below humanity[15] and elevating their power to that of the unconquerable natural world. The Old English *Genesis*, interestingly, links the virtuous Abraham and his loyal thegns with the same sub-human, superhuman power; violent force need not always be negative. In fact, according to the heroic ethic presented in literature and the historical evidence of internal struggles and Viking raids, the survival of Anglo-Saxon society depended upon it, and it is in this context that Abraham's band of warriors receives the characteristic, violent power of the natural world. At the same time, however, the power of violence is not easy to control – thus the concern expressed by the writer of *Maxims I*.[16]

The natural world's capacity for destruction renders it the ultimate model of uncontrollable power, and it thus can be used to represent the forces within society that threaten its existence, the disruptive internal forces that society must repress or at least channel in order to survive.[17] Grendel, for example, can be viewed in this way.[18] However, the natural world is more commonly represented as standing in opposition and contrast to human society, threatening it from the outside, rather than symbolising aspects of the inside, of human society itself. It appears as a backdrop against which society struggles to defend itself.[19] This apparent externality may also be deceptive, however, since the representation of the natural world as an external power may be a way of defining threats to

---

[14] It has also been argued that wolf-characteristics signal demonic allegiances: Satan is called *se awyrgda wulf* in *Christ I* (256a), and the evil king in *Daniel*, Nebuchadnezzar, may thus be linked to demonic powers through his *wulfheort* (116a, 135a and 246a). See G. D. Caie, 'The Old English *Daniel*: A Warning Against Pride', *ES* 59 (1978), 1–9 at 6, n. 17. Yet, as Nebuchadnezzar's later transformation into a beast in the wilderness indicates, his *wulfheort* may equally summon images from the natural world.

[15] Cf. pp. 34–5.

[16] And thus also the ambivalence by writers like Bede when discussing war – see J. E. Cross, 'The Ethic of War in Old English', in *England Before the Conquest*, ed. Clemoes and Hughes, pp. 269–82.

[17] Cf. Clemoes, *Interactions of Thought and Language*, p. 22; Magennis, *Images of Community*, p. 75.

[18] See below, p. 73, and cf. Berger and Leicester, 'Social Structure as Doom', pp. 41–5.

[19] Cf. Clemoes, *Interactions of Thought and Language*, p. 257.

society – a way of limiting and distancing them. Of course, the natural world *did* pose challenges for Anglo-Saxon society, and it could not help but be outside. As noted previously, however, the natural world that appears represented in Old English poetry is not an inevitable reflection of reality but rather a response to human issues: the natural world does not determine the nature of society. Instead, poets situate their society metaphorically within its grip and define their encircled society by stressing its separation from that which surrounds it.

CREATION

This definition by separation can perhaps be best illustrated by comparing the Old English rendition of the creation of the universe with Hrothgar's creation of Heorot, the centre of Danish society.[20] The similarities between these two acts have been frequently noted;[21] the comparison between Hrothgar and God both idealises the human king's achievement[22] and reveals human limitations. However, the role played by the natural world in these creations has not been fully considered. Both these accounts are myths of origins, literary creations that claim to look back to a time at which the essential nature of the structure in question came into being unqualified and uncorrupted, in order to provide a point for comparison with a later time.[23] Such accounts, deriving from the desire to anchor statements of 'truth' about the present, can reveal what a writer considers to be the central issues of his text, or, at least, their underlying assumptions. In the Old English poetic Creation and Hrothgar's creation of Heorot, the positive, constructive act involves the establishment of an enclosure within which light, order, value and safety prevail, and without which darkness, chaos and danger rage. In both cases the opposing forces define the constructions designed to withstand them.

The biblical account of Creation posits the separation of opposites as the initial creative act:

---

[20] Berger and Leicester, 'Social Structure as Doom', p. 37.

[21] See, for example, Hume, 'The Concept of the Hall', p. 74. On the other hand, the construction of Heorot has also been compared to the construction of the Tower of Babel – see Berger and Leicester, 'Social Structure as Doom', p. 38.

[22] Irving, *A Reading of 'Beowulf'*, p. 92.

[23] A. J. Frantzen, *The Desire for Origins: New Language, Old English, and Teaching the Tradition* (New Brunswick, NJ, 1990), p. 23.

In principio creavit Deus caelum et terram
terra autem erat inanis et vacua
et tenebrae super faciem abyssi
et spiritus Dei ferebatur super aquas
dixitque Deus
fiat lux et facta est lux
et vidit Deus lucem quod esset bona
et divisit lucem ac tenebras.   (Gen. I.1–4)[24]

The Old English poet reproduces the account of dividing without significant change:

Þa gesundrode   sigora waldend
ofer laguflode   leoht wið þeostrum,
sceade wið sciman.   (*Genesis* 126–8a)[25]

The Old English account of the original state of the universe, however, of the *terra ... inanis et vacua* and the *tenebrae super faciem abyssi*, contains some significant elaborations. In the beginning, the Old English poet says,

Ne wæs her þa giet   nymþe heolstersceado
wiht geworden,   ac þes wida grund
stod deop and dim,   drihtne fremde,
idel and unnyt.   On þone eagum wlat
stiðfrihþ cining,   and þa stowe beheold,
dreama lease,   geseah deorc gesweorc
semian sinnihte   sweart under roderum,
wonn and weste,   oðþæt þeos woruldgesceaft
þurh word gewearð   wuldorcyninges.

---

[24] 'In the beginning God created heaven and the earth. The earth moreover was empty and void, and [there were] shadows over the face of the abyss, and God's spirit was carried over the waters. God said, 'Let there be light', and light was made. And God saw that the light was good, and he divided light from darkness.' I cite from the Vulgate. The precise Latin version of the Bible used by the Old English poet of *Genesis* is unknown, but for discussion of which versions were available to the Anglo-Saxons, see P. G. Remley, 'The Latin Textual Basis of *Genesis A*', *ASE* 17 (1988), 163–89; Remley, *Old English Biblical Verse*, pp. 94–167; R. Marsden, *The Text of the Old Testament in Anglo-Saxon England*, CSASE 15 (Cambridge, 1995); A. Mirsky, 'On the Sources of the Anglo-Saxon *Genesis* and *Exodus*', *ES* 48 (1967), 385–97.

[25] 'Then the ruler of victories divided light from darkness, shade from shine, over the sea-flood.'

Her ærest gesceop   ece drihten,
helm eallwihta,   heofon and eorðan,
rodor arærde,   and þis rume land
gestaþelode   strangum mihtum,
frea ælmihtig.   Folde wæs þa gyta
græs ungrene;   garsecg þeahte
sweart synnihte,   side and wide,
wonne wægas.

(*Genesis* 103–19a)[26]

This uncreated world is not a void or neutral chaos. In fact, it has much in common with depictions of the natural world in poems like *The Wanderer*: the concealing darkness (*nihtscua* 'night-shadow' (104a)) and bleak hostility (*hæleþum on andan* 'in enmity against men' (105b)) that confront the Wanderer also confront the creator in the beginning. God looks upon an apparently pre-existing land that has from the beginning antagonistic power, a land that is *drihtne fremd* 'alien to the lord'. Like an uncultivated forest, this land is *rume* 'spacious' – it is a potentially rich resource – but it is still *græs ungrene* 'ungreen grass' – grass lacking any beneficial or pleasant qualities because not yet transformed from its original, natural state. Such an untransformed world is *dreama lease* 'devoid of joy' and *idel and unnyt* 'empty and useless'. Its negativity recalls the creation that occurred about seventy lines earlier as well: hell is described in similar terms, being, like the as yet uncreated world, *deop, dreama leas* 'deep, devoid of joy' (40a) and *synnihte beseald* 'covered in eternal night' (42a).

NEGATIVE LANDSCAPES

The similarities between the descriptions of the pre-Creation, the natural world, and hell do not suggest that the Anglo-Saxons thought of the natural world as hell, however unpleasant it appears in much of their

---

[26] 'Nothing existed except darkness; this wide ground stood deep and dark, hostile to the lord, empty and useless. The determined king looked on it with his eyes, beheld that place devoid of joy, and saw the dark cloud hanging in eternal night under the heavens, bleak and desolate, until this Creation was made through the word of the glorious king. Here the eternal lord, the protector of all creatures, the Lord Almighty, first made heaven and earth, raised up the sky, and established this spacious land with strong might. The land was still ungreen grass; the dark sea, the black waves, covered [it] far and wide in eternal night.'

poetry, but rather that the poets describing these three landscapes construct them in the same way.[27] All three stand in opposition to positive structures: the grim fury of the natural world in *The Wanderer* contrasts both with the happiness of the man immersed in his society and with the more stable society in heaven; the empty, painful darkness of hell and its joyless exiles stand juxtaposed with the troops of *dreamhæb-bendra* 'those possessed of joy' (*Genesis* 81b) who inhabit a *wuldres eðel* 'native land of glory' (83a) that is *beorht and geblædfæst* 'bright and securely prosperous' (89a) and *gifum growende* 'growing with gifts' (88a); and the dark, empty hostility of the pre-creation universe is eventually countered with the brightness, fullness and pleasantness of the created paradise. Although these negative landscapes are theologically distinct from each other, poetically they function so similarly that they are almost interchangeable as they contrast with and define positive creations. Paradise is thus devoid of not only the characteristics assigned to the negative pre-creation but also those ascribed to the contemporary natural world:

> Þa sceawode   scyppend ure
> his weorca wlite   and his wæstma blæd,
> niwra gesceafta.   Neorxnawong stod
> god and gastlic,   gifena gefylled
> fremum forðweardum.   Fægere leohte
> þæt liðe land   lago yrnende,

---

[27] Thus it is perhaps unsurprising to find the similarities between the depiction of hell in Blickling homily XVI and Grendel's mere in *Beowulf*, whatever the relationship between the two texts may be. For discussion of the possibility that either poet or homilist knew the other's work, see *The Blickling Homilies of the Tenth Century*, ed. R. Morris, EETS os 58, 63 and 73 (London, 1874–78; repr. as one volume, 1967), pp. vi–vii; C. Brown, '*Beowulf* and the *Blickling Homilies* and Some Textual Notes', *PMLA* 53 (1938), 905–16, at 908; *Beowulf with the Finnesburg Fragment*, ed. C. L. Wrenn, rev. edn. (London, 1958), p. 210; Chadwick, 'The Monsters and Beowulf'; P. Clemoes, 'Style as the Criterion for Dating the Composition of *Beowulf*', in *The Dating of Beowulf*, ed. Chase, pp. 173–85, at 181; R. L. Collins, 'Blickling Homily XVI and the Dating of *Beowulf*', in *Medieval Studies Conference Aachen 1983: Language and Literature*, ed. W.-D. Bald and H. Weinstock, Bamberger Beiträge zur englischen Sprachwissenschaft 15 (Frankfurt, 1984), 61–9. Cf. also the descriptions of hell in the *Visio sancti Pauli* and Vercelli homily IX; for discussion, see Wright, *Irish Tradition*, pp. 116–21. For a useful summary of these arguments, see Magennis, *Images of Community*, pp. 133–5.

> wylleburne.   Nalles wolcnu ða giet
> ofer rumne grund   regnas bæron,
> wann mid winde,   hwæðre wæstmum stod
> folde gefrætwod.   (*Genesis* 206–15a)[28]

Paradise is not only *wlite* 'bright' instead of *sweart* 'dark', *god and gastlic* 'good and holy' instead of *fremde* 'hostile' (105b) and heaven-like in its abundance of gifts instead of *idel and unnyt* 'empty and useless' (106a), but also rainless, instead of battered by precipitation like the world described in *The Wanderer* and *The Seafarer*. The absence of rain in Paradise is not a creation of the Old English poet, but it is not mentioned here to explain a theological point about the waters of the firmament or the source of Noah's flood. In fact, a similar lack of precipitation contributes to the description of the Phoenix's homeland, the earthly paradise:[29]

> Ne mæg þær ren ne snaw,
> ne forstes fnæst,   ne fyres blæst,
> ne hægles hryre,   ne hrimes dryre,
> ne sunnan hætu,   ne sincaldu,
> ne wearm weder,   ne winterscur
> wihte gewyrdan,   ac se wong seomað
> eadig ond onsund.   Is þæt æþele lond
> blostmum geblowen.   Beorgas þær ne muntas
> steape ne stondað,   ne stanclifu
> heah hlifiað,   swa her mid us,
> ne dene ne dalu   ne dunscrafu,
> hlæwas ne hlincas,   ne þær hleonað oo
> unsmeþes wiht,   ac se æþela feld
> wridað under wolcnum,   wynnum geblowen.
>   (*The Phoenix* 14b–27)[30]

---

[28] 'Then our creator looked upon the brightness of his works and the success of his productions, his new creations. Paradise stood, good and holy, filled with gifts and future benefits. Running water and springs beautifully watered that gracious land. No cloud then yet bore the rains over the broad earth, dark with wind, but the earth stood adorned with fruit.'

[29] Cf. Magennis, *Images of Community*, pp. 146–7.

[30] 'Neither rain, nor snow, nor blowing of frost, nor blast of fire, nor descent of hail, nor fall of hoar-frost, nor heat of the sun, nor perpetual cold, nor warm weather, nor wintry shower can destroy anything there, but the field remains [always] prosperous and perfect. That noble land is blooming with blossoms. Neither hills nor steep mountains stand there, nor do stony cliffs tower high, as they do here among us, nor does valley or

In both descriptions the negative traits of the natural world serve to characterise God's triumphant creation; paradise is defined not only by its riches and pleasures but by the absence of typical features of the natural world.

None of this is especially novel; the Bible contains contrasts between Paradise and the present world, and it hardly needs to be said that hell contrasts with heaven. The Old English poetic use of negative landscapes is worth mentioning in detail, however, because Creation, which in the Old English *Genesis* is more an act of transformation from dark, hostile uselessness to bright, safe fruitfulness than creation *ex nihilo*, acts as a model for human beings, especially kings. Like God, kings are imagined as builders of havens in the midst of hostility, transformers of chaos and darkness to order and light and protectors of their constructions, their societies, from the forces around them.[31] The natural world, with its links to other negative landscapes, remains the model and metaphor for those forces.

BUILDING HUMAN SOCIETY

The *Beowulf*-poet explicitly refers to the creation of the world in the process of describing Danish society (90b–98) and thus imports the divine[32] standard of power for comparison within the poem. In this case, the divine standard serves to define Hrothgar's society as a human ideal;[33] the poet depicts Hrothgar's creation of Heorot in terms that echo those of

---

gorge or hill-cave, mound or ridge, or anything rough lie there, but that noble field thrives under the clouds, blooming with delights.'

[31] Even a 'negative' king like *Daniel*'s Nebuchadnezzar is strongly identified in terms of his construction of a defensive *byrig* and his protection of that construction and his people; he is called *Babilone weard* 'guardian of Babylon' six times in the poem (104b, 117a, 167a, 448b, 460a and 487a). See R. E. Finnegan, 'The Old English *Daniel*: The King and His City', *NM* 85 (1984), 194–211, at 205.

[32] Although most critics assume that *se ælmihtiga* in this passage clearly indicates the Christian creator, Robinson argues that, within the poem, Hrothgar's scop may be referring to a specific Germanic god or perhaps 'whatever omnipotent one created the earth', even though the poet's audience would interpret the term with the benefit of their superior Christian perspective. See Robinson, *'Beowulf' and the Appositive Style*, pp. 34–7.

[33] Brennan, 'Hrothgar's Government', p. 6; Halverson, 'The World of *Beowulf*', p. 593; Irving, *A Reading of 'Beowulf'*, p. 90.

God's creation of the world in the Old English metrical *Genesis*. The *Beowulf*-poet says,

> Him on mod bearn,
> þæt healreced   hatan wolde,
> medoærn micel   men gewyrcean
> þonne yldo bearn   æfre gefrunon ...
> Ða ic wide gefrægn   weorc gebannan
> manigre mægþe   geond þisne middangeard,
> folcstede frætwan.   Him on fyrste gelomp,
> ædre mid yldum,   þæt hit wearð ealgearo,
> healærna mæst;   scop him Heort naman
> se þe his wordes geweald   wide hæfde.
> He beot ne aleh,   beagas dælde,
> sinc æt symle.   Sele hlifade
> heah ond horngeap.   (*Beowulf* 67b–70, 74–82a)[34]

Almost immediately after this glorious creation, the poet tells the story of God's creation of the world (90b–98). The inclusion of this story is suggestive, especially if its brief outline was meant to recall fuller accounts like that in the Old English metrical *Genesis*, where God's actions parallel Hrothgar's very closely:

> Heht þa lifes weard
> on mereflode   middum weorðan
> hyhtlic heofontimber.   Holmas dælde
> waldend ure   and geworhte þa
> roderas fæsten;   þæt se rica ahof
> up from eorðan   þurh his agen word,
> frea ælmihtig.   Flod wæs adæled
> under heahrodore   halgum mihtum,
> wæter of wætrum,   þam þe wuniað gyt
> under fæstenne folca hrofes.   (*Genesis* 144b–53)[35]

[34] 'It occurred to [Hrothgar] in his mind that he would command men to build a hall-building, a meadhall greater than the sons of men had ever heard of ... Then I heard far and wide that the work – to adorn the dwelling-place – was commanded of many people throughout this middle-earth. In time it happened that it was finished quickly among the people, the greatest of hall-buildings; he who exerted the power of his word widely created the name 'Hart' for it. He did not leave his boast unfulfilled: he shared out rings and treasure at the feast. The hall towered up, tall and wide-gabled.'

[35] 'Then the guardian of life commanded that a hope-filled, heavenly building be made in the midst of the sea-flood. Our ruler divided the seas and built there the stronghold of

Like God, Hrothgar first considers creation in his mind[36] after quelling his enemies (in God's case, the rebel angels; in Hrothgar's, neighbouring kingdoms); like God, Hrothgar can carry out his plan because of the power of his word. Both command a *timbred* 'timbered' structure to rise up, which both later adorn and fill with gifts.[37] These gleaming, beautiful structures tower over those dwelling securely within them. As is suggested by the close proximity of the accounts of Heorot's and the world's creation within *Beowulf* itself, Hrothgar's establishment of his kingdom is a re-enactment of God's establishment of his *eorðrice* 'kingdom of the earth' (*Genesis* 419b, 454b, 548a etc.) and the ideal human activity appears to be an imitation of God's initial assertion of order.[38]

It is possible that the Anglo-Saxons did view the Creation as a model for human undertakings; man was, after all, created in the image of God (Gen. I.26–7), especially in the image of God as Creator. It is more useful, however, to reverse the path of influence and assume that the actions and attributes of the Old English creator reflect Anglo-Saxon attitudes toward power and their position in the world – that they represent an appraisal of and response to their need for security.[39] It may be generally true that a people depicts its gods as ideal reflections of themselves;[40] certainly it is easy to see in the Old English portrayal of God an idealised portrait of an earthly lord – one like Hrothgar, who is blessed with *heresped* 'battle-victory' (*Beowulf* 64b) and who creates a beautiful, safe environment for his people. In fact, one can easily imagine an Old English poet creating for such a king a poem of praise parallel to *Cædmon's Hymn*, as J. B. Bessinger, Jr has done in this century:

the sky; the powerful one, the Lord Almighty, raised it up from the earth through his own word. The flood was divided by his holy might under the high sky, the water from the water, which remains still under the stronghold of the people's roof.'

[36] Cf. *Genesis* 92–3a: *Þa þeahtode þeoden ure / modgeþonce* 'Then our Lord thought in his mind's thoughts'.

[37] Cf. Bessinger, 'Homage to Cædmon', pp. 98–100.

[38] Halverson, 'The World of *Beowulf*', pp. 596–7. Cf. Magennis, *Images of Community*, p. 72.

[39] Cf. Magennis, *Images of Community*, p. 60.

[40] 'Any conception of a deity must consist more or less in a summation and symbolic presentation of ideals' (Skemp, 'Transformation of Scriptural Story', p. 456).

Nu sculon herian   *heall-ærnes* weard,
mann-dryhtnes meahta   and his mod-geþanc,
weorc *weorod-þeodnes*,   swa he wundra gehwæs,
eorla dryhten,   or astealde.
He ærest scop   ielda bearnum
Heorot to hrofe,   *helm scieldinga*;
þa *mæran heall*   *magu-dryhte* weard,
eorla dryhten   æfter teode –
firum *fold-bold*   *frea scieldinga*.[41]

Of course, the subject of the original Old English poem, God, though described in similar terms, is better because infinitely able to protect his thegns and achieve everlasting victory, as God does, for example, for his servants Abraham[42] and Andreas.[43] Such descriptions of God as defender are omnipresent; even in the act of Creation, before any creatures have been created, God is *helm eallwihta* 'protector of all creatures' (*Genesis*, 113a).

This depiction of God is not simply a quaint, poetic integration of Christian ideas into a secular art form, although it does exemplify Augustine's injunction in *De doctrina Christiana*[44] to absorb whatever is of use in pagan literature:

Philosophi autem qui vocantur, si qua forte vera et fidei nostrae accommodata dixerunt, maxime Platonici, non solum formidanda non sunt, sed ab eis etiam

---

[41] Bessinger, 'Homage to Cædmon', p. 91. 'Now we must praise the guardian of the hall-dwelling, the might of the lord and his thought, the work of the troop's prince, as he, the lord of men, established the beginning of each wonder. For the sons of men he, the protector of the Scyldings, first created Heorot as a roof; the guardian of the band of warriors, the lord of men, afterwards adorned the famous hall – the lord of the Scyldings [adorned] the house for men.' Italics indicate words not in *Cædmon's hymn*.

[42] Before his badly outnumbered attack on the Elamites, for example, Abraham states that God can easily grant success in battle; his faith is well founded, for, since *Him on fultum grap / heofonrices weard* 'heaven's guardian held him in his protection' (*Genesis* 2072b–3a), he puts the army to flight and gains much booty.

[43] God promises Andreas that no one can kill him without his permission (*Andreas* 1212–18) and that he will hold him in his *mundbyrde* 'protection' (1433a); eventually Andreas is delivered from captivity and torture and given a great victory over the Mermedonians.

[44] *De doctrina Christiana* is extant in a late-eleventh-century Anglo-Saxon manuscript. See Gneuss, 'Preliminary List', p. 45. For discussion of Anglo-Saxon knowledge of Augustine, see above, p. 26, n. 26.

tamquam ab iniustis possessoribus in usum nostrum vindicanda. Sicut enim Aegyptii non tantum idola habebant et onera gravia quae populus Israel detestaretur et fugeret, sed etiam vasa atque ornamenta de auro et de argento et vestem, quae ille populus exiens de Aegypto sibi potius tanquam ad usum meliorem clanculo vindicavit, non auctoritate propria, sed praecepto dei, ipsis Aegyptiis nescienter commodantibus ea quibus non bene utebantur: sic doctrinae omnes gentilium non solum simulata et superstitiosa figmenta gravesque sarcinas supervacanei laboris habent quae unusquisque sarcinas supervacanei laboris habent quae unusquisque nostrum duce Christo de societate gentilium exiens debet abominari atque devitare, sed etiam liberales disciplinas usui veritatis aptiores et quaedam morum praecepta utilissima continent, deque ipso uno deo colendo nonnulla vera inveniuntur apud eos.   (*De doctrina Christiana* II.40)[45]

Augustine refers primarily to using the wisdom discovered by the unbaptised for Christian ends, but using native poetic traditions to depict God in terms familiar to a newly converted audience has its own obvious benefits. Building an image of God within the pre-existing structures of heroic poetry also conforms to Gregory's advice to Abbot Mellitus to use native hallowed sites and occasions for Christian observances,[46] and poems like *The Dream of the Rood* show that the re-imagining of God

---

[45] 'Moreover, if the philosophers, especially those who are called Platonists, by chance should say things that are true and in accordance with our faith, not only are these things not to be feared but they are to be delivered into our use from [the philosophers] as if from unjust possessors. For, just as the Egyptians had not only idols and great burdens which the people of Israel detested and fled, but also utensils and ornaments and clothing of gold and silver, which that people, as they fled from Egypt, instead secretly delivered for a better use for themselves – not according to their own authority but by the command of God – things which were not well used by those Egyptians, who unknowingly supplied them: so all teachings of the races have not only feigned and superstitious fictions and heavy burdens of needless labour which each one of us, leaving the society of the races for [our] leader, Christ, must hate and shun, but they also contain honourable knowledge more apt for the use of truth and certain very useful precepts of behaviour, and some truths concerning worshipping the one God himself are found amongst them.' This simile became 'one of the great commonplaces of the Middle Ages', and the method of assimilating pagan literature became standard practice. See Evans, *'Paradise Lost' and the Genesis Tradition*, p. 108.

[46] See Bede, *Historia ecclesiastica* I.xxx (pp. 106–8). Many critics have noted this analogy between the conversion of shrines and poetic language to Christian use. For a summary of critical commentary, see D. H. Green, *The Carolingian Lord: Semantic Studies in Four Old High German Words: Balder, Frô, Truhtin, Hêrro* (Cambridge, 1965), pp. 289–91; for further discussion of words that had pagan associations and were transformed for Christian use, see Robinson, *'Beowulf' and the Appositive Style*, pp. 29–59.

through traditional heroic poetics produces aesthetically pleasing as well as potentially useful, evangelical results.[47] More important, however, this re-imagining of God reveals what the Anglo-Saxons valued and sought for themselves, for it describes God according to human ideals.

In depicting the original act of Creation, then, Old English poets create an idealised vision of power – a power that extends to all arenas but specifically dominates the physical world. This ideal, though unattainable, does not stand in isolation; it remains connected with the human activities from which it derives. It is also not limited to Old English poetry. In his commentary *In Genesim*, for example, Bede compares the creation of the universe to the human act of constructing a building – much like the Old English poetic vision of the universe as a structure with a timbered roof.[48] Bede says,

Nam humana fragilitas cum aliquid operatur, uerbi gratia cum domum aedificamus, in principio operis materiam preparamus et post hoc principium fodimus in altum; deinde immittimus lapides in fundamentum, deinde parietes augescentibus lapidum ordinibus apponimus; sicque paulatim ad perfectionem operis propositi proficiendo peruenimus. Deus autem cuius omnipotens manus est ad explendum onus suum, non eguit mora temporum . . .

(In Genesim I.i.8–15)[49]

As Bede's purpose is different from that of the *Beowulf*-poet, he stresses the contrast between human and divine power. God easily and immediately achieves that to which the human race aspires, sometimes in vain, through long labour: complete and permanent control over the physical world. In the Old English metrical *Genesis*, the importance and desirability of this control is stressed, for nature is shown to require an imposed order to counteract its essential character – its potentially antagonistic power. In the same way, contending with the natural world becomes a pressing issue in *Beowulf* when Grendel arrives. The conspicuous proximity of God's

[47] For further discussion of *The Dream of the Rood* and the combining of heroic and Christian traditions, see below, pp. 151–3.

[48] For further discussion of this image, see below, pp. 146–7.

[49] 'When human frailty labours at anything, when, for example, we build a house, in the beginning we prepare the material of the structure and after this beginning we dig into the depths; then we set stones in the foundation, then place the walls in increasing rows of stones; thus we arrive gradually at the completion of the work we began by progressing gradually. God, however, whose hand is omnipotent for the fulfilment of his task, did not need the delay of time.'

example to Hrothgar's creation of Heorot reveals from the beginning that the standard to be achieved and the stakes at risk are both very high: though human beings cannot presume to equal God's power, failure means a return to chaos, the disintegration of society.

The example of Hrothgar shows how the definition of divine power can overlap with the definition of human society: both take place in relation to the power of the natural world. A human king *can*, like God, assert his power and create a circle of order and light[50] in the midst of and in opposition to the natural world. However, while God's instant and irresistible power renders his definition in opposition to the natural world fairly unproblematic[51] – he is simply omnipotent – human definition is more complex, for it must both aspire to and fail to achieve the ideal. *Beowulf*, although normally characterised as a tale of a superhuman hero and supernatural monsters, provides perhaps the clearest examples of how the natural world is used to define human society. Heorot and, later, Beowulf's Geatish hall constitute the physical boundaries that divide the human circle of light from the natural world.[52] After their initial journey, Beowulf and his men thank God for allowing them to pass unscathed through the expanse separating Hygelac's from Hrothgar's kingdom; they then re-enter the circle of human society's protective confines:

> Guman onetton,
> sigon ætsomne,   oþ þæt hy sæl timbred
> geatolic ond goldfah   ongyton mihton;
> þæt wæs foremærost   foldbuendum
> receda under roderum,   on þæm se rica bad;
> lixte se leoma   ofer landa fela.   (*Beowulf* 306b–11)[53]

Hrothgar's hall provides a literal *leoma* 'light'[54] to mark society's boundaries,

---

[50] E. B. Irving Jr, *Introduction to 'Beowulf'*, (Englewood Cliffs, NJ, 1969), p. 15.

[51] For discussion of some of the problems, see below, pp. 144–77.

[52] The image of the hall in Old English poetry has been discussed at length elsewhere. For a recent, extended study of it, with helpful bibliography, see Magennis, *Images of Community, passim*, but especially pp. 35–42 and 60–2.

[53] 'The men hastened [and] advanced together until they could see the timbered hall, magnificent and adorned with gold; that was the most famous building for land-dwellers under the heavens, where the ruler dwelt; the light [from it] gleamed over many lands.'

[54] For the part this light plays in the theme of 'the traveller recognises his goal', see Clark, 'The Traveller Recognizes His Goal'.

and, in the heart of that circle, within the hall, human society at its best flourishes – loyal thegns, a good king, due ceremony and hospitality.[55] These aspects of society do not appear to require any representation of the natural world to define them, but in fact they are already positioned in a relationship with the natural world that idealises the inside and renders the outside dark (in opposition to Heorot's light) and dangerous (thus the Geats' thankfulness for their safe journey).[56] The natural world challenges and modifies the ideal outline initially presented by the poet: although Hrothgar does everything right[57] – *He beot ne aleh, beagas dælde, / sinc æt symle* 'he did not leave his boast unfulfilled, [but] shared out rings and treasure at the feast' (80–1a) – the order and security he establishes endures only temporarily. The fleeting nature of human good, of course, is a commonplace of Old English literature; *The Wanderer*, for example, states clearly that it is a condition of this world that all good things are transitory (*The Wanderer* 106–10). While *Beowulf* points ahead to the human forces that will eventually disrupt Danish (and Geatish) order and security, within the poem itself it is the power of the natural world that challenges human society. One can argue that the depredations of the natural world symbolise the incipient human power struggles, but the representation of the natural world, especially in *Beowulf*, does not present so direct an equivalence; this is not allegory.[58] Instead, the representation of the natural world embodies a general fear for society's survival.

---

[55] Though it can be argued that Heorot here symbolises the loss of all these positive things (Brennan, 'Hrothgar's Government', p. 7), the society into which Beowulf enters, though shaken by Grendel's attacks, still maintains all the structures that characterise an ideal society. See also Duncan, 'Epitaphs for Æglæcan', p. 114; Niles, *'Beowulf': The Poem*, p. 28.

[56] The creation of an inside is also the creation of an outside – see Berger and Leicester, 'Social Structure as Doom', p. 41.

[57] As he has done throughout his life – see *ibid.*, p. 44.

[58] Cf. however, the argument of Gradon, who sees each element of Grendel's landscape as symbolic of an abstract meaning; for example, the wolfslopes indicate the solitary and savage outlaw, the fenpath loneliness, the mountain stream darkness, the rimy trees winter and thus desolation and sorrow (P. Gradon, *Form and Style in Early English Literature* (London, 1971), pp. 172–3). See also the discussion in M. Whallon, M. Goldsmith and C. Donahue, 'Allegorical, Typological or Neither? Three Short Papers on the Allegorical Approach to *Beowulf* and a Discussion', *ASE* 2 (1973), 285–302. Bolton argues that, although the poem as a whole is not consistently allegorical, Grendel 'pretty surely' is: see *Alcuin and Beowulf*, p. 174.

THE AGENTS OF DESTRUCTION

Too soon after the glorious creation of Heorot[59] the natural world begins its relentless assault. An attack on the home of the Danes would be horrible enough if it were perpetrated by a human assailant,[60] but this assault is worse because the structures and punishments established to protect the central sanctuary of the hall cannot influence the world outside of human boundaries – that is, the natural world. As a result, into the hall itself are brought the miseries (the loss of kinsmen, for example) normally reserved for those who, like the Wanderer, are forced to dwell as exiles – that is, outside the protection of society, in the natural world.[61] In this case the opposing force of the natural world takes the form not of frost or hail, nor of more localised wolves, but of a particular monster, Grendel.[62] The *Beowulf*-poet associates this embodiment of nature's power with

> eotenas ond ylfe   ond orcneas,
> swylce gigantas,   þa wið Gode wunnon
> lange þrage   *(Beowulf* 112–14a)[63]

– that is, as far as a modern audience is concerned, with the supernatural world and the monstrous, the opposite of the natural world. According to

[59] The description of this glorious creation may belong to a tradition of panegyrics containing architectural matter, which extends from Pindar to late tenth century Norse poetry (for example, Úlf Uggason's *Húsdrápa*, 'A Praise Song for a House') and beyond; see Bessinger 'Homage to Cædmon', p. 93. The Old English poem, *Durham*, is a late example based on classical models; see Schlauch, 'An Old English *Encomium Urbis*'. See also C. B. Kendall, 'Let Us Now Praise a Famous City: Wordplay in the OE *Durham* and the Cult of St Cuthbert', *JEGP* 87 (1988), 507–21.

[60] The horror associated with an attack on the home (*hamsacn*) is amply demonstrated by the strict measures against it detailed in the law codes; see C. V. Colman, 'Domestic Peace and Public Order in Anglo-Saxon Law', in *The Anglo-Saxons: Synthesis and Achievement*, ed. J. D. Woods and D. A. E. Pelteret (Waterloo, 1985), pp. 49–61.

[61] For further examination of exile, see below, pp. 84–8.

[62] Cf. Robinson, *'Beowulf' and the Appositive Style*, p. 74.

[63] 'Etins and elves and ogres, likewise the giants, who strove against God for a long time'. For discussion of the word *eotenas*, see R. E. Kaske, 'The *Eotenas* in *Beowulf*', in *Old English Poetry: Fifteen Essays*, ed. Creed, pp. 285–310. On the relation of the *eotenas* to Old Testament giants, see R. E. Kaske, '*Sapientia et Fortitudo* as the Controlling Theme of *Beowulf*', *SP* 55 (1958), 423–56, at 438; Mellinkoff, 'Cain's Monstrous Progeny in *Beowulf*: Part II'.

a modern dictionary, to be 'monstrous' is to deviate greatly from the natural or normal in form, size or character.[64] Yet, despite Grendel's exceptional power, his evil, glowing eyes, his steel-hard claws, and his taste for human flesh, much of what characterises Grendel as monstrous for a modern audience parallels what characterised the natural world for the Anglo-Saxons; the modern distinction between the two does not strictly apply, just as the modern distinction between sky and heaven, between merely 'extra-terrestrial' and supernatural, is not evident in medieval texts.[65] Thus Old English poets did not describe the natural world that threatened them as natural (in the sense of normal and wholesome) but rather as *unnatural* to human tastes – unfamiliar, uncanny and unfriendly. As a result natural phenomena and monsters existed side by side in a tradition that characterised them both as fundamentally hostile to the human race.[66] This is not to say that Grendel is not 'monstrous', but that the 'monstrous' is not opposed to the 'natural'. Though feared by human beings, Grendel and his mother have their place in the natural world, just as the dragon and 'giant' in *Maxims II* do:

> Draca sceal on hlæwe,
> frod, frætwum wlanc.   Fisc sceal on wætere
> cynren cennan.   Cyning sceal on healle
> beagas dælan.   Bera sceal on hæðe,
> eald and egesfull.   Ea of dune sceal
> flodgræg feran . . .
>   Fugel uppe sceal
> lacan on lyfte.   Leax sceal on wæle
> mid sceote scriðan.   Scur sceal on heofenum,
> winde geblanden,   in þas woruld cuman.
> þeof sceal gangan þystrum wederum.   Þyrs sceal on fenne gewunian
> ana innan lande.   (*Maxims II* 26b–31a, 38b–43a)[67]

---

[64] See *OED*, s.v. 'monstrous'. Cf. also the analysis of the semantic field of the word 'monster' in Waterhouse, *'Beowulf* as "Palimpsest"'', pp. 4–5.

[65] Roberts, 'A Preliminary "Heaven" Index', p. 211; cf. also the list of terms s.v. 'Heaven(s), sky' in *A Thesaurus of Old English*, ed. Roberts, Kay and Grundy, p. 16.

[66] In contrast with his or her sources, the author of the *Liber monstrorum de diversis generibus*, possibly an Anglo-Saxon or Irishman living in the seventh century (see Lapidge, *'Beowulf*, Aldhelm, the *Liber monstrorum* and Wessex', pp. 164–5), makes it clear that monsters are hostile to the human race. See Orchard, *Pride and Prodigies*, p. 89. Cf. discussion above, pp. 31–3.

[67] 'A dragon must be in a barrow, wise, proud in its treasures. A fish must be in water to

Like the giant, Grendel and his mother naturally and fittingly live in the fens, along with their neighbours, the wolves and sea-beasts; they are not outside of nature,[68] but rather outside of human knowledge and control.[69] Grendel is a special case, but the problem he poses exemplifies the threat facing a human society attempting to survive in a hostile environment – and, in Old English poetry, given the essentially antagonistic character of the natural world posited from its creation,[70] the hostility of the environment appears almost inevitable. The problem with the natural world, what characterises it, and what gives it its huge potential as a site for the negotiation of power is its ability to exceed human control: the wind and sea, wolves, the diseases represented as attacks by witches and elves[71] and what would now be considered *super*natural monsters all possess power – power that has to be dealt with if human individuals and society are to survive, and yet power that appears intractable if not ungovernable. Thus, while it cannot be said that all of nature takes on the guise of monsters in Anglo-Saxon eyes because it lies outside of human control, the opposite is true: monsters, the worst, the most ungovernable and intractable of all forces, are a part of what we would now call the natural world, not separate entities with different rules to govern their relation to human society. There is little to distinguish between the nightmarish approach of Grendel in *Beowulf*[72] and the terrible approach of the wolf in *Maxims I*[73] except in the degree of the threat – Grendel takes thirty men at a time while the

---

conceive kindred. A king must share out rings in the hall. A bear must be on the heath, old and terrible. The flood-grey river must travel from the mountain ... The bird must play up in the air. The salmon must glide in the pool with the trout. The shower in the heavens, blended by the wind, must come into this world. The thief must travel in dark weather. The giant must dwell in the fen, alone in the land.'

[68] Cf. Niles, *'Beowulf': The Poem*, p. 7.

[69] The thief, although human, is very much a part of this group of 'creatures' living outside because of his refusal to obey human laws; for further discussion of the position of the alienated human being, the outlaw, see below, pp. 84–5.

[70] See above, pp. 58–60.   [71] See below, pp. 116–21.

[72] For the rhetorical skill displayed in this description, see S. B. Greenfield, 'Grendel's Approach to Heorot: Syntax and Poetry', in *Old English Poetry*, ed. Creed, pp. 275–84; Brodeur, *The Art of 'Beowulf'*, pp. 90–3; and Lapidge, 'Psychology of Terror'.

[73] For text and discussion, see below, p. 85.

wolf takes one. The terror elicited by the *Beowulf*-poet[74] may be especially reserved for supernatural beings, but it is not in contrast with or foreign to the depiction of the natural world, only an extreme example. Grendel and the wolf equally define the limits of society, both by stalking around the boundaries and by threatening its existence.

It has been suggested that the Danes' inability to deal with Grendel reveals flaws in the otherwise ideal, heroic society described by the poet;[75] in this sense, Grendel reflects a monstrousness within Hrothgar's people that inevitably destroys them. On the other hand, the poet provides little indication that the Danes deserve punishment,[76] and Beowulf receives no censure for freeing them. Looking at Grendel as a part of the natural world rather than as a symbolic, strictly unique individual allows for a less critical perspective on the Danes' helplessness. From this perspective, Grendel's easy domination merely reflects humanity's normal limits, since the natural world's power inevitably exceeds that of the human race. Although he must also be seen in terms of his status as a descendant of Cain,[77] Grendel *can* be seen in terms of the elemental power of the natural world: his hostility is unceasing, untiring, incomprehensible and, as far as anyone could tell for twelve years, invulnerable to human counter-attacks, for, while many vowed over beer to wait for Grendel 'with the terror of their swords',

> þone synscaðan
> ænig ofer eorþan irenna cyst,
> guðbilla nan gretan nolde. (*Beowulf* 801b–3)[78]

As regular and unstoppable as the tide, Grendel demonstrates again and again that the best that human beings can hope for is to stay out of harm's way; the nobility in Hrothgar's court hinders Grendel's destruction of life and property no more effectively than it could halt a thunderstorm.

---

[74] See Lapidge, 'Psychology of Terror' and A. Renoir, 'Point of View and Design for Terror in *Beowulf*', *NM* 63 (1962), 154–67.

[75] Fajardo-Acosta, 'Intemperance, Fratricide, and the Elusiveness of Grendel'; Goldsmith, *Mode and Meaning*, p. 112; Brennan, 'Hrothgar's Government', p. 7; Payne, 'Three Aspects of Wyrd', p. 21. Cf. also Magennis, *Images of Community*, p. 75.

[76] Berger and Leicester, 'Social Structure as Doom', p. 39.

[77] For further discussion of the many identities assigned to Grendel by critics, see below, pp. 78–9.

[78] 'The choice of irons and war-blades throughout the world – none would touch that sinful attacker.'

Of course, no one would ever expect human beings to be able to oppose the kind of power described in *Exeter Book Riddle 3*.[79] Only the foolish dare to stand up against the power of the natural world, for such an act is beyond human capabilities. Grendel's power thus demonstrates not a damnable fault in Hrothgar's people but the limitations of a human society.

DEFINITION OF AND BY GRENDEL

Grendel defines through his position outside human society: he is not only antihuman but antisocial in every sense of the word.[80] He is a *mearcstapa* 'boundary-walker' (103a); he not only lurks on the other side of the boundaries that divide the human race from the natural world, but the fact of his lurking there establishes those boundaries. His foreignness marks him both specifically as a descendant of Cain and generally as a part of that 'Other' which stands in opposition to God and the human race, and his ancestral struggle against God recalls both the rebellious angels and the state of the unmastered world in the Old English *Genesis*. His actions challenge the identity that society has established for itself[81] by transforming Heorot, the human equivalent of God's act of Creation, back into the negative state of pre-creation: the hall stands just as 'empty and useless' (and is described using the same words, *idel ond unnyt* [145b and 413a]) as chaos is in the Old English *Genesis*, with the same *sinnihte* 'eternal night' (161b) hanging overhead.

In response, human society must be redefined against his power. Physical, tangible barriers like the walls of Heorot are not effective, for Grendel easily enters and takes up a position that encapsulates the problem he poses: with such a *healðegn* 'hall-thegn' (142a) in its midst, what kind of society is this? The unexpectedness of the description of

---

[79] For discussion of the number of this riddle, see above, p. 40, n. 89. For discussion of this riddle, see below, pp. 129–30, 133, 168–9 and 176.

[80] Duncan, 'Epitaphs for Æglæcan', pp. 112–13; Hanley, 'Grendel's Humanity Again', p. 6; R. W. Hanning, '*Beowulf* as Heroic History', *Medievalia et Humanistica* ns 5 (1974), 77–102 at 93; S. B. Greenfield, 'The Extremities of the *Beowulf*ian Body Politic', in *Saints, Scholars, and Heroes*, ed. King and Stevens, pp. 1–14, at 9.

[81] Cf. Duncan, 'Epitaphs for Æglæcan', p. 113: 'Violating the social code, the Grendels extend, reverse, and parody it, to redefine themselves more fatally within its limits, but also it within theirs.' See also Waterhouse, '*Beowulf* as "Palimpsest"', p. 12.

Grendel as a *healðegn* has led some critics to doubt the authority of this word. Some, including Trautmann, Sedgefield and Holthausen, have suggested that *helðegn* is more logical, as it echoes the earlier description of Grendel as a *feond on helle* 'enemy in hell' (101b); conversely, some have argued for emending the earlier line to *feond on healle* 'the enemy in the hall'.[82] Grendel's pre-death relation to the Christian hell probably cannot be resolved. He is said to want to seek the company of devils (756a) when suffering in Beowulf's grip, implying that he is already familiar with their company and perhaps their traditional living quarters, hell. However, the place said to be his home and visited later by Beowulf cannot be unambiguously identified with hell; although dark, it is devoid of devils.[83] In addition, as is clear in *Guthlac*, even devils are permitted to live outside of hell, in lonely places like the fens and wasteland frequented by Grendel.[84] As a result, it is by no means evident that Grendel's dwelling in the fens is hell, and one might thus be reluctant to emend the manuscript in this regard. It is only after Grendel's death, after he has struggled back to his mere-home and laid down his life, that *þær him hel onfeng* 'hell received him there' (852b). On the other hand, it is easy enough to see that he is the inhabitant of a hall. Not only is the underwater cave in which Beowulf later finds Grendel's mother and corpse called a *sele* 'hall',[85] but, more important, Grendel commands the Danish hall and *Heorot eardode, / sincfage sel sweartum nihtum* 'dwell[s] in

---

[82] See ASPR IV, p. 123.

[83] As mentioned earlier, the description of Grendel's mere appears to share some characteristics of hell as described in the *Visio sancti Pauli*, Vercelli homily IX and Blickling homily XVI (see above, p. 60, n. 27). For argument that Grendel's mere is to be identified with hell rather than scenes from Norse analogues, see Malone, 'Grendel and his Abode', pp. 297–308. Schrader argues that the mere is not meant to recall hell but rather places consecrated to devil worship ('Sacred Groves', p. 81). Goldsmith points out that the place in which Beowulf finds Grendel's body, although near the fenland haunted by demons, is empty except for some treasure and the corpse on a couch (*Mode and Meaning*, pp. 115–16).

[84] For further discussion of *Guthlac*, see above, p. 44 and below, pp. 124–8.

[85] The cave is described as a *niðsele* 'hostile-hall' (1513a) and *hrofsele* 'roofed hall' 1515a); after entering it, Beowulf is described as a *selegyst* 'hall-guest' (1545a). This hall can be seen as an 'anti-hall', a reverse or parody of Heorot; see Hume, 'The Concept of the Hall', pp. 70–3. Cf. also Lee, for the idea of hell as a 'grotesque parody' of heaven (*The Guest-Hall of Eden*, p. 21). On the other hand, it has been argued that *sele* merely means 'dwelling' rather than 'hall'; see C. H. De Roo, 'Old English *Sele*', *Neophil* 64 (1980), 113–20, and Anderson, 'Uncarpentered World', p. 76. It is worth noting that

Heorot, the hall adorned with treasure, during the dark nights' (166b–7), as Hrothgar's thegns should and would do if it were not necessary for them to sleep elsewhere (138–43). Until Beowulf's arrival, Grendel remains the only dweller in the hall by night. In this sense the manuscript reading of *heal-* seems logical enough; it is only *ðegn* that requires explanation.

Although it may be dangerous to place too much emphasis on a word whose authority has been questioned, attempting to see Grendel in the role of a thegn reveals that he is to a great extent a parody of the normal human member of society – or, better, a negation of that norm.[86] Many critics have argued that the designation of Grendel as a *healðegn* indicates his envious desire to be a member of society;[87] his actions can thus be seen as grotesque attempts to imitate social behaviour. For example, like Hrothgar, Grendel rules the fens and, for twelve years, Heorot as well; he also possesses a *sele* 'hall' of his own in which there are weapons and treasure,[88] but it is a lonely, dangerous place (*niðsele* 'battle-hall' (1513a)), an inversion of the hall in which resides the friendly company described by Wealhtheow:[89]

> Her is æghwylc eorl   oþrum getrywe,
> modes milde,   mandrihtne hold,
> þegnas syndon geþwære,   þeod ealgearo. (*Beowulf* 1228–30)[90]

Grendel, of course, is in no way *modes milde* or *geþwære*; he is an *atol angengea* 'terrible solitary walker' (165a) whose mind appears perpetually *reþe* 'fierce' (122a). In addition, unlike Wealtheow's loyal thegns, Grendel

---

Heorot is called a *sele* many times (81b, 323b, 411b, 713b etc.); one cannot deny a 'dwelling' the status of a 'hall' based on this word alone.

[86] Irving, *A Reading of 'Beowulf'*, p. 18. Cf. Magennis, *Images of Community*, p. 62.

[87] Berger and Leicester, 'Social Structure as Doom', p. 52. See also Hill, 'Figures of Evil', p. 10; Baird, '"For metode": *Beowulf* 169', *ES* 49 (1968), 418–23, at 423.

[88] Taylor, 'Grendel's Monstrous Arts', p. 3.

[89] For Wealhtheow's role in the representation of this ideal society, see M. J. Enright, 'The Lady with a Mead-Cup: Ritual, Group Cohesion and Hierarchy in the Germanic Warband', *Frühmittelalterliche Studien* 22 (1988), 170–203. Cf. also J. M. Hill, *The Cultural World in 'Beowulf'* (Toronto, Buffalo, NY, and London, 1955), pp. 100–4.

[90] 'Here each man is true to each other, mild of heart, loyal to the lord; the thegns are harmonious, the people all willing.'

never renders tribute to Hrothgar after his war-like raids;[91] instead, he strives against him (151b–2a), stands *ana wið eallum* 'alone against them all' (145a) and, instead of being *getrywe* 'true' (1228a) to the members of the comitatus, he kills and eats them. It is thus fitting that Grendel is unable to approach the throne,[92] the site of the gift-giving that defines and ties a warrior-society together.[93] Because of this exclusion, Grendel *sibbe ne wolde / wið manna hwone* 'wanted no peaceful relationship with any man' (154b–5a); he does not play by human rules and pays no heed to decorum or what the human race judges to be fair.[94] As a result, the Danes neither receive recompense for the men he kills nor have any hope of paying a ransom to end the siege (157–9): one might as well bargain with the sea, or demand payment for damages done by the wind. Yet the human race always tries to do exactly that, to assimilate or coerce the natural world to comply with human rules of fairness and responsibility.[95] Before the invention of insurance, this could only be done by appealing to a superior power through sacrifice and prayer, and the Danes, as the narrator disapprovingly notes (175–83a),[96] do resort to these desperate

---

[91] Hill, 'Figures of Evil', p. 10.

[92] Although I assume that it is Grendel who cannot approach the *gifstol*, this is not the only interpretation; it has been argued that it is Hrothgar who cannot approach his own throne. For discussion, see Brodeur, *Art of 'Beowulf'*, pp. 200–5; R. M. Estrich, 'The Throne of Hrothgar – *Beowulf*, ll. 168–169', *JEGP* 43 (1944), 384–9; S. B. Greenfield, '"Gifstol" and Goldhoard in *Beowulf*', in *Old English Studies*, ed. Burlin and Irving, pp. 107–17, at 110–12; A. E. Du Bois, 'Gifstol', *MLN* 69 (1954), 546–9; R. Howren, 'A Note on *Beowulf* 168–69', *MLN* 71 (1956), 317–18; D. Clipsham, '*Beowulf* 168–169', *In Geardagum* (1974), 19–24; R. E. Kaske, 'The *Gifstol* Crux in *Beowulf*', *LSE* 16 (1985), 142–51.

[93] 'The centre of the fellowship of the comitatus, the gift-giving, is man's daring imitation of God's gifts to men.' Payne, 'Three Aspects of Wyrd', p. 27.

[94] Irving, *A Reading of 'Beowulf'*, p. 17.

[95] See, for example, *The Bee Charm*, where the speaker implores the bees to be mindful of his property as a law-abiding human being would be: *Be ge swa gemindige mines godes, / swa bið manna gehwilc metes and eþeles* 'be as mindful of my property as every man is of food and his homeland' (11–12). For explanation of the details of the charm and their reference to laws of kinship obligation, see Spamer, 'The Old English Bee Charm'.

[96] Directing human hopes and fears away from 'pagan superstition' was a struggle undertaken by the Christian church throughout its history, but for a specific example of how Christian dogma adapted to and was changed by such a challenge, see Flint, 'The Transmission of Astrology'. Cf. also the increasing use of liturgical intercession under Carolingian rule, where famine, disaster, pestilence and, eventually, human

measures, being unfortunately unaware of such texts as the Old English metrical *Genesis*, which would have shown them the proper source of power over the natural world. What is most important to note here, however, is that such negative statements about Grendel and the natural world reflect definitions of human, or specifically Anglo-Saxon, society: human beings must do what the natural world does not, must abide by rules of responsibility and, as the author of *Maxims I* states, negotiate with each other if society is to exist at all (56–8a).[97]

Grendel thus exists as an opposing and defining force; he has, at least before his fight with Beowulf, little substance of his own.[98] It is difficult to define him except in negative terms,[99] for his position outside the human circle of light places him both literally and figuratively in the dark: he inhabits a *dygel lond* 'dark land' (1357b) and is shrouded in mystery. Beowulf's description of the monster he has come to fight reveals that Grendel is, except for his threat to Danish society, an unknown quantity. He says,

> Þu wast, gif hit is
> swa we soþlice   secgan hyrdon,
> þæt mid Scyldingum   sceaðona ic nat hwylc
> deogol dædhata   deorcum nihtum
> eaweð þurh egsan   uncuðne nið
> hynðu ond hrafyl.   (*Beowulf* 272b–7a)[100]

Even at the end of *Beowulf*, even after over a century of analysis,[101] this essential ambiguity regarding what Grendel is remains.[102] Such

crises were opposed by nation-wide prayers and litanies; see M. McCormick, 'The Liturgy of War in the Early Middle Ages: Crisis, Litanies, and the Carolingian Monarchy', *Viator* 15 (1984), 1–23, at 7.

[97] For text and discussion, see above, pp. 54–5.

[98] Cf. Goldsmith, *Mode and Meaning*, p. 99; Niles, *'Beowulf': The Poem*, p. 8.

[99] Irving, *A Reading of 'Beowulf'*, p. 15. See also above, p. 38.

[100] 'You know, if it is as we truthfully heard said, that I know not which attacker, [which] mysterious perpetrator of hatred, shows unheard of hostility, humiliation and corpse-feasting, in a terrible manner during the dark nights.' For the translation of *hrafyl* as 'corpse-feasting' rather than simply 'slaughter', see Robinson, *'Beowulf' and the Appositive Style*, p. 62.

[101] It has been argued that it is the century of criticism itself that created what is now thought of as Grendel the monster. See S. M. Carlson, 'The Monsters of *Beowulf*: Creations of Literary Scholars', *JAF* 80 (1967), 357–64.

[102] Cf. O'Keeffe, *'Beowulf*, lines 202b–836', p. 489.

ambiguity allows one to identify Grendel as a devil,[103] a *draugr*,[104] one of the monstrous races which dominate the prose material accompanying the poem,[105] a descendant of the Old Testament pre-diluvian giants[106] or a human outlaw,[107] not to mention various allegorical figures.[108] Grendel is observed closely enough to establish that he has a man-like form, but the statement of his similarity to the human race is accompanied by reaffirmation of his foreignness: one receives yet another reverse or parodic

[103] The poet refers to the death of Grendel and his mother as *deofla hryre* 'the fall of devils' (1680a). Cf. also L. Malmberg, 'Grendel and the Devil', *NM* 78 (1977), 241–3; Malone, 'Grendel and His Abode', p. 298; C. J. E. Ball, '*Beowulf* 99–101', *N&Q* 216 (1971), 163; J. Smith, '*Beowulf*–II', *English* 26 (1977), 3–22, at 13.

[104] A *draugr* is a walking corpse from Norse legend; see N. K. Chadwick, 'Norse Ghosts: A Study in the *Draugr* and the *Haugbúi*', *Folk-Lore* 57 (1946), 50–65 and 106–27; N. K. Chadwick, 'The Monsters and Beowulf', in *The Anglo-Saxons: Studies in Some Aspects of their History and Culture Presented to Bruce Dickins*, ed. P. Clemoes (London, 1959), pp. 171–203; cf. also Lapidge, 'Psychology of Terror', pp. 375–7.

[105] But cf. Friedman, *The Monstrous Races*, pp. 103–6. For discussion of the relationship between *Beowulf* and the *Liber monstrorum*, see Orchard, *Pride and Prodigies*, pp. 109–14; L. G. Whitbread, 'The *Liber monstrorum* and *Beowulf*', *Mediaeval Studies* 36 (1974), 434–71; Lapidge, '*Beowulf*, Aldhelm, the *liber monstrorum* and Wessex'; A. Knock, 'The *Liber monstrorum*: An Unpublished Manuscript and Some Reconsiderations', *Scriptorium* 32 (1978), 19–28; A. Knock's review of *Liber monstrorum de diversis generibus: Libro delle Mirabili Difformità*, by C. Bologna, *MÆ* 48 (1979), 259–62, at 261.

[106] Mellinkoff, 'Cain's Monstrous Progeny in *Beowulf*: Part I, Noachic Tradition', *ASE* 8 (1979), 143–62'; 'Cain's Monstrous Progeny in *Beowulf*: Part II'; Goldsmith, *Mode and Meaning*, pp. 107–8.

[107] Hanley, 'Grendel's Humanity', pp. 5–13; J. L. Baird, 'Grendel the Exile', *NM* 67 (1966), 375–81; Bandy, 'Cain, Grendel, and the Giants of *Beowulf*', *Papers on Language and Literature*, 9 (1973), 235–49, at 241–2; R. P. Tripp, Jr, 'Grendel Polytropos', *In Geardagum* 6 (1984), 43–69, at 45; O'Keeffe, '*Beowulf*, lines 202b–836', p. 486; A. H. Olsen, 'The *Aglaeca* and the Law', *AN&Q* 20 (1982), 66–8, at 66–7. For discussion of the ironic application of human epithets to Grendel, see J. G. Johansen, 'Grendel the Brave? *Beowulf*, line 834', *ES* 63 (1982), 193–7, at 196. The possibility of crossing over from the human to the monstrous has been discussed often with reference to Grettir. See Orchard, *Pride and Prodigies*, pp. 152–68; S. L. Dragland, 'Monster-man in Beowulf', *Neophil* 61 (1977), 606–18. The discussion of the relationship between *Beowulf* and *Grettis Saga* is vast; for summaries see P. A. Jorgensen, 'Grendel, Grettir and Two Skaldic Stanzas', *Scriptia Islandica* 25 (1975), 54–61; R. L. Harris, 'The Death of Grettir and Grendel: A New Parallel', *Scripta Islandica* 24 (1973), 25–53; Orchard, *Pride and Prodigies*, pp. 140–1.

[108] For example, for Grendel as a symbol of intemperance and fratricide, see Fajardo-Acosta, 'Intemperance', pp. 205–10.

description of humanity[109] and what it should be rather than discovering much about Grendel when told that this *ellorgast* 'alien spirit' (807b, 1349a, 1617a and 1621b)[110] is *mara þonne ænig man oðer* 'larger than any other man' (1353), descends from an unknown patrilineage[111] and travels not the known ways of society but *wræclastas* 'the paths of exile' (1352b). That is, the information given about Grendel tells us primarily that he is not a member of society. Yet even this information about Grendel arrives late in the poem, after Grendel has been killed – after he has been forcefully dragged into the circle of light. Before this point Grendel is, like the natural world as a whole, vast and unknown. He comes out of the darkness, and *men ne cunnon, / hwyder helrunan hwyrftum scriþað* 'no one knows where [such] demonic sorcerers glide in their turnings' (162b–3). He has no definite shape or features; he is a *sceadugenga* 'shadow-walker' (703a), either because he is shadow-like or because he remains in shadow and is thus unseen. Even his murder of thirty men and his subsequent twelve years of raiding take place without providing an understanding of his form – although the result of his actions is *gumum undyrne* 'not hidden (i.e. clearly obvious) to men' (127b), he himself remains a mystery. It is not until Beowulf begins the process of subduing him that any concept of his form emerges, and then, in quick succession, his hand, fingers, body, shoulder, sinews and joints appear.

Beowulf's victory eliminates Grendel's vague and frightening power and 'reconciles' Grendel, if not to peace, then at least to human scale and human terms[112] – a very satisfactory renegotiation of nature's power. Grendel's defeat is a reaffirmation of the heroic society he had challenged, for Beowulf does not merely defeat an opponent; he reduces and redefines a part – and no insignificant or feeble part – of the natural world's vast power. He transforms Grendel's intractable threat into a dismembered corpse.[113] His efforts end when Grendel is fully integrated into human

---

[109] Taylor, 'Grendel's Monstrous Arts', p. 3.

[110] Cf. also *ellengæst* 'courageous spirit' (86), which various critics have emended to *ellorgæst* 'alien spirit' – see Lapidge, 'Psychology of Terror', p. 396, n. 8.

[111] Note that Hrothgar accepts Beowulf into his society on the basis of his knowledge of his father (*Beowulf* 372–4).

[112] Cf. Berger and Leicester, who argue that Beowulf's arrival makes Grendel's humanity increasingly physical and social ('Social Structure as Doom', p. 53).

[113] Note that this act of reduction and redefinition is paralleled by writers who contain and control the natural world in their descriptions; see below, pp. 190–6. Cf. also

society: 'naturalised' in human terms, but 'denatured' in terms of his place in the natural world. That is, Grendel ceases to be a limiting and defining force for human society and becomes instead an object defined by society. His arm and head are henceforth, like a hawk or ornamented horse, treasures[114] that Beowulf can bestow upon Hrothgar – counters in and tokens[115] of the system of exchange that maintains human society.[116] Beowulf's victory over Grendel, then, re-asserts the value and re-establishes the stability of the society initially created by Hrothgar.[117] Beowulf leaves Hrothgar to conduct business as usual, to preside over warriors in the meadhall, reward loyalty with treasure and arrange treaties and agreements to safeguard his kingdom. However successful Hrothgar may be in the future (Beowulf appears to doubt his chances, and the poet has already predicted that internal treachery will bring Heorot to ruin), at this point the poem describes an ideal situation: a society at peace because strong enough to defend those within it. Whatever else the poem questions, it presents this state of society as an unequivocal good.

THE DEFEAT OF SOCIETY

The attack of the dragon many years later disrupts a similarly ideal social situation: a kingdom that, after uncertainty and conflict, has been consolidated and defended by a powerful king.[118] This successful creation endured for many years but was eventually faced with the same challenge as Hrothgar's kingdom: destructive incursions from outside. Once again, the poem does look forward to *human* incursions from outside, but within

Exeter Book *Riddle 47* ('Bookmoth'), where the firm word of a man can be 'reduced' to an inanimate object (literally the dead skin of animal) and eaten by a worm.

[114] For links between the words designating 'created life' and those describing 'fashioned artifacts', see P. B. Taylor, 'The Traditional Language of Treasure in *Beowulf*', *JEGP* 85 (1986), 191–205.

[115] The poet uses 'objects of human use and exchange as metonyms of ... heroic life'. J. Thormann, 'The Poetics of Absence: "The Lament of the Sole Survivor" in *Beowulf*', in *De Gustibus*, ed. Foley, pp. 542–40, at 545.

[116] Niles, *'Beowulf': The Poem*, pp. 213–22.

[117] Robinson, *'Beowulf' and the Appositive Style*, pp. 72–3.

[118] According to Payne, such a creation is an impossible utopia. *Wyrd*, which is God's direct action to counteract the human race's interference in divine order (as a result of its free will), does not allow such creations to exist forever ('Three Aspects of Wyrd', pp. 18 and 31).

the poem external threats come from the natural world. Like Grendel, the dragon rushes into Beowulf's kingdom from the *westenne* 'the wilderness' (2298a) beyond the boundaries of human society; he is hostile to the human race, destroying life and property, including the hall, the symbolic centre of society; he is unknown and mysterious, living in a place *eldum uncúð* 'unknown to men' (2214a), until Beowulf subdues him. The dragon is thus perfectly 'natural' in the sense of being an external force opposed to society; his threat requires a defensive act on the part of Geatish society, an assertion of its existence. Similar to Grendel, the dragon can be seen to define society in reverse: he is antisocial in his solitary greed; he intends to *no ðær aht cwices ... læfan* 'leave no one there alive' (2314b–15).[119] As was the case with Grendel, the dragon's hostility and apparent impregnability pose a challenge that Geatish society must meet lest it become *idel ond unnyt* – nothing but smouldering ashes.

Although Beowulf does subdue this latest attacker from the natural world and does, in a sense, manage to assimilate and transform the dragon into treasure for his people,[120] the result is not the reaffirmation that accompanied Grendel's defeat. In destroying Beowulf, the dragon breaches the Geats' best defence,[121] leaving their society in an even worse state than that of Hrothgar's Grendel-ridden kingdom. The Danes' society, though miserable and tormented during Grendel's twelve years of siege, continued to exist because it maintained the structures that identified and ordered the individuals within it. Particularly, it retained intact the central figure of the king, the founder and defender. As centre of his society, Hrothgar suffered for the loss of his thegns, but his own position was never in danger (Grendel could never even approach the throne),[122] and so his society,

---

[119] Cf. Magennis, *Images of Community*, p. 71.

[120] This transformation should have been straightforward, since the treasure already contained 'synecdoches of hall-joys, honour and reciprocity, protection and attack' (Berger and Leicester, 'Social Structure as Doom', p. 67); all that it apparently needed to regain its value was a living community in which it could be exchanged.

[121] The poet describes Beowulf as the *epelweard* 'guardian of the homeland' (2210a) and *wigendra hleo* 'defence of warriors' (2337b), apparently without irony; I see no suggestion in the poem that Beowulf is actually a 'terrible stranger' who cunningly usurps control over his hosts and then is destroyed along with his hosts by an externalised emanation of his own evil self (i.e. the dragon), as has been argued by T. Mizuno in 'Beowulf as Terrible Stranger', *JIES* 17 (1989), 1–46.

[122] For different interpretations of this line, see above, p. 77, n. 92.

however weakened and desperate, was never doomed to dissolution as Beowulf's Geatish society is. Though the due ceremony at Beowulf's funeral indicates that the relationships of loyalty and respect that normally bind a society together still remain intact, Wiglaf predicts the complete loss of heroic society:

> Nu sceal sincþego   ond swyrdgifu,
> eall eðelwyn   eowrum cynne,
> lufen alicgean;   londrihtes mot
> þære mægburge   monna æghwylc
> idel hweorfan.   (*Beowulf* 2884–8a)[123]

The structures of society, including the exchange of gifts and the rights pertaining to land ownership, here are seen not merely as protection but also as the source of joy for the people living within, as in *Daniel*, where such structures are represented as physical buildings:

> Ða þæt gehogode   hamsittende,
> Meda aldor,   þæt ær man ne ongan,
> þæt he Babilone   abrecan wolde,
> alhstede eorla,   þær æðelingas
> under wealla hleo   welan brytnedon.
> Þæt wæs þara fæstna   folcum cuðost,
> mæst and mærost   þara þe men bun,
> Babilon burga,   oðþæt Baldazar
> þurh gylp grome   godes frasade.
> Sæton him æt wine   wealle belocene,
> ne onegdon na   orlegra nið,
> þeah ðe feonda folc   feran cwome
> herega gerædum   to þære heahbyrig
> þæt hie Babilone   abrecan mihton.   (*Daniel* 686–99)[124]

---

[123] 'Now the receiving of treasure and the giving of swords, all the joy of the homeland and the delight of your race cease; each man's, each kinsman's land-right will be allowed to become empty.'

[124] 'Then the prince of the Medes, sitting at home, thought [to do] what no man had begun before, that he would destroy Babylon, the temple of warriors, where nobles distributed wealth under the protection of walls. That [city], Babylon, was of [all] strongholds [and] fortresses the best known to the people, the greatest and most famous of those in which men dwell, until Balthazar tempted God through his fierce boast. They sat at wine, locked in by walls, [and] never dreaded the enmity of hostile ones, even though the enemy people were coming bearing battle armour to that high fortress, so that they might destroy Babylon.'

Like the kingdom of the Geats, which enjoyed fifty years of unassailable peace, the security and prosperity of Babylon seems impregnable, but even the mighty walls and fortifications of the greatest of fortresses, like the greatest and strongest of heroes, cannot prevail for ever.[125] The loss or destruction of these structures, whether physical or not, means going into exile.[126] Thus the fate from which Beowulf saved Heorot – to become empty and useless (*idel ond unnyt*) like the universe before creation – encompasses the whole of the Geatish nation, sending its inhabitants out into the natural world and transforming them into exiles.

EXILE

Because of the political instability characteristic of the period, exile was a common Anglo-Saxon fate[127] and appears widely throughout the poetry. As exile is the reverse of society, it is unsurprising that representations of the natural world feature prominently in descriptions of it. Exile draws attention to the sharp divisions between the inside and the outside, for exiles are forced to step outside the protective boundaries[128] and definitions of human society into the unmastered natural world. Their state there is precarious and miserable, for exiles lose everything: lost in the natural world, they lose their status as members of society, a status which confers upon them both power over others and the right to protection from those more powerful – including God, for Anglo-Saxon law codes indicate that exiles were also excommunicated.[129] They may even lose

---

[125] Cf. the description in *The Ruin* above, pp. 47–8.

[126] Cf. also the fate of the Israelites earlier in *Daniel*; the poet says, *Þenden hie þy rice rædan moston, / burgum wealdan, wæs him beorht wela* 'as long as they could possess the realm, rule the fortress, there was bright prosperity for them' (8–9), but very soon they lose their fortified city and are transformed into an *earme lafe* 'wretched remainder' (80b) of their former glory. See Farrell, 'The Structure of the Old English *Daniel*', p. 558.

[127] Campbell, 'Bede's *Reges* and *Principes*', p. 94.

[128] As indicated in the passage from *Daniel* above, these boundaries can be represented by physical walls. The crumbling of such walls (as in *The Ruin*) thus summons up the feelings of loss experienced by those 'No longer locked into a meaningful place in the intricate pattern of relationships' (Irving, 'Image and Meaning', p. 157); for a similar discussion of the wall depicted in *The Wanderer*, see Irving, 'Image and Meaning', p. 163.

[129] Henry, *Early English and Celtic Lyric*, p. 22. Note also that Cain is exiled both from his kin and from the sight of God (*Genesis* 1047b–50).

their identities as human beings, becoming a member of the monstrous, sub-human races as Grendel may have done[130] or, worse, a feast for a wolf:

> Wineleas, wonsælig mon   genimeð him wulfas to geferan,
> felafæcne deor.   Ful oft hine se gefera sliteð;
> gryre sceal for greggum,   græf deadum men;
> hungre heofeð,   nales þæt heafe bewindeð,
> ne huru wæl wepeð   wulf se græga,
> morþorcwealm mæcga,   ac hit a mare wile.   (*Maxims I* 146–51)[131]

Within a society, with friends,[132] a human being may have power and thus security, but the kingless Geats, like the *wineleas mon*, fearfully anticipate not only the absence of the joys of society but also the reverse of them, misery and danger.[133] As we have seen, in Old English poetry such absence and reversal are characteristically described through reference to the natural world, the negative landscape in which human constructions lose their power; the situation at the end of *Beowulf* is no exception:

---

[130] For discussion of the monstrous races, see above, pp. 33–5. The word for criminal in Old English is *wearg*; the same word can also indicate a monster or evil spirit. More interestingly, the cognate Old Icelandic word *vargr* means both wolf and outlaw; see Bosworth–Toller, s.v. *wearg*, and cf. the discussion in Jordan, *Die altenglischen Säugetiernamen*, p. 65, where 'demon' is added to the meanings of 'wolf' and 'criminal'. Evidently stepping outside the boundaries of human law, becoming an outlaw, could cause one to lose human as well as social status. With this in mind, the passage below may be read in a slightly different way: the friendless man may take criminals and outlaws, men no better than beasts or evil spirits, as companions (cf. Henry, *The Early English and Celtic Lyric*, p. 22–3). Neither interpretation should be rejected in favour of the other, for the alienation from wolves and monstrous races is of a similar kind. There may have been little to distinguish this alienation from that felt for those who had rejected or been rejected by the structures of society.

[131] 'The friendless, unhappy man takes wolves, a very deceitful beast, as his companions. Very often that companion will tear him; there must be terror for the grey ones, [and] a grave for dead men; the grey wolf laments his hunger, not at all does he raise up wailing [or] weep about the slaughter, the murderous death of men, but always wants more.'

[132] Cf. *The Wanderer*: the *anhaga* possessed joy until he lost his *winedryhten* (37b).

[133] Just as Grendel is a negative mirror image of humanity, the wolf can be seen as a parody or inversion of the friendly companion. See Larrington, *A Store of Common Sense*, p. 128.

nalles eorl wegan
maððum to gemyndum,   ne mægð scyne
habban on healse   hringweorðunge,
ac sceal geomormod,   golde bereafod
oft nalles æne   elland tredan,
nu se herewisa   hleahtor alegde,
gamen ond gleodream.   Forðon sceall gar wesan
monig morgenceald   mundum bewunden,
hæfen on handa,   nalles hearpan sweg
wigend weccean,   ac se wonna hrefn
fus ofer fægum   fela reordian,
earne secgan,   hu him æt æte speow,
þenden he wið wulf   wæl reafode.   (*Beowulf* 3015b–27)[134]

In this case, the danger anticipated is human, and the natural world depicted is a poetic convention[135] related to the theme of battle,[136] but the crossing from society to exile, from inside to outside, from the exchange of treasure and its attendant stable circle of light and warmth to the *morgenceald* where spears awaken instead of music, remains unmistakable. Leaving the positive structures of society means entering the negative landscape, means losing what is valued and instead having absence.[137] This is as true of Adam (*Genesis* 805–15) and Cain (*Genesis* 1010–53a) as it is of the Wife (in *The Wife's Lament*), where the negative landscape is specifically identified with the natural world.[138]

---

[134] 'Not at all will a man wear treasure as a reminder, nor shall the beautiful woman have ring-treasure on her neck, but miserable, deprived of gold, they must roam often, not just once, through a foreign land, now that the battle-leader has laid aside laughter, joy and music. Therefore on many a cold morning must the spear be gripped by hands, raised up in hands; not at all will the sound of the harp wake the warriors, but the dark raven, eager for the doomed, will speak many things, say to the eagle how he profited at the feast, when he plundered the corpses with the wolf.'

[135] For definition and examples of the 'Beasts of Battle', see above, p. 10, n. 50.

[136] See L. C. Ramsey, 'The Theme of Battle in Old English Poetry' (unpubl. PhD dissertation, Indiana Univ., 1965).

[137] Cf. Robinson, *'Beowulf' and the Appositive Style*, p. 74: 'Without custom, law, and ritual, man finds himself in the state of nature, where, in Hobbe's famous formulation, there is only "continuall feare, and danger of violent death; and the life of man, solitary, poore, nasty, brutish, and short"'.

[138] For discussion of this landscape, see R. W. V. Elliot, 'Form and Image in the Old English Lyrics', *Essays in Criticism* 11 (1961), 1–9, at 8–9.

The state described by the Wife clearly places her outside the structures of society: she is separated from her lord, rejected by kin, deprived of friends, alone.[139] The physical manifestation of this social absence is her position outside, in the natural world:

> Heht mec mon wunian   on wudu bearwe,
> under actreo   in þam eorðscræfe.
> Eald is þes eorðsele,   eal ic eom oflongad,
> sindon dena dimme,   duna uphea,
> bitre burgtunas,   brerum beweaxne,
> wic wynna leas.   (*The Wife's Lament* 27–32a)[140]

The darkness and joylessness of her environment, reminiscent of both hell and the pre-Creation, combined with the enclosing, overhanging, vaguely threatening mountains,[141] are depicted not for the sake of realism but because they sum up her social state.[142] The Wife's setting can be visualised, unlike that of the Geats, but once again the point is to recall a society that has been lost. The *eorðscræfe* or *eorðsele* recalls the absent meadhall;[143] the *burgtunas brerum beweaxne*, like the images in *The Ruin*,

---

[139] M. Rissanen, 'The Theme of "Exile" in *The Wife's Lament*', *NM* 70 (1969), 90–104.

[140] 'One commanded me to dwell in the forest's grove, under an oak tree in a cave. This earth-hall is old, [and] I am completely seized with longing; the hills, the tall mountains, are dark, the fortified towns painfully grown over with briars, this dwelling absent of joys.'

[141] Cf. p. 38, n. 80 above.

[142] This state shares many similarities with the more 'normal' situation of the male thegn who, like the Wanderer, has lost his lord, and thus it has been argued that the speaker is just this traditional figure rather than a woman. See R. C. Bambas, 'Another View of the Old English *Wife's Lament*', *JEGP* 62 (1963), 303–9; M. Stevens, 'The Narrator of *The Wife's Lament*', *NM* 69 (1968), 72–90; J. Mandel, *Alternative Readings in Old English Poetry*, American University Studies, series 4, English Languages and Literature 43 (New York, 1987), 153–73. For opposing views, see A. M. Lucas, 'The Narrator of *The Wife's Lament* Reconsidered', *NM* 70 (1969), 282–97 and Desmond, 'The Voice of Exile'. The ambiguity is not surprising, for Anglo-Saxon laws designated a status for a wife with respect to her husband similar to that of a thegn with respect to his lord; see *Three Old English Elegies*, ed. R. F. Leslie, rev. ed. (Exeter, 1988), pp. 4–5. See also J. Hill, who notes the similar language used to describe both exile and the 'stereotype of the woman-as-victim', in '"Þæt wæs geomuru ides!" A Female Stereotype Examined', in *New Readings on Women in Old English Literature*, ed. H. Damico and A. H. Olsen (Bloomington and Indianapolis, IN, 1990), pp. 235–47, at 242.

[143] Desmond, 'The Voice of Exile', p. 586.

recall other buildings (the works of giants in *The Wanderer* and the hall haunted by Grendel in *Beowulf*) that have returned to emptiness and uselessness (*idel hweorfan* (*Beowulf* 2888a)). They also seem similar to briars in medieval Welsh poetry, where, for example, Queen Gormflaith describes the state of her cloak after being ravaged by blackthorns and brambles.[144] Both Anglo-Saxon Wife and Welsh Queen lament their fate in the natural world. However, while the Queen feels the oppression of the natural world in a personal, physical way, the Wife's experience of the natural world denotes her deprivation, her exclusion from society; she is not physically harmed by it. The briars that grow over her joyless dwelling represent the absence of society; it is this absence that causes her misery, not the briars themselves.

The natural world does not actually symbolise anything particular in *The Wife's Lament* or any of the Old English poems discussed here, however; it is not possible to say that mountains symbolise hostile kingdoms, or that briars symbolise insidious traitors. Specific objects in the natural world are often only sparingly mentioned; instead, their attributes, such as darkness, emptiness or coldness, feature prominently. The natural world merely stands as a negative image, either as an absence of or in opposition to society. While one cannot as a result abstract much about the natural world in which Anglo-Saxon society existed, one can see from the representations of the natural world in many Old English texts that the Anglo-Saxons viewed their society both as a necessary defence for individuals and as a fragile structure always under attack, one that required a God-like founder and defender to maintain it. Although, given the constant warfare between neighbouring kingdoms and raiding of the Vikings, the most dangerous attackers in these texts – and probably also historically – were human beings, it is through the representation of the natural world as a negative landscape that Old English poets characterise their society as precious and fragile.

[144] See Jackson, *Early Celtic Nature Poetry*, pp. 112–13.

4

Standing outside, standing out:
defining the individual

> Wyrd oft nereð
> unfægne eorl,   þonne his ellen deah!
> Hwæþere me gesælde,   þæt ic mid sweorde ofsloh
> niceras nigene.   No ic on niht gefrægn
> under heofones hwealf   heardran feohtan,
> ne on egstreamum   earmran mannon;
> hwæþere ic fara feng   feore gedigde
> siþes werig.   Ða mec sæ oþbær,
> flod æfter faroðe   on Finna land,
> wadu weallendu.   No ic wiht fram þe
> swylcra searoniða   secgan hyrde,
> billa brogan.   Breca næfre git
> æt heaðolace,   ne gehwæþer incer,
> swa deorlice   dæd gefremede
> fagum sweordum   – no ic þæs fela gylpe.   (*Beowulf* 572b–86)[1]

Beowulf may not boast of it much, but his youthful adventure in the sea makes him stand out.[2] It is hardly surprising that Unferth should have failed to perform such deeds, for, in light of the experiences with the

---

[1] 'Fate often preserves an undoomed warrior, when his courage is good! Regardless, it turned out well for me, so that I slew nine sea-monsters with my sword. Never under the arch of the sky have I heard of a harder fight in the sea at night, nor of a more wretched man among water-streams; nevertheless, I survived the grasp of the hostile ones with my life, [though] weary from the journey. Then the sea bore me to the land of the Fins, the flood following the current, the welling water. Never have I heard of such strife or terror of blades with reference to you, [Unferth]. Never has either you or Breca yet performed any deed so boldly in battle-play with flashing swords – although I do not boast of it much.'

[2] See below, pp. 130–2, for further discussion of this adventure.

natural world described in previous chapters, one would expect no more from him – or from most people – than the grim endurance exemplified by the Seafarer. Beowulf's interaction with the natural world marks him off from the rest of his society and from humanity as a whole; the representation of the natural world serves to define him, not as a member of a weak human race or a threatened society, but as a powerful individual. While the previous two chapters have suggested how descriptions of the natural world's power reflect Anglo-Saxon ideas about humanity and society – how representations of the natural world define the human and social conditions seen by Old English poets – this chapter will examine the representation of the natural world as it relates to individuals – both like and unlike Beowulf – rather than formal or abstract groups.

The most immediate problem in such an examination lies in defining the difference between individual as opposed to group interaction, for, while the difference between Beowulf and his peers is evident,[3] other characters are less easy to isolate. Most of these Anglo-Saxon 'individuals' can interact with the natural world as an individual, or as a representative of the human race, or as a representative of a society; the Anglo-Saxon use of characters like Adam[4] and Hrothgar[5] – named, historical individuals who nevertheless symbolise the groups to which they belong – renders it very difficult to distinguish between a representative of humanity or society facing the natural world and an individual facing the natural world.[6] In many cases it may be unnecessary or impossible to isolate members from groups, since the same bleak description of helplessness appears to be the conclusion of any confrontation between the looming power of the natural world and human beings struggling to maintain

---

[3] The coastguard can see that Beowulf is exceptional from first glance; he says, *Næfre ic maran geseah / eorla ofer eorþan* 'I have never seen a greater man throughout the earth' (247b–8a).

[4] For discussion of how Adam's plight in relation to the natural world characterises that of all humanity, see above, pp. 19–22. Of course, Adam is more than a characteristic example of humanity, since he actually contains in himself the whole of the future human race; his sin subjects humanity as a whole to both sin and the natural world (cf. Rom. V.17–19).

[5] For discussion of Hrothgar's role in constructing and preserving society from hostile incursions from outside, see above, pp. 57 and 62–9.

[6] This difficulty in distinguishing between the individual and the general is not restricted to dealings with the natural world. See Clemoes, *Interactions of Thought and Language*, pp. 120–1.

defensive postures. This lack of distinction in Old English poetic texts raises an interesting question: if it is not possible to isolate the individual from the abstract group that he or she supposedly represents – if, for example, the society represented by Hrothgar cannot be described except through Hrothgar – can one claim that such an apparently synecdochical individual truly refers back to a realised abstract concept at all? This question, though an issue in its own right, is of interest here because of the ramifications that the absence of concepts like 'humanity' and 'society' in Anglo-Saxon thought would have for the arguments in the previous two chapters: if there is no 'humanity' or 'society' in Anglo-Saxon minds, what is defined by the natural world in the texts described above? It has, in fact, been argued that the concepts of both 'humanity' and 'society' are abstractions imposed by modern patterns of cognition upon texts written by people without a real understanding of them,[7] and it is true that nowhere in Anglo-Saxon texts do 'humanity' (*menniscnes*) and 'society' (*geferscipe*) literally struggle against nature. Instead, laments for the general human condition of helplessness before the power of the natural world are uttered not by 'Man' but by individual voices – Adam's, the Wanderer's, the Seafarer's, the Wife's and the Last Survivor's.[8] Likewise, Grendel's threat to Danish society is summed up with the phrase *Grendel wan / hwile wið Hroþgar* 'Grendel strove against Hrothgar for a time' (*Beowulf* 151b–2a), not *Grendel wan hwile wið geferscipe Gardena* 'Grendel strove against Danish society for a time', nor even *Grendel wan hwile wið folc Gardena* 'Grendel strove against the Danish people for a time.'

One might thus argue that Anglo-Saxon writers may have had little inclination to conceive of an entity like humanity, or to consider the collective relationships between an individual lord and his thegns as a thing in itself, despite the importance ascribed to it by modern investigators into Anglo-Saxon society. The 'lord–thegn relationship' is now almost a synonym for 'Anglo-Saxon society', for most Anglo-Saxon social structures are seen to derive from this complicated system of reciprocal obligations and privileges, which, by the tenth century, controlled the issues of military obligation, public works, taxation, inheritance and

---

[7] Radding, *A World Made by Men*, pp. 42–5 and 84–90.
[8] Cf., however, the view of U. Schaefer, 'The Fictionalized Dilemma: Old English Poems at the Crossroads of Orality and Literacy', in *Mündlichkeit und Schriftlichkeit*, ed. Erzgräber and Volk, pp. 39–51, at 45.

criminal activity.[9] Yet one could argue that the Anglo-Saxons themselves might not have considered their individual relationships to be part of such a system, and one could summon in support the fact that the words *menniscnes* and *geferscipe* are strikingly absent from all Old English poetry, not just poetry describing conflicts between the natural world and the human race.[10]

ORAL-FORMULAIC CONSIDERATIONS

However, the language of this poetry is characteristically concrete, not abstract,[11] and one must thus be careful when interpreting the absence of words for humanity and society; a poetic convention does not necessarily indicate an intellectual gap.[12] The conservative nature[13] of an oral-formulaic poetic vocabulary might go far to account for a lack of abstract words in Old English poetry, and, despite the fact that this poetry appears only in written and thus literate texts, and despite the fact that many Old English poems display much more than a passing acquaintance with books,[14] the form employed in these poems does appear to refer back to

---

[9] Abels, *Lordship and Military Obligation*, pp. 44, 52–6 and 88–9.

[10] *Menniscnes* does not appear at all in poetry, and even in prose many of its appearances are in the form of glosses of the bible. The occurrences of *geferscipe* in poetry are limited to a translation of a Latin text, *The Metres of Boethius XI* (47a, 82a and 93a), and there it is evident that the word does not mean 'society' in the abstract sense but rather 'company'.

[11] Cf., however, Shippey's view in *Old English Verse*, p. 13: 'the determination with which the eye is taken off the object, the utter lack of concern about visible unity, these prove only that Anglo-Saxon poets were not interested in externals'. Yet the undeniable Anglo-Saxon 'carelessness' (*ibid.*) regarding external details does not correspond to abstraction: the *Beowulf*-poet may only discuss objects like Wiglaf's sword when they have 'representative significance' (*ibid.*), but he/she does not require that these objects stand for abstract concepts such as, for example, the history of conflict. It could be argued that swords come close to such a symbolic meaning, however; cf. D. Cronan, 'The Rescuing Sword', *Neophil* 77 (1993), 467–78.

[12] Old English poetic diction similarly blurs the line between factual and figurative narrative. See E. G. Stanley, 'Old English Poetic Diction and the Interpretation of *The Wanderer, The Seafarer,* and *The Penitent's Prayer*', *Anglia* 73 (1955), 413–66 (reprinted in his *A Collection of Papers with Emphasis on Old English Literature* (Toronto, 1987), pp. 234–80).

[13] Ong, *Orality and Literacy*, p. 41. Cf. Hill, 'The Soldier of Christ', p. 57.

[14] For example, Old English poets may have known and used classical rhetorical figures.

oral-formulaic composition,[15] a method of creating poetry apparently described by the *Beowulf*-poet[16] as he or she narrates the Danes' exultation following their confirmation of Grendel's death:

> Hwilum heaþorofe   hleapan leton,
> on geflit faran   fealwe mearas,
> ðær him foldwegas   fægere þuhton,
> cystum cuðe.   Hwilum cyninges þegn,
> guma gilphlæden,   gidda gemyndig,
> se ðe ealfela   ealdgesegena
> worn gemunde,   word oþer fand
> soðe gebunden;   secg eft ongan
> sið Beowulfes   snyttrum styrian,
> ond on sped wrecan   spel gerade,
> wordum wrixlan.   (*Beowulf* 864–74a)[17]

See L. D. Benson, 'The Literary Character of Anglo-Saxon Formulaic Poetry', *PMLA* 81 (1966), 334–41; J. J. Campbell, 'Learned Rhetoric in Old English Poetry', *MP* 63 (1966), 189–201; J. J. Campbell, 'Knowledge of Rhetorical Figures in Anglo-Saxon England', *JEGP* 66 (1967), 1–20; J. J. Campbell, 'Adaptation of Classical Rhetoric in Old English Literature', in *Medieval Eloquence: Studies in the Theory and Practice of Medieval Rhetoric*, ed. J. J. Murphy (Berkeley, CA, 1978), pp. 173–97; Frank, 'Some Uses of Paronomasia'; W. H. Beale, 'Rhetoric in the Old English Verse-Paragraph', *NM* 80 (1979), 133–42; M. Nelson, 'The Rhetoric of the Exeter Book Riddles', *Speculum* 49 (1974), 421–40.

[15] The idea of oral-formulaic composition in Old English poetry has been discussed intensively since it first arose. The article that instigated the debate is F. P. Magoun, Jr, 'The Oral-Formulaic Character of Anglo-Saxon Narrative Poetry', *Speculum* 28 (1953), 446–67. For a summary of the development of the field from the mid-nineteenth century to 1981, see J. M. Foley, *The Theory of Oral Composition: History and Methodology* (Bloomington, 1988), pp. 65–74. Additional useful summaries appear in A. H. Olsen, 'Oral-Formulaic Research in Old English Studies: I', *Oral Tradition* 1 (1986), 548–606 and 'Oral-Formulaic Research in Old English Studies: II', *Oral Tradition* 3 (1988), 138–90; and D. H. Green, 'Orality and Reading: The State of Research in Medieval Studies', *Speculum* 65 (1990), 267–80.

[16] And perhaps also a method echoed in the *Beowulf*-poet's own text. See H.-J. Diller, 'Literacy and Orality in *Beowulf*: The Problem of Reference', in *Mündlichkeit und Schriftlichkeit*, ed. Erzgräber and Volk, pp. 15–25, at 25.

[17] 'Sometimes those brave in battle [i.e. the Danes] let their glossy horses gallop and run in competition where the paths seemed good [and were] known for their excellence. Sometimes a thegn of the king, a man laden with boasts, [was] mindful of songs, he who remembered a great number of the old traditions; a word found another truly bound together; the man again began to tell Beowulf's journey wisely, and skilfully to

The context of this skilfully woven tale is important: the Danish *scop* composes his story about Beowulf minutes after ascertaining its truth as he rides back from the mere. That is, the composition of the tale takes place spontaneously, without the use of writing.[18] Whether any of the Old English poems presently extant derive from such an event is impossible to determine,[19] but they do share some characteristics with oral-formulaic poetry as defined by scholars.[20] For example, many poems appear to contain standard, traditional descriptions of situations or scenes that are used as building blocks – themes[21] and type-scenes[22] like the 'Beasts of Battle'[23] and 'The Hero on the Beach'.[24]

make a clever story, to exchange words.' For the translation of *fealu* as 'glossy', see Barley, 'Old English Colour Classification', pp. 21–4.

[18] For more discussion of this passage, see Opland, 'From Horseback to Monastic Cell', pp. 30–3; N. E. Eliason, 'The "Improvised Lay" in *Beowulf* ', *PQ* 31 (1952), 171–9; R. P. Creed, ' "... Wel-Hwelc Gecwæþ ...": The Singer as Architect', *Tennessee Studies in Literature* 11 (1966), 131–43; R. E. Kaske, 'The Sigemund-Heremod and Hama-Hygelac Passages in *Beowulf* ', *PMLA* 74 (1959), 489–94.

[19] Bede's account of *Cædmon's Hymn*, however, does contain another example of apparently spontaneous, oral composition. See *Historia ecclesiastica* IV.24 (pp. 414–20). For discussion of this account, see A. Orchard, 'Poetic Inspiration and Prosaic Translation'; in *Doubt Wisely: Papers in Language and Literature for E. G. Stanley*, eds. M. J. Toswell and E. M. Tyler (London, 1996); Wrenn, 'The Poetry of Cædmon'; F. P. Magoun, Jr, 'Bede's Story of Cædmon: The Case History of an Anglo-Saxon Oral Singer', *Speculum* 30 (1955), 49–63; Huppé, *Doctrine and Poetry*, pp. 99–130; G. H. Brown, 'Old English Verse as a Medium for Christian Theology', in *Modes of Interpretation*, ed. Brown, Crampton and Robinson, pp. 15–28.

[20] See especially A. B. Lord, *The Singer of Tales*, Harvard Studies in Comparative Literature 24 (Cambridge, MA, 1960). See also J. M. Foley, *Oral-Formulaic Theory and Research: An Introduction and Annotated Bibliography* (New York, 1985), pp. 3–70.

[21] A theme has been defined as 'a subject unit, a group of ideas, regularly employed by a singer, not merely in any given poem, but in the poetry as a whole'. A. B. Lord, 'Homer and Huso II: Narrative Inconsistencies in Homer and Oral Poetry', *Transactions and Proceedings of the American Philological Society* 69 (1938), 439–45, at 440.

[22] D. K. Fry, 'Old English Formulaic Themes and Type-Scenes', *Neophil* 52 (1968), 48–54.

[23] For discussion of the 'Beasts of Battle', see above, p. 10, n. 50.

[24] For definition of this theme, see D. K. Crowne, 'The Hero on the Beach: An Example of Composition by Theme in Anglo-Saxon Poetry', *NM* 61 (1960), 362–72. This theme has been identified in a number of poems; see, for example, J. Thormann, 'Variations on the Theme of "The Hero on the Beach" in *The Phoenix*', *NM* 71 (1970), 187–90; D. K. Fry, 'The Hero on the Beach in *Finnsburh*', *NM* 67 (1966), 27–31; D. K. Fry, 'The Heroine on the Beach in *Judith*', *NM* 68 (1967), 168–84;

These themes or type-scenes may be merely stylistic remnants of an earlier poetic tradition, but they may also indicate a continuing pattern of thought and interaction based upon orality, despite the prevailing literate conditions.[25] One of the characteristics of oral thought patterns is an absence of abstractions,[26] and one might thus ascribe Old English poetry's concreteness to such a pattern of thought. However, while a prevailing orality in Old English poetry could account for the absence of words like *geferscipe*, the fact that the texts – and the culture from which they arise – are literate means that one cannot claim an inability to conceive of abstractions on the part of Old English poets merely based on their participation in a residual oral culture. A lack of abstractions, like type-scenes, may simply be a stylistic characteristic of Old English poetry[27] and not prove anything about the Anglo-Saxon understanding of concepts like humanity and society.

THE VISUAL ARTS AND THE LAW

One might thus turn to other sources and texts to gain confirmation or negation of the existence of the concepts said to be defined by the representation of the natural world. For example, the visual arts offer evidence regarding how Anglo-Saxons viewed not only their relationship with the natural world[28] but also their understanding of abstract ideas

D. Hamilton, '*Andreas* and *Beowulf*: Placing the Hero', in *Anglo-Saxon Poetry: Essays in Appreciation for John C. McGalliard*, ed. Nicholson and Frese, pp. 81–98, at 94; Higley, '*Aldor on Ofre*, or the Reluctant Hart'.

25 Clanchy, *From Memory to Written Record*, pp. 1, 224 and 254; Ong, *Orality and Literacy*, p. 26. The consequences of the transformation from orality to literacy for both Anglo-Saxon literature and society have been discussed in detail elsewhere. See, for example, Bäuml, 'Varieties and Consequences of Medieval Literacy and Illiteracy', *Speculum* 55 (1980), 237–65; H. J. Chaytor, *From Script to Print: An Introduction to Medieval Literature* (Cambridge, 1945), pp. 5–21; Kelly, 'Anglo-Saxon Lay Society and the Written Word'; A. Renoir, 'Oral-Formulaic Context: Implications for the Comparative Criticism of Medieval Texts', in *Oral Traditional Literature: A Festschrift for Albert Bates Lord*, ed. J. M. Foley (Columbus, OH, 1980), pp. 416–39; O'Keeffe, *Visible Song*, pp. 1–22. Cf. also Lerer, who suggests that symptoms of orality in Old English texts are literary fictions, *Literacy and Power*, p. 4.

26 Ong, *Orality and Literacy*, pp. 50–5.   27 Frank, '"Mere" and "Sund"', p. 154.

28 See, for example, Friedman, 'The Marvels-of-the-East Tradition', pp. 327–34 and 338; V. I. J. Flint, 'Monsters and the Antipodes in the Early Middle Ages and Enlightenment', *Viator* 15 (1984), 65–80; P. Testini, 'Il Simbolismo degli Animali nell'Arte

like the structure of the universe.[29] Law codes similarly have the potential
to offer much information, especially regarding Anglo-Saxon ideas about
society. In fact, in both cases one finds contradictory evidence. Although
the illustrations of the Creation in the Junius manuscript,[30] like illustrations of the Creation cycle elsewhere, contain reflections of exegetical
interpretations of the biblical text,[31] they do not abstract these interpretations into the form of the later 'Genesis initial', a design that unites the
events of the Creation not only with depictions of the Fall and redemption
but also with representations of the Platonic schema of the universe
(including the relationship between the four elements).[32] Such
illustrations indicate both that the Anglo-Saxon illustrator(s) sought to
incorporate non-literal interpretations into the depiction of the events of
the Creation, and that he or she or they[33] did not go so far as to reduce
the act of Creation to an abstract, geometric scheme, as later artists
did. Perhaps the Anglo-Saxon artist(s), still participating in an oral
framework, could not see the chronology of the Creation as later artists
did; perhaps there was a choice of style based on other criteria.[34] That is,

Figurativa Paleocristiana', *Settimane* 31 (1985), 1107–68. Cf. also F. Klingender, who
argues that the 'barbaric art' of this age 'was inadequate to provide the monumental
symbols of authority and the representational imagery through which urban civiliza-
tions seek to express a richer content of ideas' (*Animals in Art and Thought to the End of
the Middle Ages*, ed. E. Antal and J. Harthan (London, 1971), p. 141).

[29] Glass, '*In Principio*'; Blum, 'Cryptic Creation Cycle'. For further discussion of Anglo-
Saxon ideas of the structure of the universe, see below, pp. 145–8 and 153–63.

[30] For some discussion of these illustrations, see Ohlgren, 'Five New Drawings';
T. Ohlgren, 'Visual Language in the Old English *Caedmonian Genesis*', *Visible Language*
6 (1972), 253–76; T. Ohlgren, 'The Illustrations of the *Caedmonian Genesis*: Literary
Criticism through Art', *Medievalia et Humanistica: Studies in Medieval and Renaissance
Culture* ns 3 (1972), 199–212.

[31] Glass, '*In Principio*', p. 97; Blum, 'Cryptic Creation Cycle', pp. 211 and 215.

[32] Blum, 'Cryptic Creation Cycle', pp. 220–1.

[33] For discussion of how many illustrators were involved in the manuscript, see
M. Rickert, *Painting in Britain: The Middle Ages* (Harmondsworth, 1954), p. 45;
Ohlgren, 'Five New Drawings', pp. 231–2; G. Henderson, 'The Programme of
Illustrations in Bodleian Ms. Junius XI', in *Studies in Memory of David Talbot Rice*, eds.
G. Robertson and G. Henderson (Edinburgh, 1975), pp. 113–45, at 144–5.

[34] Novel illustrations in the Old English Hexateuch, for example, can derive from a
'literal rendering of the Old English text into images', but also from ideas coming
from the 'Anglo-Saxon milieu' – that is, from ideas outside the text. See Mellinkoff,
'Serpent Imagery', p. 51.

one cannot be certain about either the extent of abstraction or the understanding of cosmological structure that contributed to the production of
the illustration.

In the same way, in Anglo-Saxon law codes one finds that there is little
sign of a 'society' or public order,[35] but rather a great deal of interest in
the compensation that individual malefactors had to pay to their victims
and lords.[36] On the other hand, one can also find that the laws deal not so
much with individuals at all, but rather with the kindred group to which
they belong,[37] and one might thus interpret the *Anglo-Saxon Chronicle*'s
naming of kindred groups, such as *Angelcynn*, as evidence of the self-
awareness of a nation or political community.[38] That is, one finds
inconclusive evidence both for and against Anglo-Saxon awareness of the
abstract idea of society.

A full discussion of either Anglo-Saxon visual art or law lies beyond
the scope of this investigation, as does examination of many other,
potentially informative texts, particularly those contained in the corpus of
Latin literature, which provides a much larger range of styles, genres and
subjects than that preserved in Old English poetry;[39] it is not possible
here to examine the representation of the natural world in all these texts
and other sources, much less determine the Anglo-Saxons' cognitive
abilities.[40] However, it is possible to surmise that additional investigation
into Anglo-Saxon ideas regarding humanity and society would uncover

---

[35] Jolliffe, *Constitutional History*, p. 45, n. 1.

[36] Radding, *A World Made by Men*, pp. 84–90.

[37] J. W. Earl, *Thinking about 'Beowulf'* (Stanford, CA, 1994), p. 108.

[38] Jolliffe, *Constitutional History*, p. 2. See also Wormald, 'Bede, the *Bretwaldas* and the
Origins of the *Gens Anglorum*' and S. Foot, 'The Making of Angelcynn: English
Identity before the Norman Conquest', *TRHS* 6th ser. 6 (1996), 637–52, at 638–9.

[39] For some idea of the range of Latin texts available, see M. Lapidge, 'The Anglo-Latin
Background', in *A New Critical Review of Old English Literature*, ed. S. B. Greenfield and
D. G. Calder (New York, 1986), pp. 5–37; M. Lapidge, 'Surviving Booklists from
Anglo-Saxon England', in *Learning and Literature in Anglo-Saxon England: Studies
Presented to Peter Clemoes on the Occasion of his Sixty-Fifth Birthday*, ed. M. Lapidge and
H. Gneuss, pp. 33–89; T. J. Brown, 'An Historical Introduction to the Use of Classical
Latin Authors in the British Isles from the Fifth to the Eleventh Century', *Settimane*
22 (1974), 237–93. For discussion of Latin learning, see Lapidge, *Anglo-Latin
Literature 900–1066* and *Anglo-Latin Literature 600–899* (London and Rio Grande,
OH, 1996).

[40] But see Radding, *A World Made by Men* and Gurevich, *Categories of Medieval Culture*,
p. 13.

further uncertainties and contradictions, if for no other reason than that the centuries constituting the Anglo-Saxon period saw many changes and developments in, for example, the social structure.[41] One might also expect parallel developments in depictions of the natural world, even though most critics argue that there was little development in approaches to the natural world in this period:[42] Isidore is said to copy and corrupt Pliny and his other sources unquestioningly,[43] and later writers are said to copy and corrupt Isidore[44] and the few other sources to which they had access.[45] The representation of the natural world in Old English poetry may lend indirect confirmation for this lack of development, for there is no discernible chronology of ideas about the natural world in the undatable body of extant texts.[46] This may not mean that there was no development; it may merely be impossible to trace it through time now. On the other hand, there may simply have been diversity without development. Whatever the case, the same is probably true of Anglo-Saxon ideas regarding society and humanity.

As a result, this excursion in search of confirmation or negation of the

---

[41] For description of the development in ideas behind military organisation in Anglo-Saxon England, for example, see Abels, *Lordship and Military Obligation*. For some of the changes in the institutions of law, see Jolliffe, *Constitutional History*, pp. 57–138. One might also note one critic's assertion that there were as many distinct major philosophies during the Middle Ages as there were major philosophers (attributed to E. Gilson, in R. S. Crane, 'On Hypotheses in "Historical Criticism": Apropos of Certain Contemporary Medievalists', in his *The Idea of the Humanities and Other Essays Critical and Historical*, 2 (Chicago, 1967), II, 251). It has been argued, however, that changes in the 'medieval world picture' were so slow as to be negligible – see Gurevich, *Categories of Medieval Culture*, pp. 18–19.

[42] See above, pp. 13–14. One exception is Flint, 'The Transmission of Astrology'.

[43] Brehaut, *Encyclopedist of the Dark Ages*, p. 16.

[44] Seventh-century Irish sources may be an exception to this generalisation, since the Irish apparently received little ancient scientific writing and thus were able to develop their own ideas about the natural world. See Smyth, 'Isidore of Seville and Early Irish Cosmography', p. 69; M. Smyth, 'The Physical World in Seventh-Century Hiberno-Latin Texts'; *Peritia* 5 (1986), 201–34; M. Smyth, *Understanding the Universe in Seventh-Century Ireland*, Studies in Celtic History 15 (Woodbridge, 1996).

[45] This complaint is widespread. See, for example, Jones, 'Some Introductory Remarks', p. 118; C. Kappler, *Monstres, Démons et Merveilles à la Fin du Moyen Age* (Paris, 1980), p. 19; Singer, *A Short History of Scientific Ideas to 1900*, pp. 138–9; Abrams, 'The Development of Medieval Astronomy', p. 194.

[46] For further discussion, see below, pp. 144–5.

constructs defined in the previous two chapters ends by reaffirming what was stated early in chapter 2: since the Anglo-Saxons have left behind little direct commentary on the state of humanity and society, the representation of the natural world not only has much to offer to an understanding of how the Anglo-Saxons viewed themselves, but is one of the few sources available for the investigation of it. This source, however, unavoidably leaves room for doubt about how much Anglo-Saxon writers thought about abstractions like humanity and society and how clearly they imagined them.

IMPRECISION AND AMBIGUITY

The issues raised above, though not resolvable, point to an important characteristic of the representation of the natural world in Old English poetry. Whether or not the ambiguity between individual and collective relations to the natural world reflects an inability to grasp abstractions, the uncertainty reveals that the representation of the natural world in Anglo-Saxon writing is uneven: it is not always developed sufficiently to allow for much comment beyond rather banal observations, such as 'life is hard'. In fact, although the previous chapters have focused as much as possible upon specific, concrete representations of the natural world – storms, seas, monsters, wolves – very often the natural world appears as nothing more than an undefined danger.[47] That is, it can hardly be said to 'appear' at all. For example, in *Journey Charm* a fearful individual appeals to a higher power for protection from a range of undefined threats:

> Ic me on þisse gyrde beluce and on godes helde bebeode
> wið þane sara stice, wið þane sara slege,
> wið þane grymma gryre,
> wið ðane micela egsa þa bið eghwam lað,
> and wið eal þæt lað þe in to land fare.
> Sygegealdor ic begale, sigegyrd ic me wege,
> wordsige and worcsige. Se me dege;
> ne me mere ne gemyrre, ne me maga ne geswence,
> ne me næfre minum feore forht ne gewurþe,
> ac gehæle me ælmihtig and sunu and frofre gast,

---

[47] This lack of 'reference to spatial or visual shape', like the lack of abstraction mentioned earlier, is characteristic of Old English poetic language. See Frank, '"Mere" and "Sund"', p. 153.

ealles wuldres   wyrðig dryhten,
swa swa ic gehyrde   heofna scyppende ...
Forð ic gefare,   frind ic gemete,
eall engla blæd,   eadiges lare.
Bidde ic nu sigeres god   godes miltse,
siðfæt godne,   smylte and lihte
windas on waroþum.   Windas gefran,
circinde wæter   simble gehælede
wið eallum feondum.   Freond ic gemete wið,
þæt ic on þæs ælmihtgian frið   wunian mote,
belocun wið þam laþan,   se me lyfes eht,
on engla blæd   gestaþelod,
and inna halre hand   heofna rices,
þa hwile þe ic on þis life   wunian mote. Amen.

(The Journey Charm 1–12, 31–42)[48]

It can be argued that the 'journey' described in the poem is a metaphor for the general concept of 'life' and that the poem itself is a prayer for spiritual protection and guidance until the time of departure to heaven.[49] Yet, although it is possible to read the poem entirely in terms of protection from the temptations of the devil, the poem does not provide much evidence of a spiritual contest. Its language is physical; its concern is with the speaker's life, not his or her soul. In fact, the literal context of the poem is of someone stepping out into the natural world and journeying through it.

[48] 'I protect myself with this rod and under God's protection proclaim against the painful sting, against the painful blow, against the grim terror, against the great horror which is hostile to everyone, and against everything hostile that travels into the land. A victory-charm I chant, a victory-rod I carry, word-victory and work-victory. May it be strong for me; may no harmer/nightmare harm me, nor my stomach torment me, nor there ever be any fear for my life; rather may the almighty and his son and the consoling spirit heal me, the lord worthy of all glory, as I obey the creator of the heavens ... I travel forth: may I meet friends, all the splendour of angels, the teaching of the blessed/prosperous. I ask now the God of victory for God's mercy, a good road, mild and light winds on the shores. I have heard the winds, the roaring water, [while I was] always protected from all enemies. May I meet with friends, so that I might dwell in the almighty's security, locked up against the hostile one who attacks my life, made firm in the splendour of angels, and inside the healing hand of the ruler of heaven, as long as I might dwell in this life.'

[49] H. Stuart, '"Ic me on þisse gyrde beluce": The Structure and Meaning of the Old English *Journey Charm*', *MÆ* 50 (1981), 259–73, at 268–9.

It is difficult, however, to determine exactly what the charm is warding against. Given the appositive nature of Old English poetry, it is difficult even to know how many separate 'things' are discussed in the charm – whether there are clear distinctions between a *stice* and a *slege*, whether the *grymma gryre* is responsible for them or represents a separate cause for concern, whether the *micela egsa* is merely another designation for the *gryre* and whether all the *lað* things travelling through the land are further entities or a summary of those preceding them. Also, it is possible that the charm intends to ward off any blow, any grim terror, any hostile thing that travels through the land. That is, it is possible that particular identities were never intended for these nouns. This may be true despite the impression given by *þane*, which may have a meaning as strong as 'that'. If *þane* does mean 'that', however, the charm may be very specific in its reference to '*that* great horror, which everyone knows is hostile to everyone' and '*that* thing, commonly called the grim terror', in the same way that 'Grendel' was the name known by people for the grim terror stalking through the land near Heorot.

Unfortunately, the evidence of other texts only increases the ambiguity. *Gryre* is used elsewhere to describe both the Grendelkin and *Maxims I*'s wolf,[50] and there is nothing in the poem to disqualify *lað* 'the hostile thing' or *gryre* 'the terror' from being either a Grendel-type monster or a wolf. On the other hand, there is also not much other than these very common words to provide an idea of what the speaker fears. Within *Beowulf* alone, *lað* is used to designate human beings six times, inanimate objects or abstract concepts six times, monsters fourteen times and the weather once.[51] Also in *Beowulf*, *gryre* and its compounds describe monsters most often (eleven times), but this word is also applied to the actions and attributes of human beings (twice).[52] That is, the words refer often enough to human beings and other things to show that their use is not limited to a particular type of creature.

---

[50] *Beowulf* 384a, 478a, 591b and 1282b; *Maxims I* 148a.

[51] Human beings: 242b, 440a, 511a, 815a, 2432b and 2672a. Inanimate objects or abstract concepts: 83a, 134a, 192a, 1061a, 2467a and 3029a. Monsters: 132a, 440a, 550a, 841a, 929b, 938a, 1257a, 1505b, 2008b, 2305a, 2315a, 2354a, 2910a and 3040a. The weather: 1375a.

[52] Monsters: 174a, 384a, 478b, 591b, 786a, 1282b, 1284a, 1441a, 2136a, 2560a and 3041a. Actions or attributes of human beings: 324a and 483b.

THE NIGHTMARE

Mere, although more specific, is even more difficult to identify, since the uncertainty of its minimal context in *The Journey Charm* is compounded by the uncertainty of the word's meaning elsewhere. Given its company in its half-line, the potentially tormenting *maga* 'stomach', it seems logical to look to Anglo-Saxon medical texts for enlightenment. There treatments are suggested that are *gode* 'good' against *mære* and *nihtgengan* 'night-visitors'.[53] In this context, it appears that a *mere* or *mære* is a nightmare.

One need not doubt that a traveller might seek to protect him or herself from nightmares. One might even note the close association of the tormenting stomach in the same half-line as the *mære* as an indication that the Anglo-Saxons were aware of the link between over-eating before sleep and bad dreams, as Chaucer certainly was.[54] However, while Chaucer has left behind a discussion of the nature of dreams, Old English poets have not.[55] One can assume that they did not have a modern, psychological concept of the bad dream, but all one can tell about 'mares' from *The Journey Charm* is that they can 'harm', apparently physically. To get closer to the meaning of this word than the limited context of *The Journey Charm* allows, I shall pursue two lines of inquiry: an exploration of the Indo-European and Germanic roots of the word, and an examination of the Latin and Old English words that Anglo-Saxon glossators associated with it. An awareness of the ambiguities underlying *mære* provides a useful perspective for approaching not only famous monsters like Grendel but also Old English representations of the natural world more generally: the *mære* demonstrates that what is important is the opposing power that these entities possess, rather than their specific identities.

---

[53] *Leechdoms, Wortcunning and Starcraft*, ed. Cockayne, p. 306.

[54] See, for example, *The Nun's Priest's Tale* 2921–3156, where the cock and hen debate whether his dream came from *replecciouns* 'over-eating' or divine wisdom; for the sources of dream lore that Chaucer might have consulted, see *The Riverside Chaucer*, ed. L. D. Benson, 3rd edn (Boston, MA, 1987), p. 937.

[55] They did apparently have access to classical dream-theory, however. See A. Harbus, 'Nebuchadnessar's Dreams in the Old English *Daniel*', *ES* 75 (1994), 489–508, at 495.

Etymologies and Medical Associations

The Indo-European root of *mære* suggests a range of hostile, dangerous associations: *mer-* indicates pushing, destroying,[56] forcing down, crushing[57] or harming, and gave rise to a Germanic word, **maron* 'goblin'.[58] This root is possibly related to another *mer-*, whose derivatives refer to death and to human beings as subject to death.[59] Related words include words for witch, ghost, Morrigain (queen of the elves),[60] a Norwegian giant[61] and the mysterious lights in swamps, the will-o'-the-wisp.[62] In addition, the German word for nightmare, although not etymologically related to *mære*, is *alptraum* 'elf-dream',[63] and so it, too, associates bad dreams with this 'family' of hostile creatures. Although the Anglo-Saxons did not necessarily believe in all these creatures, there is evidence for belief in some of them. The reference to elves in the German word for nightmare is particularly suggestive, since it recalls the Old English elves who shoot disease-causing arrows.[64]

One might also note the *dweorh* 'dwarf' in the Old English charm, *Wiþ Dweorh*, as dwarves and elves are closely related,[65] and it has been argued that the charm is intended to ward off a nightmare:[66]

---

[56] *Isländisches Etymologisches Wörterbuch*, ed. Jóhannesson, s.v. *mer-* (p. 669).

[57] *Vergleichendes Wörterbuch*, ed. Walde, s.v. *mer-* (vol. 2, p. 277).

[58] *Dictionary of Indo-European Roots*, ed. Watkins, s.v. *mer-* (p. 42).

[59] *Ibid.*, s.v. *mer-* (p. 42). See also *Vergleichendes Wörterbuch*, ed. Walde, s.v. *mer-* (p. 277): 'Auch *mer-* "sterben" ist urspr[ün]gl[ich] = *mer* "aufreiben"'.

[60] *Vergleichendes Wörterbuch*, ed. Walde, s.v. *mer-* (p. 277); *Altenglisches Etymologisches Wörterbuch*, ed. F. Holthausen, (Heidelberg, 1934) s.v. *mare* (p. 215).

[61] She was named *Morn*, 'the crusher'. *Isländisches Etymologisches Wörterbuch*, ed. Jóhannesson, s.v. *mer-* (p. 670).

[62] Icelandic *maurildi*, Danish *marild, morild*, Norwegian *morild* and Swiss *mareld* refer to 'meerleuchten', 'phosphoreszierendes leuchten in verfaulten stoffen, morschem holz, rohem fisch'. *Ibid.*, s.v. *mer-* (p. 670).

[63] Grimm, *Teutonic Mythology*, p. 443.

[64] For further discussion of disease, see below, pp. 115–21.

[65] See the discussion in Grimm, *Teutonic Mythology*, pp. 443–72.

[66] Nelson, 'An Old English Charm Against Nightmare'. Cf., however, Stuart, who suggests that dwarf- or *mære*-riding refers to epileptic fits and other spasms, including those caused by asthma ('The Anglo-Saxon Elf', pp. 314–15). Cf. also Jamborn, *'Peri Didaxeon'*, pp. 149–53.

Her com in gangan,   in spiderwiht,
hæfde him his haman on handa,   cwæð þæt þu his hæncgest wære,
legde þe his teage an sweoran.   Ongunnan him of þæm lande liþan;
sona swa hy of þæm lande coman,   þa ongunnan him ða liþu colian.
Þa com in gangan   dweores sweostar;
Þa geændade heo   and aðas swor
ðæt næfre þis ðæm adlegan   derian ne moste,
ne þæm þe þis galdor   begytan mihte,
oððe þe þis galdor   ongalan cuþe. Amen. Fiað.   *(Against a Dwarf)*[67]

Some of the details of the action are difficult to explain, but the 'garment' and 'fetters' seem to derive from dwarves' associations with spiders and spinning. In general, the charm seems to describe a dwarf that 'rides' its victims, like the traditional nightmare. It has also been suggested that dwarf- and *mære*-riding refers to epileptic fits and other spasms, including those caused by asthma.[68] For my purposes it is not crucial to determine whether the ailment is epilepsy or a nightmare; it is possible that the feelings of paralysis common to both were seen by the Anglo-Saxons as similar or identical problems. What is of interest to me here are the perceived sources of the problems, all of which seem to be associated in one way or another with the *mære*. It seems clear that the *mære* was some kind of supernatural creature, like an elf or dwarf, which was hostile to human beings and could afflict them physically in some way, most likely in the same way as the dwarf in the charm.

With the introduction of Christianity, devils took over the elfish habit of shooting invisible, health-impairing arrows and the dwarfish habit of oppressing people in their sleep,[69] and so the *mære* may have gained devilish characteristics as well. Devils do not, however, appear to have

---

[67] 'A spider-creature came in here; he had his garment in his hands. He said that you were his horse and laid his fetters on your neck. They began to travel from the land; as soon as they came from the land, their limbs began to cool. Then the dwarf's sister came in; she ended this and swore oaths that this would never be permitted to hurt the sick one, neither one who could receive this song nor one who knew how to sing this song. Amen. So be it.'

[68] Stuart, 'The Anglo-Saxon Elf', pp. 314–15. Cf. also Jamborn, *'Peri Didaxeon'*, pp. 149–53.

[69] See Bonser, 'Magical Practices against Elves', *Folklore* 37 (1926), 350–63, at 359. He cites as evidence for the equation of elves and devils the following line from London, British Library, Royal 2 A XX, 45v: *Adiuro te Satanae diabulus aelfae*. The charm is printed in Storms, *Anglo-Saxon Magic*, p. 294. See also Grattan and Singer, *Anglo-Saxon*

supplanted the previous inhabitants of the Anglo-Saxon landscape altogether; elves, dwarves and devils seem to have tormented their unfortunate victims side by side. The presence of these devils in the natural world can be explained by the tradition that the fallen angels were not all confined to hell and that some were assigned residences in the sky, water and woods, like the demons who had taken up residence in Guthlac's fens.[70]

The Evidence of Glossaries

Old English glossaries offer a different set of associations. The Latin word most commonly defined by *mære* is *incuba*.[71] From classical Latin onwards, *incubo* or *incubus* was used to designate a nightmare; in the Middle Ages, the creature that 'lay upon' (*incubare*) its victims was described as:

a feigned evil spirit or demon (originating in personified representations of the nightmare) supposed to descend upon persons in their sleep, and especially to seek carnal intercourse with women.[72]

Mære appears to be a good translation of *incuba*, especially since the roots of both words (*mer-*, *incubare*) suggest the act of forcing down.[73] It is possible, therefore, that the Anglo-Saxons possessed a native tradition of an evil creature that sat on people during their sleep and that, when the Anglo-Saxons discovered the Latin word *incuba*, they easily recognised their own 'crusher' despite the foreign name.[74] The Old English *mære* does not, however, appear to have the sexual nature of the *incuba*, although other traditions do maintain a clear connection between elves, goblins

Magic and Medicine, p. 50, and Meaney, 'The Anglo-Saxon View of the Causes of Illness', p. 18.

[70] See also *The Prose 'Solomon and Saturn'*, ed. Cross and Hill, pp. 97–8.

[71] The Epinal, Erfurt, Corpus and Leiden glossaries all supply some variation of *mære* for *incuba*. See *Old English Glosses*, ed. Pheifer, p. 30 (line 558).

[72] See *OED*, s.v. *incubus*.

[73] See *Vergleichendes Wörterbuch*, ed. Walde, s.v. *mer-* (p. 277), which defines *mære* as: 'übernatürliches weibliches Wesen, das sich in der Nacht den Schlafende auf die Brust setzt'. Cf. also the French word *cauchemar* 'nightmare', whose first element derives from *calcare* 'to tread, trample'. *Isländisches Etymologisches Wörterbuch*, ed. Jóhannesson, s.v. *mer-* (p. 670).

[74] See Thun, 'The Malignant Elves', pp. 388–9. Cf. also Kiessling's discussion of Grendel in his chapter entitled, 'The Germanic North: From Monster to Sex Demon', in *Incubus in English Literature*, pp. 16–20.

and sexuality. Some Old English charms mention *ælfsidene* 'elfish influence' in conjunction with *feondes costunga* 'temptation of the devil', but they do not explicitly link this temptation or influence with sexuality.

The relation between *mære* and *incuba* is complicated by the glossaries' inclusion of other creatures to supplement the definition of *incuba*: satyrs and perhaps a classical deity, Saturn.[75] It seems probable that the glossator of the Erfurt Glossary did not mean to include Saturn and merely misspelled *satyr*, given the Leiden glossator's spelling of it as *saturus*. The yoking of *incuba* and *satyrus*, however, indicates that the glossators were not interested in fine distinctions between classical words for supernatural powers, and so the pagan god may indeed have reminded an Anglo-Saxon of a *mære* – particularly this pagan god, since Saturn is linked with the Tower of Babel and the kin of Cain in *Solomon and Saturn II*.[76] Despite the difference apparent to a modern reader between a spirit or demon who sits upon sleeping people, a partly human, partly bestial woodland creature and a god of agriculture, Old English glossators apparently felt that one word, *mære*, could serve for all. The lack of distinction may in fact have arisen much earlier, since Pliny describes a remedy (made from the tongue, eyes, gall and intestines of a snake) designed to help people troubled by the gods of the night and by *fauni*[77] – that is, apparently, plagued by nightmares. It is also interesting to note that later translations of the bible into English call the hairy, desert-dwelling demons of Semitic tradition 'satyrs'.[78]

There is yet another word associated with *mære* and *incuba* in the glossaries, however. Two glossaries, the Cleopatra A3 and Corpus Glossaries, supply *faecce* or *fecce* for *mære*.[79] The word does not appear in Latin

---

[75] The Epinal Glossary includes *satyrus*; the Erfurt Glossary substitutes *saturnus*; the Leiden Glossary has *saturus*. The Corpus Glossary has *maere* only. *Old English Glosses*, ed. Pheifer, p. 30 (line 558, and note to line 558).

[76] Orchard, *Pride and Prodigies*, p. 83. For further discussion of *Solomon and Saturn*, see below, pp. 197–8.

[77] *Naturalis historia* XXX.xxiv.

[78] See *OED*, s.v. *satyr*. 'In the English Bible the word is applied (without precedent either in the [Septuagint] or the Vulgate) to the hairy demons or monsters ... of Semitic superstition, supposed to inhabit deserts.'

[79] *Old English Glosses*, ed. Pheifer, does not mention the word, but for the Corpus Glossary see J. H. Hessels, *An Eighth-Century Latin-Anglo-Saxon Glossary preserved in the Library of Corpus Christi College, Cambridge* (Cambridge, 1890), p. 6 (line 135); for the

dictionaries and may thus be an Old English word, the origin of the word 'fetch', which is defined as

the apparition, double or wraith of a living person; ... the supernatural facsimile of some individual, which comes to ensure to its original a happy longevity, or immediate dissolution.[80]

It would be unusual for an Old English word to gloss another Old English word, and so it may be that *faecce* was an Irish word; 'fetch' appears only to have been in popular use in Ireland.[81] The Old English glossator, however, seems to have considered it a Latin word, even if no Latin texts remain that contain it. One possibility is that it is related to the modern word 'fetish' or 'fetich', whose meanings include inanimate objects worshipped by savages, charms and sorcery in general, and which appears to derive from the Latin word *factitius* 'created, factitious'.[82] It is difficult, however, to see how such an apparently Christian and derogatory word (almost 'fake') came to be applied to an apparition with power over life and death (thus the modern variant 'fetch-life').[83]

Alien Harmers

The lack of a certain meaning for *faecce*, however, is almost to be expected, given its context. The examination of *mære* undertaken above, far from identifying and limiting the meaning of the word, shows above all that *mære* possessed a wide range of associations and concepts. These include not only the elves, dwarves, ghosts, giants, witches, goblins, satyrs and pagan gods that have been mentioned above but also extend to fauns,[84]

Cleopatra Glossary, see W. G. Stryker, 'The Latin–Old English Glossary in MS Cotton Cleopatra A3' (unpubl. PhD dissertation, Stanford Univ., 1951), line 2459; or see T. Wright, *A Second Volume of Vocabularies* (privately printed, 1873), pp. 35 (line 26) and 108 (line 44), as cited in Bosworth–Toller, s.v. *mære*.

[80] See *OED* s.v. *fetch*.   [81] See *ibid.*

[82] *The Oxford Dictionary of English Etymology*, ed. C. T. Onions with G. W. S. Friedrichsen and R. W. Burchfield (Oxford, 1966), s.v. *fetish* (p. 352).

[83] See *OED*, s.v. *fetch*.

[84] Fauns were assimilated to satyrs during Roman times (see *OED*, s.v. *faun* and *satyr*). *Faunus* originally was a woodland god much like Pan, and with the same nocturnal habits as the *incubae*; satyrs were close associates of both Pan and Dionysus and shared their hedonistic associations. See *The Oxford Classical Dictionary*, ed. S. Hornblower and A. Spawforth, 3rd ed. (Oxford and New York, 1996), s.v. *Faunus* and *satyrs* (pp. 590

naiads, dryads, hamadryads, muses[85] and devils.[86] One might also note that *mære*'s close companion in medical texts, the *nihtgenga*, is elsewhere used to gloss *hyena*:[87] terms like *nihtgenga* may literally describe a creature's habits rather than stand as names. *Mære* could be such a term; it could, like the Norwegian giant's name, simply mean 'crusher' or 'destroyer'. It may thus be best to take the word in its most general sense and translate it as 'harmer'. This translation has the advantage of maintaining the echo (almost a pun) in the original Old English line: *ne me mere ne gemyrre* 'may no harmer harm me' (*The Journey Charm* 8a). Certainly it is impossible to identify the one 'species' to which it belongs and separate it from the web of links to other creatures.[88]

On the other hand, it is clear that the Anglo-Saxons had some kind of creature in mind when they worried about a *mære*. It is also clear that it is not a human harmer: no *mære*, elf or demon lives within the human circle of light; all reside outside, in the natural world, like the giant living in the fens in *Maxims II*. Their place in and connection with the natural world is further suggested by another occurrence of *mære* in an Old English word: *wudumær*. In the glossaries, the word translates 'echo'.[89] Unfortunately it does not appear in any Old English poetic texts, but its

and 1361). In Old High German, 'faun' was translated by the word for 'elf' (Grimm, *Teutonic Mythology*, p. 1408).

[85] The names of these classical entities tended to be glossed with terms for different types of elves: *sæelfen, wuduelfen, wylde elfen*, and *dunælfa*. Stuart, 'The Anglo-Saxon Elf', pp. 317–19.

[86] See p. 104, n. 69 above. There is also a tradition that the fallen angels were not all confined to hell and that some were assigned residences in the sky, water, and woods. See *The Prose 'Solomon and Saturn'*, ed. Cross and Hill, pp. 97–8. See also the discussion of *Guthlac*'s demons below, pp. 125–8.

[87] Jordan, *Die altenglischen Säugertiernamen*, p. 45.

[88] One might also note that the Anglo-Saxons were similarly imprecise in their meaning for the word *wyrm*; although it seems to mean 'dragon' or 'snake' in poetry, in medical texts like the *Herbarium* it is also applied to spiders and scorpions (Meaney, 'The Anglo-Saxon View of the Causes of Illness', p. 27, n. 15); Isidore, too, was broad in his definition of *serpens* 'serpent' and *vermis* 'worm'. See *Etymologiae* XII.iv and XII.v.

[89] See *Old English Glosses*, ed. Pheifer, p. 19 (line 347). He translates the word as 'woodsprite' and refers to the Junius Glossary, which lists not only *satiri* and *fauni* but also a new term, *wudewasan* (*ibid.*, p. 83). Bosworth–Toller defines *wuduwasa* straightforwardly as a satyr or faun, but notes also *silvanus* and the occurrences of *wodwos* in *Sir Gawain and the Green Knight* (721) and *The Alliterative Romance of Alexander* (1540), where they appear to be barbarous men or wild beasts.

appearance in other Germanic texts suggests that it represents the voice of the creatures – elves, dwarves, nymphs, fauns, even the hills and woods themselves[90] – that, like Grendel, dwell on the other side of the *mearc*. 'Natural harmer' obviously does not do justice to the associations implicit in *mære*, but perhaps 'alien harmer' may serve as a general definition.

This definition recalls a very specific monster, Grendel, who is both an *ellorgæst* 'alien spirit' (807b, 1349a and 1621b) and a *scynscaþa* 'demonic harmer' (707a), who is related through Cain to the elves (*Beowulf* 104b–14), whose mother shares with the *incuba* the technique of sitting on human victims (*Beowulf* 1545a)[91] and whose name may mean 'the grinder', thus recalling the crushing aspects of the Indo-European root *mer-*. It has also been argued that Grendel has a direct connection to the word *mære* itself and that, when Grendel is introduced as a *mære mearcstapa*, one should translate as 'mare' in apposition with 'boundary-walker', rather than as 'notorious boundary-walker'. Likewise, when the poet says that *se mæra* wanted to flee from Beowulf's grip, perhaps one should understand it to mean 'the mare' rather than 'the notorious one'. That is, the word *mære* (with a long vowel) meaning 'famous' or 'notorious' may have become confused over time with the *mære* meaning 'harmer'.[92] The metrical problems with such an interpretation make one hesitate to pursue this possibility, but having followed the trail of *mære* through some of its many permutations, one might now approach the seemingly incompatible list of epithets for Grendel (spirit, demon, man, monster, giant etc.)[93] as not simply a poetic technique for increasing suspense and terror[94] but also a reflection of the fluid nature of many of these terms.

The identity and nature of such threats were perhaps more evident to the original audience than they are now, but within the poems themselves, as in *The Journey Charm*, they are not explicitly described. In such cases it would be truer to say that the natural world in the poem

---

[90] Grimm, *Teutonic Mythology*, pp. 452 and 1412–13.

[91] But cf. F. C. Robinson, who argues that Grendel's mother does not actually sit on Beowulf but rather 'besets' him. 'Did Grendel's Mother Sit on Beowulf?' in *From Anglo-Saxon to Early Middle English: Studies Presented to E. G. Stanley*, ed. M. Godden, D. Gray and T. Hoad (Oxford, 1994), pp. 1–7.

[92] See Kiessling, *Incubus in English Literature*, pp. 16–18. For a rejection of this theory, see Lapidge, 'Psychology of Terror', p. 396, n. 11.

[93] For discussion of Grendel's ambiguous nature, see above, pp. 78–80.

[94] Cf. Lapidge, 'Psychology of Terror', pp. 391–4.

represents a general threat of danger from outside than that the natural world is represented in the poem: not only is the *mære* constitutionally vague, but the perpetrators of the *sare stice* 'painful sting' and *sare slege* 'painful blow' are not identified, much less described, and the single image, *circinde wæter* 'roaring water', hardly offers ground for discussion. Yet even when the representation of the natural world is limited and vague it is not devoid of significance, for, as such empty references to the natural world do not contribute to a setting, they must function in other ways. In this case, the lack of detail makes the role of the natural world in reflecting concerns with power and powerlessness more clear.

INDIVIDUALS AGAINST THE NATURAL WORLD

The 'representation' of the natural world in *The Journey Charm* – or, rather, its non-specific, non-descriptive reference to the natural world – provides a useful background for examination of the depiction of individuals in Anglo-Saxon poetry, for in most cases the 'individual' is similarly non-specific and anonymous, and the natural world is similarly non-representational. In such cases the representation of the natural world does not refer to the external environment so much as to the individual's power or lack of power. For example, *Judgement Day II* uses the description of the environment to establish the speaker's precarious and powerless position before the Apocalypse:

> Hwæt! Ic ana sæt   innan bearwe,
> mid helme beþeht,   holte tomiddes,
> þær þa wæterburnan   swegdon and urnon
> on middan gehæge,   eal swa ic secge.
> Eac þær wynwyrta   weoxon and bleowon
> innon þam gemonge   on ænlicum wonge,
> and þa wudubeamas   wagedon and swegdon
> þurh winda gryre;   wolcn wæs gehrered,
> and min earme mod   eal wæs gedrefed.[95]

> (*Judgement Day II* 1–9)

[95] 'Listen! I sat alone in a grove, sheltered by the covering [of the trees], in the midst of a wood, where a stream resounded and ran through a meadow – all just as I say. Also pleasant plants grew and bloomed there in a multitude on the splendid field. And then the trees swayed and resounded from the terror of the winds; the cloud[s were] disturbed, and my miserable mind was troubled.'

110

The Old English poet expands and increases the vividness of the natural setting that appeared in the Latin source of this poem, Bede's *De die iudicii*:[96]

> Inter florigeras fecundi cespitis herbas,
> Flamine ventorum resonantibus undique ramis,
> Arboris umbriferae mæstus sub tegmine solus,
> Dum sedi, subito planctu turbatus amaro. (*De die iudicii* 1–4)[97]

Perhaps most significant among the Old English poet's modifications is the change in the weather. In the Latin poem, the speaker's lament is contrasted with a pleasant garden scene; in the Old English poem, it is the *gryre* 'terror' of the increasingly rough weather that stimulates the speaker's mental distress. The effort that the Old English poet expends on this aspect of the poem reflects the associations latent in the representation of the natural world: the frightening storm is an easy, because traditional, poetic expansion, but it is also entirely appropriate to the message of the original poem. As in many other Old English poems, this individual's interaction with the natural world reveals the same insecurity discussed with reference to the definition of humanity and society. In this case, the realisation of need is designed to impel readers toward a superior source of power. *Christ II* uses the simile of life being like a dangerous sea journey in the same way:

> Nu is þon gelicost   swa we on laguflode
> ofer cald wæter   ceolum liðan
> geond sidne sæ,   sundhendgestum,
> flodwudu fergen.   Is þæt frecne stream
> yða ofermæta   þe we her on lacað
> geond þas wacan woruld,   windge holmas
> ofer deop gelad.   Wæs se drohtað strong
> ærþon we to londe   geliden hæfdon
> ofer hreone hrycg.   (*Christ II* 850–8a)[98]

---

[96] Cf. Magennis, *Images of Community*, pp. 139–40.

[97] 'Among the flowering plants of the fruitful grassy field, with the branches rustling everywhere from the gusts of the winds, under the cover of a shady tree, I, while I sat troubled and alone, [was] suddenly disturbed by a bitter lament.'

[98] 'Now it is most like sailing on the sea-flood, over the cold water, in ships, sea-horses, throughout the wide sea, travelling in sea-wood. That stream is hostile and the waves on which we sway throughout this weak world are beyond measure; the waters on the

Though common to classical traditions[99] as well as Insular Latin texts,[100] the figure of the dangerous sea journey exemplifies the use of the natural world in Old English poetry: the natural world, largely stripped of particularity and imagery, instils a physical insecurity that represents not the effect of the environment but the more profound insecurity of the human individual.[101]

The representation of the natural world does not always, however, send the Anglo-Saxons straight to God. In *Maxims I*, for example, mental self-discipline contrasts with the juxtaposed image of the raging sea: *Styran sceal mon strongum mode* 'one must steer one's mind firmly' (*Maxims I* 50a) lest one be, like the sea before the winds, helplessly forced into *grimmum sælum* 'grim conditions' (51a). The Wanderer, facing the *waþema gebind* 'the binding of the waves' (24b), likewise endorses firm control over one's thoughts and words:

> Ic to soþe wat
> þæt biþ in eorle   indryhten þeaw,
> þæt he his ferðlocan   fæste binde,
> healde his hordcofan,   hycge swa he wille.
>
> (*The Wanderer* 11b–14)[102]

Again, it is difficult to make significant distinctions between the Wanderer as an individual and the Wanderer as a representative of humanity; the *indryhten þeaw* 'noble custom' (12b) practised by this individual as he *gesæt him sundor æt rune* 'sat apart in secret thought' (111b) reflects the passive

---

awful journey are windy. The situation was severe before we had sailed to land over the angry surface.'

[99] For discussion of nautical metaphors, including the tempest at sea, throughout Latin literature, see E. de Saint-Denis, *Le rôle de la mer dans la poésie latine* (Paris, 1935).

[100] Aldhelm (in his prose *De virginitate*), Alcuin (in his poem on York) and the author of the *Liber monstrorum*, for example, combine the nautical metaphor of literary composition as used by Virgil with the Christian metaphor of life in the secular world as a dangerous journey. For discussion and texts of these passages, see Orchard, *Pride and Prodigies*, pp. 96–8.

[101] The connection between the representation of the physical world and the expression of Christian doctrine, especially apocalyptic, can also be seen in Exeter Book *Riddle 1*; see Foley, '"Riddle I" of the *Exeter Book*', pp. 352–4. Foley considers *Riddle 1* to be a unit distinct from *Riddles 2* and *3*, which he groups together; for evidence that the three are one riddle, see above, p. 40, n. 89.

[102] 'I know as a truth that it is a noble custom in a man to bind his life's chest firmly, hold the contents of his heart, however he thinks.' See also *The Wanderer* 112–13.

endurance to which the power of the natural world characteristically limits the human race.[103] Yet, although containment and restriction are at issue here just as they are in defining humanity, and although the poem almost immediately denies the efficacy of even this effort,[104] the binding is performed *by* the individual, not upon him. Against the backdrop of loss, chaos and deterioration represented by the absence of human society and the presence of the natural world, the individual maintains himself through the exercise of control over his mind – a limited kind of power, but still valuable.

Elsewhere it is evident that control is expected to be external as well as internal. Given the limitations of both humanity and society evident in the representations of the natural world discussed earlier, it is hardly surprising that the power to control conditions posited for individuals is not extensive, but the power is of the same kind as the ideal power ascribed to God in the Creation, the power to transform hostile useless-ness (*fremde, unnyt* (*Genesis* 105b and 106a)) into productive artefacts (the human equivalent of the *giefa* 'gifts' in God's *niwra gesceafta* 'new creations,' Paradise (*Genesis* 208–9)).[105] For example, Exeter Book *Riddle 26* describes an object made from a former 'member' of the natural world. The fabrication of this object is a violent assault and defeat – a successful exercise of human power over the natural world:

> Mec feonda sum feore besnyþede,
> woruldstrenga binom, wætte siþþan,
> dyfde on wætre, dyde eft þonan,
> sette on sunnan, þær ic swiþe beleas
> herum þam þe ic hæfde. Heard mec siþþan
> snað seaxses ecg, sindrum begrunden;
> fingras feoldan. (Exeter Book *Riddle 26*, 1–7a)[106]

---

[103] See above, pp. 40–7.

[104] It is a noble custom to maintain mental discipline, but even then *Ne mæg werig mod wyrde wiðstondan, / ne se hreo hyge helpe gefremman* 'the weary spirit cannot withstand fate, nor can the troubled mind perform any help' (*The Wanderer* 15–16).

[105] See above, pp. 57–9.

[106] 'Some enemy robbed me of life, stripped away my physical strength, then wet and dipped me in water, then did it again, set me in the sun, where I was violently deprived of the hair that I had. Afterwards the hard edge of a knife slashed me, and I was ground down with ashes and folded by fingers.'

Although the riddle focuses on marvellous transformations within both the object itself and the people using it,[107] and although it does not specify that the object was originally dangerous or hostile (*fremde*) to God, humanity, human society or any individual, its initial premise is the antagonistic relationship between the parchment-producing animal and human craftsmen, the knife-bearing *feond* 'enemy' who seizes and deprives it of strength. The result of this violent human action is unquestionably positive: in the end, the completed book, probably a Gospel book,[108] is like other beautifully adorned treasures that enhance human life,[109] but also like the Paradise that God created out of useless darkness and chaos and like Grendel's arm once Beowulf has forcibly subdued its originally hostile owner and brought it into the system of human exchange in Hrothgar's hall.[110]

Other riddles also offer descriptions of human triumphs over members of the natural world. The reed pen in Exeter Book *Riddle 60*, though not a treasure like the Gospel book, is transformed from a lonely inhabitant of a wasteland (*anæd*) by the sea into something marvellous through human ingenuity and force:

> Þæt is wundres dæl,
> on sefan searolic   þam þe swylc ne conn,
> hu mec seaxes ord   ond seo swiþre hond,
> eorles ingeþonc   ond ord somod,
> þingum geþydan,   þæt ic wiþ þe sceolde
> for unc anum twam   ærendspræce
> abeodan bealdlice   (Exeter Book *Riddle 60*, 10b–16a)[111]

---

[107] *Gif min bearn wera brucan willað, / hy beoð þy gesundran ond þy sigefæstran* 'if the children of men wish to use me, they will be healthier and firmer in victory as a result' (Exeter Book *Riddle 26*, 18–19). For further discussion of this riddle, see below, p. 198.

[108] ASPR III, p. 335.

[109] A man *gierede mec mid golde; forþon me gliwedon / wrætlic weorc smiþa, wire bifongen* 'clothed me with gold; therefore the wondrous work of the smith adorned me, encased with wire' (Exeter Book *Riddle 26*, 13–14). Cf. the description of the treasures given to Beowulf and those guarded by the dragon in *Beowulf: feower madmas / golde gegyred* 'four treasures adorned with gold' (1027b–8a), a helmet *wirum bewunden* 'wound about with wires' (1031a), *wrætta ond wira* 'ornaments and wires' (2413a).

[110] See above, pp. 80–1.

[111] 'It is a great wonder, an intricate [puzzle] of the mind for one who does not know such things, how the knife's point and the right hand, the man's thought and the

114

Although the 'wonder' underlying the riddle is the ability of the pen to speak silently, the poem recounts the same kind of transformation as that involved in the making of a book: the object, after being removed from its place outside the human circle of light, *be sonde, sæwealle neah, / æt merefarobe* 'by the shore, near the sea-wall, by the surging of the waves' (1–2a), becomes something useful, beautiful or wonderful through the agency of a human individual. Similar processes take place in Exeter Book *Riddles* 53 and 88, where a tree and the antler of a deer, both dwelling happily and naturally in the forest (*bearu, holt*), are seized, removed from their environment, wounded and used by human beings; as tools, as battering rams and ink-horns, they are forced *on wera æhtum* 'into the possessions of men' (Exeter Book *Riddle* 88, 23b). Like Grendel's arm, these objects become valuable when they have been forcibly 'denatured'; that is, when their natural state, characteristics and power have been removed and replaced by traits conferred by human art and skill.[112]

MEDICINE AND MAGIC

The triumphs described in these riddles are modest, in keeping with the limited power possessed by the human race in general; their modesty reinforces rather than contradicts the overwhelming power usually ascribed to the natural world. When great claims to power over the environment are made, on the other hand, they are made in the context of an appeal to a higher power – for example, in the charms, where the focus is on co-opting non-human power for human uses.[113] In these cases the characteristically uneven struggle between human beings and the natural world reappears in the representation of diseases as attacks by elves or dwarves – members of the same threatening 'family' to which the *mære* and *wudumære* belong. It is this parallel between some Anglo-Saxon medical texts and the representation of the natural world that suggests that disease might be included in this discussion; one might otherwise

point together, stabbed me purposefully, so that I might boldly declare a message to you, for us two alone.'

[112] Cf. also the 'pleasure and reassurance' derived from the imposition of order and geometric symmetry on the 'menacing forces of the natural world' by Anglo-Saxon pictorial artists. Robinson, *'Beowulf' and the Appositive Style*, p. 72.

[113] This co-opting of power is the underlying idea of magic in general. See Storms, *Anglo-Saxon Magic*, p. 36.

consider medical texts to be irrelevant to an investigation of the natural world. As with the distinction between 'monstrous' and 'natural',[114] however, one cannot assume that modern divisions (between medicine and natural history, for example) apply to Anglo-Saxon writing, or that what appears to be a different issue (human health) does not offer insight into the representation of the natural world. As has been discussed above, the creatures associated with disease are connected with monsters like Grendel, who lurk outside the boundaries of human society and threaten those within.

As my intention is to investigate the representation of the natural world in Old English poetry and not the nature of Anglo-Saxon medicine itself,[115] I do not pretend to consider the majority of Anglo-Saxon medical writing here. I consider a very small part of it, the charms and recipes that mention elves or other 'supernatural' agents. These medical writings are interesting not only because they apparently contain traces of earlier, pagan beliefs,[116] but because, unlike most Anglo-Saxon medicine, they contain an explanation of the causes of ailments. The Anglo-Saxons' lack of understanding of the origin of disease hampered their attempts to counteract it;[117] like most early practitioners of medicine, they could only react to symptoms,[118] not to imperceptible, microscopic causes.

---

[114] See above, pp. 2–3 and 70–4; cf. also V. Fumagalli, *Landscapes of Fear: Perceptions of Nature and the City in the Middle Ages*, trans. S. Mitchell (Cambridge, 1994), p. 9.

[115] The major medical texts are contained in Cockayne, *Leechdoms, Wortcunning and Starcraft*. For a discussion of Anglo-Saxon medicine centred on its magical characteristics, see Grattan and Singer, *Anglo-Saxon Magic and Medicine* and Storms, *Anglo-Saxon Magic*. For investigation of the learned aspects of Anglo-Saxon medicine and its sources, see C. H. Talbot, 'Some Notes on Anglo-Saxon Medicine', *Medical History* 9 (1965), 156–69; C. H. Talbot, *Medicine in Medieval England* (London, 1967); M. L. Cameron, 'The Sources of Medical Knowledge in Anglo-Saxon England', *ASE* 11 (1983), 135–55; M. L. Cameron, 'Bald's *Leechbook*: Its Sources and their Use in its Compilation', *ASE* 12 (1983), 153–82; M. L. Cameron, 'Anglo-Saxon Medicine and Magic', *ASE* 17 (1988), 191–215; M. L. Cameron, *Anglo-Saxon Medicine*, pp. 65–73; M. A. D'Aronco, 'The Botanical Lexicon of the Old English *Herbarium*', *ASE* 17 (1988), 15–33.

[116] Grendon, 'The Anglo-Saxon Charms', pp. 154–7; Vaughan-Sterling, 'The Anglo-Saxon *Metrical Charms*', pp. 188–9; Grattan and Singer, *Anglo-Saxon Magic and Medicine*, pp. 52–63; Storms, *Anglo-Saxon Magic*, pp. 6–11.

[117] Yet there is evidence that the Anglo-Saxons did react intelligently and observantly in many cases. See Meaney, 'The Anglo-Saxon View of the Causes of Illness', pp. 12–33.

[118] Grattan and Singer, *Anglo-Saxon Magic and Medicine*, p. 92.

Their usual lack of comment on the subject of causes[119] reflects their lack of information, but the absence of facts did not always silence them, and a cause is occasionally cited with little basis that can be perceived from a modern point of view[120] – flying venom, for example, or projectiles shot by elves. Interestingly, just as symptoms often are described without causes,[121] remedies *with* explanations of causes often lack a description of symptoms. For example, the remedies *Wiþ Dweorh* 'Against a Dwarf', *Wiþ fleogendan attre* 'Against Flying Venom', and *Wiþ ylfa gescotum* 'Against Elf-shot'[122] provide no description of the ailments ascribed to supernatural agents – in the case of *Wiþ Dweorh*, for example, critics have attempted to 'solve' the charm as if it were a riddle.[123] The paucity of clear lines of cause and effect leaves modern scholars too free to speculate about whether elves and witches were blamed even when the remedy does not specify a cause,[124] or whether the mention of elves is merely a relic of language and does not represent Anglo-Saxon beliefs about the source of disease at all.[125] However, while one may never determine the extent to which the Anglo-Saxons consciously imagined elves when they spoke of *wæterælf-adl* 'water-elf

---

[119] Cameron, *Anglo-Saxon Medicine*, p. 41.

[120] The options chosen by the Anglo-Saxons appear to have included: the invasion of the body by alien matter, the loss of something inherent, and the disruption of the natural order within the body. See N. F. Barley, 'Anglo-Saxon Magico-Medicine', *Journal of the Anthropological Society of Oxford* 3 (1972), 67–76, at 68.

[121] For example, although one remedy describes how ritualistic use of a beetle can aid *wiþ wambe wærce and rysel wærce* 'against stomach ache and pain in the abdomen' (Storms, *Anglo-Saxon Magic*, p. 262), it mentions nothing of where or why the pain originates.

[122] Storms, *Anglo-Saxon Magic*, pp. 166, 254 and 248.

[123] Nelson, 'An Old English Charm Against Nightmare', pp. 17–18.

[124] Consider, for example, the following charm: 'Wið wina fær steorfan, do a in heora mete, seoð glidan, syle etan. Nim eac elehtran, bisceopwyrt and cassuc, ðefeþorn, hegerifan, haranspricel, sing ofer feower mæssan. Drif on fald, hoh ða wyrte on feower healfe and on þan dore, bærn, do recels to, læt yrnan ofer ðone rec.' 'Against the sudden death of pigs, always put this in their food – boil glide and give it to them to eat. Take also lupine, bishop's-wort, sedge, buckthorn, goose grass, viper's bugloss; sing four masses over them. Drive [the pigs] into the pen, hang the herbs on four sides and on the door, burn them, add incense, and let the smoke run over them.' Storms comments: 'The sudden and mysterious death of pigs was, of course, ascribed to elvish influence and the remedy consists in the attempts to drive out the elf.' *Anglo-Saxon Magic*, p. 254. The charm itself does not mention elves in any way.

[125] Cameron, *Anglo-Saxon Medicine*, p. 142; Thun, 'The Malignant Elves', p. 386.

disease',[126] the ascription of disease to hostile agents is consistent with their other representations of the natural world: *ælf-adl* and other diseases belong to the same antagonistic natural world[127] that sends wind, wolves and monsters against the human race. It is thus unsurprising to find that herbs like *stune* are expected to be effective against 'natural' dangers like venomous snakes[128] as well as more 'supernatural' dangers like flying venom and the unspecified enemy roaming throughout the land:

> Þis is seo wyrt,   seo wiþ wyrm gefeaht,
> þeos mæg wið attre,   heo mæg wið onflyge,
> heo mæg wið þa laþan   ðe geond lond fereþ.
>
> (*Nine Herbs Charm* 18–20)[129]

The exact identity of the *onflyge* is uncertain; although usually interpreted as flying venom or infection,[130] it could be a further reference to the *wyrm* in the first line. If this *wyrm* is of the same kind as the dragon in *Beowulf*, it would be logical to describe it as a poisonous[131] *onflyge* 'flyer'[132] and a *laþ ðe geond lond fereþ* 'hostile one who travels through the land'.[133] However, like the *laþ* in *The Journey Charm*, the 'hostile one' here has no identifying characteristics; it could be a dragon, but it could be the devil,[134] and it could equally well be a disease or elf – or even a wolf. In

---

[126] Storms, *Anglo-Saxon Magic*, p. 158.

[127] This lively, apparently conscious, teeming hostility also suggests a lingering animistic world-view. See Glosecki, *Shamanism and Old English Poetry*, p. 66.

[128] Snake venom, although now considered 'natural', was held to be inherently magical; otherwise the dire consequences of such a small bite could not be explained (Storms, *Anglo-Saxon Magic*, p. 193). Once again it is impossible to distinguish between 'natural' and 'supernatural' phenomena. There were few poisonous snakes in Anglo-Saxon England (as there are still few today – see above, p. 6), but the Anglo-Saxons could have inherited ideas about them from elsewhere; snakes have been considered magical in both positive and negative ways in a large number of traditions. Mellinkoff, 'Serpent Imagery', pp. 59–60.

[129] 'This is the herb that fought against the serpent; this prevails against poison; it prevails against the flyer; it prevails against the hostile one who roams throughout the land.'

[130] Storms translates *onflyge* as 'infection' (*Anglo-Saxon Magic*, pp. 187 and 195).

[131] Beowulf's dragon is called an *attorsceaða* 'poisonous harmer' (2839a); additional reference is made to its poison at 2523a and 2715a.

[132] Beowulf's dragon is called a *lyftfloga* 'air-flyer' (2315a) and *widfloga* 'far-flyer' (2346a).

[133] Beowulf's dragon is called *lað* at 2305a, 2315a, 2672a, 2910a and 3040a.

[134] Note, however, that the word is normally but not invariably feminine in the *Nine Herbs Charm* (at 6 and 20, but masculine at 13); the creature is also identified as *heo*

118

fact, given the associations of all these creatures,[135] it could be all of them at once. The *laþ ðe geond lond fereþ* may thus be a literal reference to the collection of hostile entities that inhabit and constitute the natural world rather than the ambiguous reference that it appears to be.

While the modern environment contains its share of insidious dangers, including ultraviolet radiation, electromagnetic fields and food additives, all of which *may*, in largely unknown ways, cause painful ailments, dread for the physical environment has been greatly alleviated since Anglo-Saxon times by a dramatic increase in both the understanding of and ability to defend against disease. The resources and efforts still devoted to medical research bear witness to the continuing need for security. The Anglo-Saxons, of course, were not as successful as modern healers, and their approach to disease could ill afford complacency. Worse than the wolf, which can be held at bay by sufficient numbers, worse than the wind, which human structures can *usually* withstand, and worse than Grendel, who only threatens at night and can be avoided by sleeping out of the way (*Beowulf* 138–43), disease reaches across all barriers erected to keep out the natural world, striking invisibly and, often, fatally. However daunting other physical conditions might appear, disease poses a particularly difficult problem for human defences. This was especially true during the Anglo-Saxon period: Anglo-Saxon England was a 'medically dangerous and helpless world'.[136] Yet it was not, apparently, hopeless. The resources and efforts devoted by the Anglo-Saxons to medicine bear witness not only to the need for security but also to a belief in the potency of the attempts: a thousand pages of medical writing remain,[137] and the contents of those pages[138] indicate an energetic pursuit of remedies of all kinds, including both genuinely efficacious herbal concoctions[139] and superstitious or magical combinations of herbs, amulets, rituals and charms.

'she' (35). See Storms, *Anglo-Saxon Magic*, p. 197. This would weigh against identifying the *laþ* as either the devil or a dragon; the obvious, immediate choices, *onflyge* and *attor*, are likewise disqualified, since they are both neuter. *Mære*, however, is feminine.

135 Dragons and wolves were both associated with the devil (in the *Physiologus*, for example); as discussed above, devils were associated with elves (p. 104).

136 Cameron, *Anglo-Saxon Medicine*, p. 40.   137 *Ibid.*, p. 2.

138 Anglo-Saxon medical texts contain an 'extraordinarily large number' of 'prescribed drugs'. *Ibid.*, p. 100.

139 *Ibid.*, pp. 177–29; M. L. Cameron, 'Anglo-Saxon Medicine and Magic', *ASE* 17 (1988), 191–215.

The most important part of any attempt to improve health is probably understanding the nature and source of the ailment. While the Anglo-Saxons' medical texts, especially those that posit elves or other super-natural agents as causes, reveal them to have been particularly weak in this crucial area, their writing about elves also reveals them working to penetrate and handle this problem of incomprehensible sources for disease. They did not merely apply herbal concoctions in response to visible symptoms as directed by classical medical texts; they reorganised, simplified and recast the texts they received on the basis of their own experience.[140] They also created – in writing if nowhere else – structures in which the mysterious onslaught of disease could be explained and handled. For example, writers with didactic, Christian aims inscribed disease into the context of divine interference in human affairs; Bede, in his commentary *In Ezram et Neemiam*, suggests that the proper response to disease is not physical treatment but rather thankfulness for received blessings and concern and penance for sins – that is, he sees disease to be linked to divine will and punishment for immoral behaviour.[141] In such a literary construction, it was possible to bring apparently intangible, invisible phenomena – the source of infection, for example – within the sphere of human understanding and perhaps even human action: after suitable penance, one could hope for divine forgiveness and thus the removal of the affliction.

Old English poetic texts likewise construct situations in which disease is brought within the sphere of human understanding and action and thus made subject to defence if not counterattack. For example, the charm, *For a Sudden Stitch*, describes the onslaught of a sharp, perhaps arthritic pain caused by the armed attack of *mihtigan wif* 'mighty women', *esa* 'gods', *ylfa* 'elves' or *hægtessan* 'witches':

> Hlude wæran hy, la, hlude,   ða hy ofer þone hlæw ridan,
> wæran anmode,   ða hy ofer land ridan.
> Scyld ðu ðe nu,   þu ðysne nið   genesan mote.
> Ut, lytel spere,   gif her inne sie!
> Stod under linde,   under leohtum scylde,

---

[140] The evidence of *Bald's Leechbook* indicates that some healers, at least, attempted to experiment and develop beyond what they received (Cameron, *Anglo-Saxon Medicine*, pp. 82–3); see also Meaney, 'The Anglo-Saxon View of the Causes of Illness', p. 24.

[141] *In Ezram et Neemiam Libri III*, ed. D. Hurst, CCSL 119A, 237–392. For commentary, see McCready, *Miracles and the Venerable Bede*, pp. 26–7.

þær ða mihtigan wif   hyra mægen beræddon
and hy gyllende   garas sændan.   (*For a Sudden Stitch* 3–9)[142]

The charm represents the unexplainable in terms of the explainable, an apparently sourceless pain in terms of the familiar, expected, well-understood wound inflicted by a spear.[143] This representation supplies what the Anglo-Saxons, lacking the technology since developed by modern advances in medicine, could not otherwise grasp: the source and nature of the ailment. The advantage conveyed by this knowledge is immediately evident, for it provides the possibility of evading attack by interposing a shield: *Stod under linde* 'I stood under a linden shield' (7). It also describes a further simple remedy if the shield should fail to block a missile: the removal of the foreign body, either through a direct command – *Ut, lytel spere, gif her inne sie!* 'Out, little spear, if you are in here!' (6, 15) – or through its destruction – *Gif her inne sy isernes dæl, / hægtessan geweorc, hit sceal myltan* 'if a bit of iron is in here, the work of a witch, it shall melt' (18–19). In addition, and most important in the context of bringing the natural world within human grasp, the charm suggests that the source of hostility is vulnerable to human retaliation: in response to the spears sent earlier, the speaker says, *ic him oðerne eft wille sændan, / fleogende flane forane togeanes* 'I will send them back another, a flying arrow against those opposite' (10–11).

Such representation is an act of assimilation.[144] Just as Beowulf reduces Grendel from a relentless, unknowable hostility to a hunting trophy, so the charm reduces the incomprehensible attack of disease to human scale, transforming a frighteningly unknown danger – like Grendel, featureless except for the damage it inflicts – to a limited list of creatures that attack and can be dealt with in much the same way as human opponents. While modern readers may remain sceptical about the medical success attainable by such a remedy, within the literary sphere of the charm itself the strategy is victorious,[145] for it allows an individual to assert power and

---

[142] 'They were loud, indeed loud, when they rode over the mound; they were fierce when they rode over the land. Shield yourself now, [and] you might survive this attack. Out, little spear, if you are in here! I stood under a linden shield, under a light shield, when the mighty women betrayed their might and, yelling, sent spears.'

[143] Grattan and Singer, *Anglo-Saxon Magic and Medicine*, p. 3.

[144] Cf. above, pp. 10–13.

[145] The charm might also be victorious in 'real life' as well, since its words could have had a psychotherapeutic effect on its hearers. See W. Nöth, 'Semiotics of the Old

121

control over the natural world and achieve a victory like that in the Exeter Book *Riddles* discussed above.

HEROIC SAINTS IN THE NATURAL WORLD

The individual in the charm is anonymous; he or she could potentially be anyone who has been taught the words or who can read the text. By the agency of the charm, however, this individual is transformed into someone extraordinary, a hero who can confidently boast, *nu ic wille ðin helpan* 'now I will help you' (24 and 26).[146] The word 'hero' is apt, although it is not what a modern reader tends to associate with medical texts.[147] The speaker of the charm inscribes him or herself into the literary world of military heroism through the language of weapons, battle and boasts,[148] but, more

English Charm', *Semiotica* 19 (1977), 59–83, at 74; B. Malinowski, *Magic, Science and Religion, and Other Essays* (Garden City, NY, 1954), p. 90; Vaughan-Sterling, 'The Anglo-Saxon *Metrical Charms*', p. 199.

[146] The *beot* or 'heroic vaunt' in itself is characteristic of heroic tradition; it is the promise that the hero utters before performing his/her deed of valour (the word is derived from *be-* and *hatan* 'promise'). See Harris, 'Beowulf's Last Words', p. 26. See also B. Nolan and M. W. Bloomfield, '*Beotword, Gilpcwidas*, and the *Gilphlæden* Scop of *Beowulf* ', *JEGP* 79 (1980), 499–516; S. Einarsson, 'Old English *beot* and Old Icelandic *heitstrenging*', *PMLA* 49 (1934), 975–93; M. Nelson, 'The *Battle of Maldon* and *Juliana*: The Language of Confrontation', in *Modes of Interpretation*, pp. 137–50. The importance of the boast to the idea of the hero may be seen in some of the words for hero or warrior, which contain the same root as *beot*. *Oretta* and *oretmæcg* originally derived from **or-hat* 'ultimate vow'. See Robinson, *'Beowulf' and the Appositive Style*, p. 67. The *Beowulf*-poet was apparently aware of the root meaning of this word; see C. Brady, ' "Warriors" in *Beowulf*: an Analysis of the Nominal Compounds and an Evaluation of the Poet's Use of them', *ASE* 11 (1982), 210–14.

[147] A heroic aspect is, however, consistent with shamanism; the charm suggests that, like a gifted shaman, 'the trained doctor was credited with the ability to coerce the invisible powers of the spirit realm' (Glosecki, *Shamanism and Old English Poetry*, p. 66). Cf. also G. Hübener, '*Beowulf* and Germanic Exorcism', *RES* 11 (1935), 163–81.

[148] In fact, the boast itself, the spoken charm, is the weapon through which the speaker does battle. This, too, is characteristic of heroic action – see E. Jager, 'Speech and the Chest in Old English Poetry: Orality or Pectorality?', *Speculum* 65 (1990), 845–59, at 851, who argues that such boasts are reified as weapons (referring to Beowulf's challenge to the dragon). See also W. J. Ong, *The Presence of the Word: Some Prolegomena for Cultural and Religious History*, Terry Lectures 34 (New Haven, 1967), 113; cf. B. R. Straus, 'Women's Words as Weapons: Speech as Action in *The Wife's Lament*', *Texas*

importantly, he or she claims powers beyond the abilities of an ordinary armed warrior – the ability to assert power over the hostile agents of the natural world. This ability is commonly ascribed to heroes and saints, who proclaim and demonstrate their power both in the context of and in opposition to the natural world.[149]

A modern audience might not immediately see the connection between a saint and a hero, but Anglo-Saxon writers describe them in similar terms, even if a saint's military prowess is metaphorical rather than physical.[150] This characterisation of saints as heroes occurs widely and has received much comment.[151] A full discussion of saints' lives lies beyond the scope of this investigation, but the opening of *Andreas* can provide an idea of the technique used to glorify saints:

> Hwæt! We gefrunan   on fyrndagum
> twelfe under tunglum   tireadige hæleð,
> þeodnes þegnas.   No hira þrym alæg
> camprædenne   þonne cumbol hneotan,
> syððan hie gedældon,   swa him dryhten sylf,
> heofona heahcyning,   hlyt getæhte.
> Þæt wæron mære   men ofer eorðan,
> frome folctogan   ond fyrdhwate,
> rofe rincas,   þonne rond ond hand
> on herefelda   helm ealgodon,
> on meotudwange.   (*Andreas* 1–11a)[152]

This description of the apostles clearly recalls descriptions of secular

---

Studies in Literature and Language 23 (1981), 268–85, and E. R. Anderson, 'Flyting in *The Battle of Maldon*', *NM* 71 (1970), 197–202, at 202.

[149] Cf. Clemoes, *Interactions of Thought*, p. 20.

[150] Skemp, 'Transformation of Scriptural Story', p. 437.

[151] See M. A. Dalbey, 'The Good Shepherd and the Soldier of God: Old English Homilies on St Martin of Tours', *NM* 85 (1984), 422–34; Hill, 'The Soldier of Christ'; S. Morrison, 'OE *cempa* in Cynewulf's *Juliana* and the Figure of the *Miles Christi*', *ELN* 17 (1979), 81–4; J. P. Hermann, 'The Recurrent Motifs of Spiritual Warfare in Old English Poetry', *Annuale Mediævale* 22 (1982), 7–35.

[152] 'Listen, we have heard of twelve glory-blessed heroes under the stars in days of yore, lord's thegns. Their power in warfare did not lessen when banners clashed, after they separated, as the lord himself, the high-king of heaven, assigned their lot to them. They were famous men throughout the earth, bold folk-leaders and warlike, brave warriors, when shield and hand defended the helmet on the battlefields, on the plain of fate.'

heroes; it also appears to echo *Beowulf* directly.[153] Although the nature of the relationship between *Beowulf* and *Andreas* is much disputed,[154] it is clear that poets like the *Andreas*-poet found the heroic language associated with *Beowulf* suitable for more spiritual exploits. This perceived suitability, probably deriving from the Christian Latin tradition of using military language in religious contexts,[155] may have been reinforced by another basic characteristic shared by heroes and saints: the arena in which they distinguish themselves, the natural world. These individuals are literally 'outstanding', for they prevail against the natural world without the aid of society – they stand outside.[156] They are also literary, defined by the poets' use of the natural world. Though there are other criteria as well, within the conventions of Old English poetry the ability to stand outside independently – out in the natural world, outside the shelter of society – is a necessary requirement for a character to be considered either a hero or a saint.

For example, *Guthlac*[157] introduces its hero by first describing the

---

[153] Cf. *Beowulf* 1–2: *Hwæt, we Gardena in geardagum, / þeodcyninga þrym gefrunon* 'Listen, we have heard of the glory of the folk-kings of the Spear-Danes in days of yore.' Such verbal echoes occur throughout *Andreas*. The first critic to link the two poems was A. Fritzche, 'Das angelsächsische Gedicht Andreas und Cynewulf', *Anglia* 2 (1879), 441–96; some kind of connection between the poems has been assumed ever since.

[154] It is not possible to provide more than a sample of the scholarship here, but see L. J. Peters, 'The Relationship of the Old English *Andreas* to *Beowulf*', *PMLA* 66 (1951), 844–63; D. Hamilton, 'The Diet and Digestion of Allegory in *Andreas*', *ASE* 1 (1972), 147–58; A. Renoir, 'Old English Formulas and Themes as Tools for Contextual Interpretation', in *Modes of Interpretation*, ed. Brown, Crampton and Robinson, pp. 65–79; A. G. Brodeur, 'A Study of Diction and Style in Three Anglo-Saxon Narrative Poems', in *Nordica et Anglica: Studies in Honor of Stefán Einarsson*, ed. A. H. Orrick (The Hague and Paris, 1968), pp. 97–114; A. R. Riedinger, 'The Formulaic Relationship Between *Beowulf* and *Andreas*', in *Heroic Poetry in the Anglo-Saxon Period*, ed. Damico and Leyerle, pp. 283–312; Shippey, *Old English Verse* (London, 1972), pp. 92–6 and 115–18; D. Pearsall, *Old and Middle English Poetry*, The Routledge History of English Poetry 1 (London, 1977), 41.

[155] Hill, 'Soldier of Christ', pp. 58–64.

[156] In *Beowulf* especially, heroic stature is established by stepping out, by crossing boundaries into unfamiliar realms. See below, pp. 129–38, but see also Higley, '*Aldor on Ofre*', pp. 343 and 346.

[157] I do not distinguish between *Guthlac A* and *Guthlac B* in my discussion, since their approach to the natural world does not appear different, but for distinctions in other areas see Calder, '*Guthlac A* and *Guthlac B*'. For an argument that *Guthlac A*, like *Guthlac B*, is based mainly on Felix's *Life of Saint Guthlac*, see G. H. Gerould, 'The

many *hadas under heofonum* 'conditions under the heavens' (31a),[158] some of which provide profitable examples for imitation. Of these, the poem singles out that of those who

> wuniað on westennum,
> secað ond gesittað sylfra willum
> hamas on heolstrum. *(Guthlac* 81–3a)[159]

The choice of habitation of such saints (*halige*) distinguishes them from another kind of *had* described by the poem, that of those for whom *eorðwela* 'worldly wealth' (62a) is *hyhta hyhst* 'the highest of hopes' (63a); it identifies saints, not only to those searching for role models but also to devils seeking to persecute them, as *þa gecostan cempan þa þam cyninge þeowað* 'the proven warriors who serve the king' (91). It is in this context that Guthlac is finally mentioned, and he immediately conforms to the pattern just established: his *halig had* 'holy condition' (94), the inner saintliness of his thoughts (fixed on heaven and renouncing earthly things), results in his choosing a lonely *beorgseþel* 'mountain dwelling' (102a) for himself:

> Þær he mongum wearð
> bysen on Brytene, siþþan biorg gestah
> eadig oretta, ondwiges heard. *(Guthlac* 174b–6)[160]

Guthlac thus leaves the pleasures and safety of human society to live in the dangerous *westen*, the normal habitat of monsters according to *Maxims II* and *Beowulf*. The vague terrors listed in *The Journey Charm* are here solidified[161] and specifically identified as devils, but in both poems the

---

Old English Poems on St Guthlac and their Latin Source', *MLN* 32 (1917), 77–89. For the Latin text, see *Felix's Life of Saint Guthlac*, ed. B. Colgrave (Cambridge, 1956). For an argument that *Guthlac A* is mainly based on popular traditions, see F. R. Lipp, 'Guthlac A: An Interpretation', *MS* 33 (1971), 46–52, at 51; C. Schaar, *Critical Studies in the Cynewulf Group*, Lund Studies in English 17 (Lund, 1949), 39–41.

[158] For the changing meaning of *had* in the poem, see Calder, 'Guthlac A and Guthlac B', pp. 67–9.

[159] 'dwell in the wasteland, seek and inhabit homes in the darkness out of their own free will'.

[160] 'There he became an example for many in Britain, after the blessed champion, firm in resistance, ascended the mountain.'

[161] But cf. Calder, who argues that the devils in *Guthlac A* do not have an external reality but rather are projections of Guthlac's mind ('Guthlac A and Guthlac B', p. 72).

premise is the same: the individual going out into the natural world inevitably meets enemies. The poet allows no time between Guthlac's settling into his dwelling and the arrival of antagonists from the countryside; within the same line the *bold* 'house' is visited by *broga* 'terror' (140). This terror takes many forms, but initially, at least, it includes images from the natural world – representations of enemies that even a modern audience might expect a hero to meet in the wilderness:

> Dryhtnes cempa,
> from folctoga,   feonda þreatum
> wiðstod stronglice.   Næs seo stund latu
> earmra gæsta,   ne þæt onbid long,
> þæt þa wrohtsmiðas   wop ahofun,
> hreopun hreðlease,   hleoþrum brugdon.
> Hwilum wedende   swa wilde deor
> cirmdon on corðre,   hwilum cyrdon eft
> minne mansceaþan   on mennisc hiw
> breahtma mæste,   hwilum brugdon eft
> awyrgde wærlogan   on wyrmes bleo,
> earme adloman   attre spiowdon.
> Symle hy Guðlac   gearene fundon,
> þonces gleawne.   He geþyldum bad,
> þeah him feonda hloð   feorhcwealm bude.

(*Guthlac* 901b–15)[162]

It has been argued that the description of such conflicts represents tentative steps toward a fully allegorical psychomachia.[163] In this regard one might recall the *wudumare*, the echo or 'forest-harmer' that cries out from the wilderness; 'demon' is easily within *mære's* semantic range, and *wudu* 'wood' may well have been used to describe the place whence the demons come, since it has already been called a *bearwe* 'grove, wood' (148a).[164] One

---

[162] 'The lord's warrior, the bold leader, strongly withstood the throngs of enemies. There was no time of delay by the wretched spirits, nor did he wait for long until the crime-smiths raised up shrieks, the inglorious ones howled and were transformed with noises. Sometimes like wild beasts they shrieked in multitudes, sometimes the evil criminals changed again into human shape with the greatest of cries, sometimes again the cursed traitors were transformed into the appearance of dragons – crippled by fire the wretched ones spewed poison. Always they found Guthlac ready, wise in thought. He endured patiently, although the crowd of enemies threatened murder.'

[163] Calder, '*Guthlac A* and *Guthlac B*', pp. 76–7.

[164] *Wudu-* can also simply indicate 'wild'. See Bosworth–Toller, s.v. *wudu*.

might then describe an external 'psychomachia' taking place out in the open air, with Guthlac assaulted by the howling and shrieking of his own echo. However, by the time the demons arrive God has already settled the strife between Guthlac's guardian angel and the devil (*Guthlac* 133–40); the poem presents no inkling of self-doubt and inner conflict in the course of Guthlac's encounters with the demonic swarms – Guthlac is always steadfast and firm – and so the presence of a psychomachia in the poem seems unlikely. Instead, what seems most evident is the external nature of Guthlac's attackers and their association with the natural world.

When the demons arrive, neither the poet nor Guthlac expresses any surprise. They appear to assume that this lonely spot in the natural world, like any other isolated from human settlement, will naturally contain devils. Guthlac says:

> Wid is þes westen, wræcsetla fela,
> eardas onhæle earmra gæsta.
> Sindon wærlogan þe þa wic bugað.   (*Guthlac* 296–8)[165]

As in *The Journey Charm*, these enemies are both physical and spiritual, and although a modern audience considers devils unambiguously super-natural, these ones are equally connected with the spiritual and natural world. What they want from Guthlac is not his soul but his land.[166] Their initial objection to Guthlac is not his goodness, but his squatting on the site of their homes.

> wæron teonsmiðas tornes fulle,
> cwædon þæt him Guðlac eac gode sylfum
> earfeþa mæst ana gefremede,
> siþþan he for wlence on westenne
> beorgas bræce, þær hy bidinge,
> earme ondsacan, æror mostun
> æfter tintergum tidum brucan,

---

[165] 'This wilderness is wide – [there are] many places of exile and secret dwelling places of wretched spirits. They are devils who dwell in this place.' See also the poet's assertion that the devils had *þær ær fela / setla gesæton* 'previously inhabited many homes there' (*Guthlac* 143b–4a).

[166] L. K. Shook, 'The Burial Ground in *Guthlac A*', *MP* 58 (1960), 1–10, at 9. Cf., however, Calder, '*Guthlac A* and *Guthlac B*', p. 77 and P. F. Reichardt, '*Guthlac A* and the Landscape of Spiritual Perfection', *Neophil* 58 (1974), 331–8, where it is argued that the landscape represents Guthlac's soul.

ðonne hy of waþum werge cwoman
restan ryneþragum,   rowe gefegon.   (*Guthlac* 205–13)[167]

Of course, as has been indicated above, Guthlac's choice of habitat is intimately connected with his saintly status. The devils' habitat is likewise a part of their devilish status – like the monster in *Maxims II*, devils have their natural place in the natural world.

Other than the presence of demons, there is very little description of this landscape which Guthlac has chosen to colonise for God. The minimal details regarding the natural setting that the poet does provide cannot be separated from the representation of the supernatural, nor can they be separated from the poem's didactic purpose. As a result, of all the non-demonic elements that the poet could have depicted from the setting, only birds appear; once again, however, the focus is not on what they are like but rather how they interact with Guthlac.

Hine bletsadon
monge mægwlitas,   meaglum reordum,
treofugla tuddor,   tacnum cyðdon
eadges eftcyme.   Oft he him æte heold,
þonne hy him hungrige   ymb hond flugon
grædum gifre,   geoce gefegon.   (*Guthlac* 733b–8)[168]

Like his miraculous triumph over the demons, the anomalous respect that Guthlac receives in these interactions marks the saint off from the rest of humanity;[169] they are considered proof of his sainthood. They appear only for this purpose.[170]

---

[167] 'The malice-smiths were full of indignation; they said that, besides God himself, Guthlac alone committed the greatest of torments against them, after he broke into the mountains in the wasteland out of pride, where they, wretched enemies, [were] dwelling, [and] previously were allowed to enjoy some time after tortures, when the outlaws came from their journeys to rest for a space of time [and] enjoy quietness.'

[168] 'Many species blessed him with strong voices; the offspring of tree-birds made known the return of the blessed one with signs. Often he held out food for them, when, hungry and greedily eager, they flew around his hand, rejoiced in his help.' See also *Guthlac* 916–19a.

[169] It has also been argued, however, that figures like Guthlac represent mankind as a whole – see W. F. Bolton, 'The Background and Meaning of *Guthlac*', *JEGP* 61 (1962), 595–603, at 597–9. Such contradictory critical interpretations raise once again the problem of distinguishing between individuals and representatives discussed earlier in this chapter – see above, pp. 90–2.

[170] This is true also of the miracles that Bede ascribes to Saint Cuthbert; they appear

BEOWULF OUTSIDE

Beowulf's interactions with the natural world similarly reveal his singularity, his distinction from normal humanity. From his first presentation of himself to Hrothgar to his choice of burial place, Beowulf is circumscribed – both 'written about' and limited – by the natural world. Although he is defined within society by his relationships and contrasts with characters like Hrothgar and Hygelac, he is also and perhaps most importantly defined by his interactions with the natural world – that is, by his actions *outside* society, *beyond* the normal capacities of humanity. Like Guthlac, Beowulf is able to leave the protective sphere of human society, penetrate into the midst of nature's power and survive; unlike the 'friendless, unhappy man' in *Maxims I*, who falls prey to the wolf upon entering the forest, Beowulf not only enters but characteristically immerses himself – alone – in the natural world. One can ascribe this ability either to exceptional strength or exceptional good luck, but it is important to note that it is a different thing from being a very strong or very lucky participant in human conflicts. Beowulf does, of course, participate in human battles on behalf of Hygelac (2354b–66), but these are circumstantial; by the time we hear about them, Beowulf's status has already been fully established through his other exploits. Perhaps more important, the tale of Beowulf's human battles is immediately supplemented by a tale of his triumph over the sea (2359–68). The implication is that success in battle is not enough to distinguish Beowulf from other strong warriors. Such distinction requires success against the natural world's superior power.

The poet places the hero in the natural world from the start. Beowulf's easy crossing from Geatland to Hrothgar's kingdom is indicative of his luck in the natural world's embrace, for it is always possible that, as in Exeter Book *Riddle 3*,

> Þær bið ceole wen
> sliþre sæcce,   gif hine sæ byreð
> on þa grimman tid,   gæsta fulne,
> þæt he scyle rice   birofen weorþan

merely as evidence of sanctity. See McCready, *Miracles and the Venerable Bede*, pp. 152–3.

129

feore bifohten   fæmig ridan
yþa hrycgum.   (Exeter Book *Riddle 3* 28b–33a)[171]

In Old English poetry, a safe sea-voyage is in no way to be taken for granted, and Beowulf's successful passage should thus not be passed over too quickly. Though not a crucial thing in itself, it sets the pattern for Beowulf's interactions with the natural world.

The swimming[172] competition with Breca displays much more clearly the exceptional nature of Beowulf's relation to the natural world and the contrast with that of ordinary mortals. It is also the first opportunity for the poet to define the hero at length, both for the internal and external audience.[173] Beowulf and Unferth[174] tell different versions of this story, the most important disparity being who emerged victorious from the competition.[175] Unferth's version also contains additional information: the views that people other than Beowulf held about the contest. From the perspective of normal people living within the protective boundaries of society, Beowulf and Breca's proposal to swim in the ocean is a *dolgilp* 'foolish boast' (509a); normal people do not embark upon such a painful journey and risk their lives against the power of the natural world needlessly. This is something, however, that Beowulf does throughout his life. It is something that defines him as surely as Unferth's refusal to do so later defines Unferth.[176] For this contest Beowulf willingly, even wilfully, leaves the protected place created by people grouped defensively together and places himself in the grip of nature: he is surrounded by

[171] 'There will be the expectation of savage strife for the ship, if the sea takes it away in a grim time, full of souls, so that it is bereft of power, fought out of life, [and] the foamy one rides [alone] on the backs of the waves.' For further discussion of this riddle, see above, p. 40 n. 89 and below, pp. 113, 168–9 and 176.

[172] Or rowing – for a convincing argument that Beowulf and Breca rowed rather than swam for seven days, as well as bibliography concerning the poetic and prosaic meanings of 'sund', see Frank, '"Mere" and "Sund"', pp. 158–72.

[173] Pope, '*Beowulf* 505', p. 182.

[174] Or perhaps Hunferth; the name appears in the poem four times with an initial 'H'. See L. E. Nicholson, 'Hunlafing and the Point of the Sword', in *Anglo-Saxon Poetry*, ed. Nicholson and Frese, pp. 50–61, at 51–4.

[175] For discussion of the differences in the two accounts and the meaning of the episode, see F. C. Robinson, 'Elements of the Marvellous in the Characterization of Beowulf: A Reconsideration of the Textual Evidence', in *Old English Studies*, ed. Burlin and Irving, pp. 119–37, at 126–32. Cf. also Frank, '"Mere" and "Sund"', pp. 161–2.

[176] See *Beowulf* 1465–72.

wado weallende,   wedera cealdost,
nipende niht,   ond norþanwind
heaðogrim.   (*Beowulf* 546–8a)[177]

More dangerous than the elements and equally anticipated are the attacks of the *hronfixas* 'whales' (540b).[178] Like the wolf-infested forest in *Maxims I*, the ocean contains *aglæcan* 'combatants' (556a) waiting for those who stray into their territory. Normally these brave few venture out only in groups, and only within the protective walls of a ship; even so, previously the *niceras* 'sea-monsters' (575a) *brimliðende / lade … letton* 'impeded sailors in their journey' (568b–9a). When Beowulf, however, alone and protected only by a sword and mail shirt, finds himself in the grip of a savage sea-beast, he both defends himself and successfully counterattacks, much to the unpleasant surprise of the ill-intentioned whales:

Næs hie ðære fylle   gefean hæfdon,
manfordædlan,   þæt hie me þegon,
symbel ymbsæton   sægrunde neah;
ac on mergenne   mecum wunde
be yðlafe   uppe lægon,
sweordum aswefede.   (*Beowulf* 562–7a)[179]

Unferth's comments are meant to be subversive, not reasonable,[180] but the view he presents is, in fact, common-sense – it *is* silly to swim in the ocean during dangerous weather, especially if you know that you could be eaten. It is obvious, however, that the story does not operate under the

[177] 'the tossing sea, the coldest of weather, darkening night, and the battle-fierce north wind'.

[178] For further discussion of the *hronfixas*, see below, pp. 191–2.

[179] 'By no means did those crime-workers have joy in that feast, that they should partake of me, sitting around the feast near the sea-bottom; but in the morning they lay upon the leavings of the waves [i.e. the beach] wounded by my blade, put to sleep by the sword.'

[180] For Unferth's role in the poem, see J. L. Rosier, 'Design for Treachery: The Unferth Intrigue', *PMLA* 77 (1962), 1–7; N. E. Eliason, 'The *Þyle* and *Scop* in *Beowulf*', *Speculum* 38 (1963), 267–84; I. M. Hollowell, 'Unferth the *Þyle* in *Beowulf*', *SP* 73 (1976), 239–65; C. J. Clover, 'The Germanic Context of the Unferþ Episode', *Speculum* 55 (1980), 444–68; Frank, '"Mere" and "Sund"', pp. 161–3; Pope, '*Beowulf* 505', pp. 173–87; J. D. A. Ogilvy, 'Unferth: Foil to Beowulf?' *PMLA* 79 (1964), 370–5; G. Hughes, 'Beowulf, Unferth and Hrunting: An Interpretation', *ES* 58 (1977), 385–95.

limitations of normal human expectations and thus does not function to disqualify Beowulf from respect. From Beowulf's, the Danes' and, presumably, an Anglo-Saxon audience's perspective, this triumph over the natural world positively distinguishes him from other people[181] and is used as an item on Beowulf's heroic *curriculum vitae* to identify him as someone whom Hrothgar should take seriously. Although the poet also defines Beowulf's strength in human terms – he has the strength of thirty men in his hands – and although he has to hop through many hoops of decorum to be acknowledged as a paragon of heroic ideals, he initially proves himself by pitting his strength against the power of the natural world. The Danish society within the poem – and, presumably, an Anglo-Saxon audience – receive this account of confrontation with the natural world as acceptable evidence of heroism; upon hearing this story, Hrothgar recognises, rejoices and believes (*Beowulf* 607–10).[182]

Beowulf's ability to accomplish such feats, to challenge the power of the natural world, defines him as an ideal, a unique human being. The poet ensures that his uniqueness is set off again and again by contrast with ordinary people's experience of the natural world: Bronding (i.e. Breca), Dane and Geat alike, individually and in groups, fail to do what Beowulf does alone and often unarmed. His success with Grendel is his crowning effort. This battle may appear on the surface to be generically different from his triumph in the sea, since Grendel's ancestry and association with devils seem to differentiate him from the natural world, but, as the examination of *mære* has indicated, the Anglo-Saxons do not make clear distinctions in this regard: the wealth of argument on the subject of Grendel's status likewise suggests that the categories used by modern critics are too rigid,[183] and the association of devils with wild, natural places (as in *Guthlac*) reveals that the supernatural and natural, at least, were not mutually exclusive.[184] Instead, Grendel's

---

[181] But cf. Orchard, *Pride and Prodigies*, p. 171; Beowulf's exploits may also identify him as a figure of the prodigious pride that can make monsters out of men.

[182] Cf. Pope, 'Beowulf 505', p. 183.

[183] For some of these opinions, see above, pp. 78–9.

[184] Likewise, the inclusion of *Beowulf* in a manuscript with *The Wonders of the East*, *The Letter of Alexander to Aristotle* and *The Legend of Saint Christopher* may suggest that the compiler considered the poem 'history' and its monsters part of a real, though exotic,

status is 'epistemologically doubtful', shifting and suggestively multiple.[185]

THE PLACE OF THE GRENDELKIN

Grendel's function in the poem thus parallels the representation of the natural world in *Beowulf* and elsewhere. His attacks on Heorot are unrelenting, untiring, non-negotiable and invulnerable to human counter-attacks, like the elements in Exeter Book *Riddle 3*:

> Winnende fareð
> atol eoredþreat,   egsa astigeð,
> micel modþrea   monna cynne,
> brogan on burgum,   þonne blace scotiað
> scriþende scin   scearpum wæpnum.
> Dol him ne ondrædeð   ða deaðsperu,
> swylteð hwæþre,   gif him soð meotud
> on geryhtu   þurh regn ufan
> of gestune læteð   stræle fleogan,
> farende flan.   Fea þæt gedygað,
> þara þe geræceð   rynegiestes wæpen.
>
> (Exeter Book *Riddle 3* 48b–58)[186]

Again, there is nothing to prevent one from identifying this *scriþende scin* as yet another *laþ ðe geond lond fereþ* 'hostile thing which travels through the land'; one might also note that this creature shoots arrows at human beings like elves do.[187] Grendel does not appear out of place in such company; he is merely one more of a number of entities from the

---

landscape. (Brynteson, '*Beowulf*, Monsters, and Manuscripts'.) Cf., however, the different interpretation of the manuscript collection in Orchard, *Pride and Prodigies*.

[185] Duncan, 'Epitaphs for Æglæcan', p. 120.

[186] 'Raging, the terrible troop advances, terror [and] great mind-anguish mounts up for mankind, dread in the towns, when the flashing, gliding evil spirit shoots with its sharp weapons. The foolish one does not dread the death-spears; he will perish, nevertheless, if the true creator rightly lets missiles, travelling arrows, fly through the rain from above, out of the whirlwind. Few of those whom the weapon of the running spirit reaches survive that.' For further discussion of this passage, see below, pp. 168–9.

[187] Another connection is suggested by the fact that stone hammers and knives found in ancient tombs were associated with lightning and elf-shot. Grimm, *Teutonic Mythology*, pp. 179–87.

dangerous outside which attack human structures. As a result of his attacks, Heorot itself was in danger of becoming another glorious ruin, eaten away by the elements, with its human defenders lying dead by the wall, like the previous inhabitants of the *eald enta geweorc* 'old works of giants' in *The Wanderer* (87a), the builders of the *wrætlic ... wealstan* 'ornamented wall-stone' in *The Ruin* (1) and the kin of the Last Survivor in *Beowulf* (2247–66).[188] In this context Beowulf's defeat of Grendel may appear to be even more extraordinary than a monster fight, for it is a reversal of the helplessness depicted as the inescapable lot of the human race in the face of the incursions of the natural world.

The reaction to Grendel's mother's attack reiterates the normal human incapacity to handle the hostile power of the natural world: a lament is raised up and grief is renewed, but no remedy other than the demonstrably exceptional Beowulf can be imagined. If a human assassin had crept into the hall and killed Æschere, even if the murder were justified by a long-standing feud, the Danes would not have lacked ideas of what to do about it – Hrothgar has to think and work hard to end self-propagating feuds, not spur them on. This situation is different; it is beyond human society and beyond its power to cope. Thus Grendel's mother, although entirely human in her motivation,[189] remains *outside*, a member of that vague family of elves, *mæran*, dwarves, fauns and demons, and there is no thought of negotiating a settlement of this feud.[190] As before, and as usual when faced with the power of the natural world, the Danes are powerless to act against her without the help of a superior power. With Beowulf's encouragement, however, Hrothgar and the Scyldings go out in pursuit of Grendel's mother and enter into the frightening landscape around Grendel's mere.

---

[188] See above, pp. 47–8.

[189] K. S. Kiernan argues not only that Grendel's mother's motivation is human but that she acts in accordance with Anglo-Saxon laws regarding feuds ('Grendel's Heroic Mother', *In Geardagum* 6 (1984), 13–33). Cf. M. K. Temple, '*Beowulf* 1258–1266: Grendel's Lady-Mother', *ELN* 23.3 (1986), 10–15. See also Orchard, *Pride and Prodigies*, p. 30: Grendel's mother is 'driven to avenge the killing of her son by motives which would tug at the hearts of any Germanic audience'. On the other hand, the poet does not ascribe any thoughts or feelings to Grendel's mother, and she thus appears more bestial than her son. Irving, *A Reading of 'Beowulf'*, p. 114.

[190] The poet raises the idea of wergild with respect to Grendel only to deny that it would be paid – see above, p. 77. The idea is not even suggested with respect to Grendel's mother.

This landscape[191] is inextricably involved with its inhabitants, and the fear it inspires depends on who is lurking in it: for the Danes joyfully following Grendel's bloody tracks in the sunshine (*morgenleoht* (917b)) it holds no terror, but for a similar group anticipating Grendel's mother it appears frightening and inhospitable.[192] Like Grendel, it is strange and *uncuð* 'unknown'.[193] Its position on the other side of the *mearc* – outside the boundaries of human society – previously defined him as a *mearcstapa*. It also complements his hostility toward the human race, being, in the eyes of the human beings observing it fearfully, a *frecne fengelad* 'a dangerous fen-tract' (1359a). The party that enters this territory is defined with reference to the threat: it is armed and defensive, a throng of *lindhæbbendra* 'shield-carriers' (1402a), for, like the wolves' wood and *hronfixas*' sea, this is hostile territory, complete with the same hostile agents found in other Old English poems – wolves, wind, *yðgeblond* 'tossing waves' (1373a) and *lað gewidru* 'hostile weather' (1375a) – and patrolled by even more powerful guardians: Grendel and his mother, the 'sea-wolf'. Though they do venture this far, the Scyldings and Geats stop

---

[191] For discussion of the mere's relation to hell based on the similarities between the poem's description and that in the *Visio sancti Pauli*, Vercelli homily IX and Blicking homily XVI, see above, p. 60, n. 27. The description of the mere may also be compared to descriptions in classical literature. See A. Renoir, 'The Terror of the Dark Waters: A Note on Virgilian and Beowulfian Techniques', in *The Learned and the Lewed: Studies in Chaucer and Medieval Literature*, ed. L. D. Benson, Harvard English Studies 5 (Cambridge, MA, 1974), 147–60; T. M. Andersson, 'The Virgilian Heritage in *Beowulf*', in his *Early Epic Scenery: Homer, Virgil, and the Medieval Legacy* (Ithaca, NY, and London, 1976), pp. 145–59; T. B. Haber, *A Comparative Study of the 'Beowulf' and the 'Aeneid'* (Princeton, NJ, 1931), pp. 92–6; R. D. Cornelius, 'Palus inamabilis', *Speculum* 2 (1927), 321–5; Magennis, *Images of Community*, pp. 135–41.

[192] Thus this landscape can also be read as less an external than an internal topography, a description of 'men's imaginative and psychological response to Grendel' rather than an actual physical place. R. Butts, 'The Analogical Mere: Landscape and Terror in *Beowulf*', *ES* 68 (1987), 113–21. See also Goldsmith, *Mode and Meaning*, pp. 113–23; R. Waterhouse, 'Spatial Perception and Conceptions in the (Re-)presenting and (Re-)constructing of Old English Texts', *Parergon* ns 9 (1991), 87–102, at 98; Schrader, 'Sacred Groves', p. 77. Cf. Magennis, *Images of Community*, pp. 142–3.

[193] The actual nature of Grendel's dwelling – freshwater marshy pool or part of the sea? – remains a puzzle for modern readers as well. For summary of the arguments, see Frank, '"Mere" and "Sund"', pp. 154–6. Cf. also Malone, 'Grendel and his Abode' and W. W. Lawrence, 'The Haunted Mere in *Beowulf*', *PMLA* 27 (1912), 208–45.

short of entering the mere itself and penetrating the 'heart of darkness', the centre of the natural world's hostility. Though presumably brave enough in human confrontations, in this environment they do not pursue the heroic ideal of unflinching advancement in the face of all opposition – the ideal expressed, for example, in the futile bravery of Byrhtnoth's men in *The Battle of Maldon*:

> Ic þæt gehate, þæt ic heonon nelle
> fleon fotes trym, ac wille furðor gan.
>
> (*The Battle of Maldon* 246–7)[194]

Here, however, when *Horn stundum song / fuslic fyrdleoð* 'the horn sang an eager battle-song' (1423b–4a), the surprising response is: *Feþa eal gesæt* 'the foot-soldiers all sat down' (1424b). Normal human exploits stop at the boundaries of human society.

The Danes sit like spectators in an amphitheatre; their sitting down is 'the collective gesture of a group', like that of Beowulf's cowardly retainers later, and provides a contrast with the dramatic, singular standing of the heroic individual.[195] Beowulf seizes this opportunity to prove himself against the power of the natural world and once again immerses himself and puts himself in nature's grasp: first *brimwylm onfeng / hilderince* 'the ocean surge receive[s] the warrior' (1494b–5a), and then Grendel's mother, the *brimwylf* 'sea-wolf' (1506a, 1599a) *guðrinc gefeng / atolan clommum* 'seize[s] the warrior with her terrible grip' (1501b–2a). Once again Beowulf emerges victorious, having transformed a veritable soup of monsters (*wyrmcynnes fela* 'many of the serpent-kind' (1425b), *nicras* 'water monsters' (1427b),[196] *wyrmas* 'serpents' (1430a), *wildeor* 'wild beast' (1430a), *gryrelicne gist* 'terrible visitor' (1441a), *sædeor* 'sea-beast' (1510b), not to mention Grendel's mother, the *brymwylf* 'sea-wolf') into ordinary surging waves:

> Sona wæs on sunde se þe ær æt sæcce gebad
> wighryre wraðra, wæter up þurhdeaf;

---

[194] 'I promise that I will not flee a footstep from here, but will proceed further.'

[195] Harris, 'Beowulf's Last Words', p. 24.

[196] This rare word also appears in an episode in *The Letter of Alexander to Aristotle* (§15), which shares similarities with this one; Alexander finds a river with *nicra mengeo* 'a multitude of water monsters', which drag swimming men down to the bottom. It is interesting to note that there is a sounding of a trumpet in this episode as well. See Orchard, *Pride and Prodigies*, pp. 45–6.

wæron ýðgebland   eal gefælsod,
eacne eardas,   þa se ellorgast
oflet lifdagas   ond þas lænan gesceaft.   (*Beowulf* 1618–22)[197]

A BEACON IN THE DARKNESS

Many years later, as king of Geatland, Beowulf faces another hostile incursion of the natural world: the overwhelming, unrelenting, non-negotiable attack of the dragon. Beowulf responds as the definition of his character throughout the poem demands; he cannot do otherwise, regardless of his role as king. Once again he leads an armed party out into the natural world; once again, however, his defence of a society is an assertion of his own identity as a hero, and so he leaves the safety of the armed group to penetrate hostile territory alone. Once again he overcomes his foe. This time, however, he cannot immerse himself and escape unscathed: encircled, not by surging waves but *wælfyre* 'slaughter-fire' (2582a) and *hildeleoman* 'battle-flames' (2583a), and then engulfed by the dragon's mouth (2691b), he suffers mortal wounds. In this last battle, the inescapable human condition finally reasserts itself so that Beowulf becomes yet another victim of the natural world. One could even argue that, in the end, Beowulf loses his distinction as a conqueror of the natural world's power and is redefined to be the same as everyone else; despite his heroic stature, he, like all human beings, finally must succumb to nature's unrelenting attacks.

This may appear to support the gloomy theme of vanity, monstrous pride,[198] or fatalism that some believe is the poet's final message. There is not really, however, so coherent a message to be discerned in the poet's representation of the natural world. The natural world in Old English poetry does not have an independent identity or meaning as it often does in later poetry like Alan of Lille's *De planctu naturae*;[199] its meaning is determined by its role, and its role is always a supporting, even a minor, one. In the end, in fact, the natural world is employed again, not to define Beowulf as mortal, but rather to define him both as worthy of commemoration and

---

[197] 'Immediately he who previously brought about his foes' destruction in battle was swimming, diving up through the water; the surging waves and the vast region were completely cleansed after the alien spirit left behind her life's days and this loaned existence.'

[198] Orchard, *Pride and Prodigies*, pp. 56 and 171.   [199] See below, p. 204.

once again as a strong actor against the natural world. Beowulf asks that his name and remains be placed out on the windy cliffs near the sea, out in the midst of the natural world against which he defined himself while living. He tells Wiglaf:

> Hatað heaðomære   hlæw gewyrcean
> beorhtne æfter bæle   æt brimes nosan;
> se scel to gemyndum   minum leodum
> heah hlifian   on Hronesnæsse,
> þæt hit sæliðend   syððan hatan
> Biowulfes biorh,   ða ðe brentingas
> ofer floda genipu   feorran drifað.   (*Beowulf* 2802–8)[200]

Beowulf seeks to transform himself into a kind of lighthouse[201] to counteract the darkness,[202] a defender or *helm*,[203] now inanimate, that will continue to guide his people and protect them from the natural world. Thus in the end Beowulf is still standing upright against the natural world, still standing out in the natural world, still standing out in comparison with other mortals, still outstanding. As in many other Old English poems, the definition of this outstanding individual owes much to the representation of the natural world.

---

[200] 'Command those renowned in battle to build a bright barrow after the pyre on the promontory of the ocean; it must tower high on "Whale's Bluff" as a reminder to my people, so that afterwards seafarers will call it "Beowulf's Barrow", when they drive their ships from afar over the darkness of the waters.'

[201] Aldhelm, at least, was familiar with the concept of the lighthouse, as he wrote a riddle about one (*XCII: Farus Editissima* 'Most Lofty Lighthouse'). It has also been suggested that Aldhelm may have based his riddle on a lighthouse that he had seen; see *The Riddles of Aldhelm*, ed. J. H. Pitman, Yale Studies in English 67 (New Haven, 1925), 78.

[202] The natural world is explicitly identified with darkness in *Guthlac* (83a).

[203] For discussion of the use of this word to describe the ideal protector and ruler, God, see above, p. 25, n. 21.

5

Representing God: power in and against nature

Þæt wearð underne   eorðbuendum,
þæt meotod hæfde   miht and strengðo
ða he gefestnade   foldan sceatas.
Seolfa he gesette   sunnan and monan,
stanas and eorðan,   stream ut on sæ,
wæter and wolcn,   ðurh his wundra miht.
Deopne ymblyt   clene ymbhaldeð
meotod on mihtum,   and alne middangeard.
He selfa mæg   sæ geondwlitan,
grundas in geofene,   godes agen bearn,
and he ariman mæg   rægnas scuran,
dropena gehwelcne.   Daga enderim
seolua he gesette   þurh his soðan miht.
Swa se wyrhta   þurh his wuldres gast
serede and sette   on six dagum
eorðan dæles,   up on heofonum,
and heanne holm.   Hwa is þæt ðe cunne
orðonc clene   nymðe ece god?   *(Christ and Satan* 1–18)[1]

---

[1] 'It became revealed to earth-dwellers that the creator had might and strength when he made firm the corners of the earth. He himself set the sun and moon, the stones and earth, the current out in the sea, water and cloud, through the might of his wonders. The creator in his might completely enfolds the whole circle and all middle-earth. He himself can scan the sea, the bottom of the ocean, and he, God's own son, can count the showers' downpours, every drop. He himself set the limit of the days through his true might. Thus the maker in six days devised and set the region of the earth, the upper heavens, and the deep ocean. Who is it who knows that skilful plan completely except eternal God?'

The question posed by the poet of *Christ and Satan* is a common one; the natural world inspired more than one Old English poet to see it as a riddle that the human mind could not hope to solve.[2] In this passage, however, the incomprehensibility appears to be satisfactorily resolved: the vast expanse of the natural world, from heaven to the bottom of the sea, is evidence of God's power. The act of creating the natural world itself is presented as a demonstration of divine strength, a way by which this strength 'became revealed to earth-dwellers', even though those earth-dwellers did not exist when the demonstration took place. This demonstration of power fundamentally defines God in Old English poetry: although Old English poets imagined God's role and his relationships with his followers in terms derived from their own human rulers,[3] it is through the vastness of the natural world that they indicate the extent of divine power. That is, Old English poets defined God qualitatively in terms of their society but quantitatively in terms of the natural world. This definition of God as one who has the *miht and strengðo* to control[4] the natural world is used as the basis for other descriptions of his ineffable works.[5]

It is important to note here that the use of the natural world to define God is a poetic technique. The contradictions and ambiguities that arise from this use are a part of the Old English poetic tradition; they are not necessarily the bottom line on Anglo-Saxon belief. Homiletic texts, for example, contain other ways of describing God's power; the natural world may not have played a crucial role in the Anglo-Saxons' relationship with their God. In their poetry, however, it does appear to have been an important aspect of the definition of God, and the desire to describe a power beyond human comprehension motivates a large number of Old

---

[2] See also Exeter Book *Riddles 1* (Storm), *3* (Wind), *40* (Creation), *66* (Creation) and Aldhelm's *Enigma C: Creatura*.

[3] See above, pp. 64–7.

[4] Although the passage describes God creating the universe, the verbs used – *fæstnian, settan, ymbhealdan, geondwlitan* – suggest control and restriction rather than Creation *ex nihilo*. This is consistent with the description of creation in the Old English poetic *Genesis*; for discussion of this passage, see above, pp. 57–61.

[5] In *Christ and Satan*, for example, the power demonstrated at Creation underlies and justifies God's ease in casting out Satan and his followers. This act, too, is described as a demonstration of power: *He þæt gecydde þæt he mægencræft hæfde, / mihta miccle, þa he þa mænego adraf* 'He made known that he had powerful skill, great might, when he drove out that multitude' (199–200).

English representations of the natural world.[6] For example, the *Daniel*-poet, who normally 'tones down' the descriptions of his or her biblical source,[7] elaborates the description of God's miraculous defence of his thegns in Nebuchadnezzar's oven. Where the biblical text[8] briefly indicates coolness in contrast with the uncontrollable inferno,[9] the Old English poet adds more positive associations – God's power brings to the oven not merely relief but the best of weather:

> Þa wæs on þam ofne, þær se engel becwom,
> windig and wynsum, wedere gelicost
> þonne hit on sumeres tid sended weorðeð
> dropena drearung on dæges hwile,
> wearmlic wolcna scur. Swylc bið wedera cyst,
> swylc wæs on þam fyre frean mihtum
> halgum to helpe. (*Daniel* 345–51a)[10]

The subsequent exhortation of creation to praise God (362–408) follows the biblical text (Dan. III.52–90) closely and so includes in its

---

[6] Many of these representations, like that in *Christ and Satan*, refer specifically to the natural world at the Creation – see *Cædmon's Hymn*, *Beowulf* (92–8), *Genesis* (97–168), *Andreas* (797–9), *Elene* (725–30), *Juliana* (111b–13a) and *The Order of the World* (38–85).

[7] E. R. Anderson, 'Style and Theme in the Old English *Daniel*', *ES* 68 (1987), 1–23, at 13. See also R. E. Bjork, 'Oppressed Hebrews and the Song of Azarias in the Old English *Daniel*, *SP* 77 (1980), 213–26, at 219, n.20; N. D. Isaacs, '*Daniel* and the Change of Pace', in his *Structural Principles in Old English Poetry* (Knoxville, TN, 1968), pp. 145–51.

[8] The Old English poet may have used an Old Latin version of the bible. For discussion of which biblical text and what other sources were used, see Remley, *Old English Biblical Verse*, pp. 231–333; D. A. Jost, 'Biblical Sources of Old English *Daniel* 1–78', *ELN* 15 (1978), 257–63; R. T. Farrell, 'The Structure of Old English *Daniel*', 535; R. T. Farrell, 'A Possible Source for Old English *Daniel*', *NM* 70 (1969), 84–90.

[9] The angel fans in to the captives 'a coolness such as wind and dew will bring' (Dan. III.50).

[10] 'When the angel came, then the weather in the oven was breezy and pleasant and most like when in summer time the weather sends the sprinkling of drops, a warm shower from the clouds, in the day time. Such as is the best of weather was [brought] into the fire by the power of the lord as a help to the holy ones.' These lines are part of 'The Song of the Three Children', sometimes seen as an interpolation and called *Daniel B*. For discussion, see W. J. Craigie, 'Interpolations and Omissions in Anglo-Saxon Poetical Texts', *Philologia* 2 (1923), 5–19; ASPR I, p. xxxii. For a contrary argument, see R. T. Farrell, 'The Unity of Old English *Daniel*', *RES* 18 (1967), 117–35.

chorus of praise some unlikely voices: frost, snow, lightning, whales and wild beasts. These are sources of discomfort, fear and danger in other Old English poems,[11] but it is evident that, in the context of praising the deity, the traditional, negative associations with these entities could be forgotten.

Representing God and representing the natural world are closely related in such texts. They are so closely related, in fact, that these particular descriptions offer perhaps the clearest proof of what I have argued above: the representation of the natural world is included specifically to manifest and make physical a non-physical, culturally constructed idea. In this case, the construction is the abstract truth of God's power.

POETIC STRATEGIES

In previous chapters, the relationship between God and the natural world has been discussed only insofar as it provides a contrast with the relationship between human entities and the natural world. For example, God's easy victory over the chaotic natural world in the beginning and his construction of a light-filled, secure, permanent structure stands as an impossible ideal toward which Hrothgar strives when he creates Heorot and his society in the midst of hostile forces and darkness.[12] In this context, God's surpassing power makes his relationship with the natural world uncomplicated. A Christian poet should have no need to represent God in any other way, since he or she could not allow a depiction of God that revealed him to be threatened or limited by the power of the natural world.

This absolute constraint on the representation of the relationship between God and the natural world goes far to explain the uniformity of the representation of the natural world in texts mentioning the Creation. Almost always there is mention of the trio of sea, earth and heaven, with an emphasis on spaciousness. For example, *Elene* refers to *heofon ond eorðan ond holmþræce, / sæs sidne fæðm, samod ealle gesceaft* 'heaven and earth and rushing ocean, the broad expanse of the sea, all creation together'

---

[11] See, for example, *The Seafarer* 9b, *The Wanderer* 48a, Exeter Book *Riddle 3*, 51b–8, *The Whale* and *The Rune Poem* 5a respectively.

[12] See above, pp. 62–9.

(727–8). Describing or even merely listing the wonders of Creation by way of introducing God's ineffable power was evidently a standard poetic strategy for Old English poets,[13] one which they could introduce either extremely briefly and elliptically, as in *Elene*'s two lines, or at great length, as in Exeter Book *Riddle 40*'s 107 lines.[14] Such a standardised pattern for the description of God participated in the traditional Old English poetic system of expression[15] and was an element of composition, like the theme or type-scene of the 'Beasts of Battle',[16] that could be isolated as an identifiable unit even as it was integrated into its context.[17] The pattern, once recognised, could both summon echoes from other, similarly patterned texts and establish the present text as truthful because traditional.[18] The benefits of describing the deity using such a pattern are obvious: whether a poet chose to be brief or to display poetic dexterity by elaborating at length, he or she could be sure that the audience would recognise and accept this particular passage, at least, as poetic *and* true. One might go so far as to say that this pattern of describing God was a poetic strategy for garnering authority and acceptance. The importance of such a pattern lies deeper, however: since there were no (human)[19]

---

[13] A similar poetic strategy can be observed in the connection of descriptions of the zodiacal series to the nature and power of God; this technique, though used briefly by Bede in *De natura rerum*, had become 'habitual' by the twelfth century. R. Tuve, *Seasons and Months: Studies in a Tradition of Middle English Poetry* (Cambridge, 1933), p. 130.

[14] The text as it stands is incomplete and was probably intended to be much longer. Its source, Aldhelm's *Enigma C: Creatura*, is eighty-three lines long; as the Old English translator used approximately two lines to translate each one of Aldhelm's, the Old English poem could have extended to 166 lines.

[15] R. Quirk, 'Poetic Language and Old English Metre', in *Early English and Norse Studies Presented to Hugh Smith in Honour of his Sixtieth Birthday*, ed. A. Brown and P. Foote (London, 1963), pp. 150–71.

[16] For discussion and bibliography of this theme, see above, p. 10, n. 50; for additional examples of themes, see Cross, 'The Old English Poetic Theme of "The Gifts of Men"' *Neophil* 46 (1962), 66–70, Clark, 'The Traveller Recognises his Goal'; for discussion of 'The Hero on the Beach' type-scene, see above, p. 94, n. 24.

[17] Griffith, 'Convention and Originality', p. 197.

[18] Pasternack, *Textuality of Old English Poetry*, pp. 77 and 88–9.

[19] It appeared likely but not certain that the angels were there to witness the Creation; since the bible does not explicitly mention the creation of the angels, some patristic writers, including Augustine, argued that they were included in the creation of light on the first day (*De civitate Dei* XI.xix). Bede, however, assumed that they already existed at this point. See *In Genesim* I.i.3.164–6.

witnesses to the act of Creation, the poetic description itself *is* the demonstration of God's power. That a poetic unit with such an important burden should be stable and consistent is unsurprising. It is also unsurprising that this is not the whole story.

A STRUCTURE BUILT ON SAND

If the pattern described above contained all the information that the representation of the natural world has to offer regarding Anglo-Saxon ideas about God, there would be little need for further commentary, but the representation of the natural world with respect to God is not so simple. In fact, as the passage from *Daniel* has suggested and as the discussion below will show, it contributes more ambiguity and incon- sistency to that found in the representations of the natural world described earlier, which served the shifting needs of poets defining the human condition, the state of society, and the power of individuals. Not only can frost and wild beasts carry radically different connotations when used with reference to God's consummate power rather than a human being's struggle to survive, but different Old English poems posit conflicting accounts of God's relationship with the natural world.[20] One could account for this inconsistency by assuming that contradictory views derive from different poets writing in different schools or different times, but one could never prove it, for it is not possible to identify the dates,[21] authors[22] or even areas of origin[23] for most of these

[20] For example, *The Order of the World*, *The Meters of Boethius*, *The Wanderer*, *Maxims I*, Exeter Book *Riddle 3*, *Genesis* and *Exodus*, which will be discussed below.

[21] For a summary of attempts to date Old English texts on linguistic grounds, see Amos, *Linguistic Means*, pp. 1–12 and *passim*.

[22] Besides Cædmon's hymn and Cynewulf's signed poems, it has proven impossible to determine the authorship of Old English poems. Pasternack argues that the nature of Old English poetry itself renders questions of authorship redundant, because the texts we have are collaborations of tradition, scribes and readers, not authors in the modern sense (*Textuality of Old English Poetry*, pp. 17 and 199–200). Similarly, Desmond argues that Old English poems were not so much authored as performed; what mattered was not originality or ownership but the rhetorical dexterity of a particular performer, and thus the surviving poems are pervasively anonymous. ('The Voice of Exile', pp. 582–3).

[23] It is generally accepted that most Old English poetic texts contain a mixture of dialects that renders locating their place of origin extremely problematic. See, for example,

poems.[24] The debate that has raged over the date and provenance of *Beowulf* is an extreme example,[25] but the inability to establish any aspect of a poem's origins conclusively is not unique: the efforts to establish a canon of works even for named poets like Cædmon and Cynewulf have largely failed to command acceptance.[26] In the same way, it is not possible to discern groups of texts that might represent a 'school of thought' or chronological trend.[27]

Yet another difficulty in approaching the issue of God's relation to the natural world is the absence of an identifiable cosmological system in Old English texts. Although it is possible that the loss of many Anglo-Saxon manuscripts has deprived modern critics of enough texts to see an overall pattern, it is not possible to make any assumptions about such a pattern –

A. Campbell, *Old English Grammar* (1959; Oxford, 1983), pp. 9–10, §18. For a discussion of some reasons for the difficulty, see R. M. Hogg, 'On the Impossibility of Old English Dialectology', in *Luick Revisited*, ed. D. Kastovsky and G. Bauer, Tübingen Beiträge zur Linguistik 288 (Tübingen, 1988), 183–203.

[24] But see Hill, who argues that study of the Latin sources of Anglo-Saxon literature provides another method for solving the problem of origins. T. D. Hill, 'Literary History and Old English Poetry: the Case of *Christ I, II, and III*', in *Sources of Anglo-Saxon Culture*, ed. P. E. Szarmach and V. D. Oggins, SMC 20 (Kalamazoo, MI, 1986), 3–22.

[25] The amount of scholarship on this debate is daunting; it is not possible to provide more than a sample of it here. For a summary ranging from the 'patchwork' theory of *Beowulf* 's origins, to the reconstitution of the poem as a pagan construction marred by Christian interpolations, to grammatical investigations of the text, to comparisons with other poems, to considerations of cultural history, see the introduction to the poem in ASPR IV, pp. liii–lviii. Later scholarship has covered much of the same ground again and again and not attained much more certainty. See, for example, the collection of essays published in *The Dating of Beowulf*, ed. C. Chase, especially the summary in his chapter, 'Opinions on the Date of *Beowulf*, 1815–1980', pp. 3–8. For the more radical view that the manuscript itself (datable to the eleventh century) contains the original version of the poem, see K. S. Kiernan, *'Beowulf' and the 'Beowulf' Manuscript*. For a recent argument for an eighth century, Anglian provenance, see Newton, *The Origins of 'Beowulf'*; see also Clemoes, *Interactions of Thought and Language*, pp. 3–67. For a summary of the arguments for an eighth-century Northumbrian provenance and a contrary proposal for a southern, pre-Conquest provenance, see Lapidge, *'Beowulf*, Aldhelm, the *Liber monstrorum* and Wessex'.

[26] See ASPR I, p. ix and Wrenn, 'The Poetry of Cædmon', pp. 407–10. For Cynewulf, see Anderson, *Cynewulf*, p. 20.

[27] For a brief summary and dismissal of scholarly efforts to establish a 'Cynewulfian school', see Anderson, *Cynewulf*, pp. 21–2.

not even that there was one. One can look for hints of how the Anglo-Saxons visualised the shape of the cosmos, but there is little evidence, in poetry at least, that they visualised it at all.[28] An exception may be the image used to describe the newly-constructed world in the Old English poetic *Genesis*, that of the *hyhtlic heofontimber* 'hope-filled heavenly building' (146a), the *fæsten folca hrofes* 'stronghold of the people's roof' (153).[29] At least one critic has considered this image of the world-hall in the midst of the ocean, roofed by the heavens, to be a 'distinctively Germanic' contribution to the Genesis-myth,[30] and, given its appearance in *Cædmon's Hymn*[31] and Bede's comparison of the creation of the world to the construction of a building,[32] it is possible that these brief instances[33] do reflect a specifically Anglo-Saxon image of the universe.

On the other hand, the image of the hall might recall Cosmas Indicopleustes's image of the world as a tabernacle;[34] his work may have

---

[28] The Anglo-Saxons produced no detailed description of the idea of the Seven Heavens, for example – see Roberts, 'A Preliminary "Heaven" Index', p. 211. For a text from an Old English homily that does contain a brief account of the Seven Heavens, see *Two Apocrypha in Old English Homilies*, ed. R. Willard, Beiträge zur Englischen Philologie 30 (Leipzig, 1935), pp. 4–6; commentary pp. 6–36. Illustrations from Junius 11 similarly show no evidence of the Seven Heavens, although they arguably do constitute an attempt to visualise the cosmos. For discussion of these illustrations, see above, p. 96. See also M. Bridges, 'Of Myths and Maps: the Anglo-Saxon Cosmographer's Europe', in *Writing and Culture*, ed. B. Engler (Tübingen, 1992), pp. 69–84, for the evidence offered by cartography, which suggests that the Anglo-Saxons had an ambiguous notion of their place in the world.

[29] For discussion of the similarities between this image and that of Hrothgar's Heorot, see above, pp. 62–5.

[30] Lee, *The Guest-Hall of Eden*, p. 24.

[31] *He ærest sceop eorþan bearnum / heofon to hrofe, halig scyppend* 'The holy creator first created the earth for men, [with] heaven as its roof' (5–6).

[32] *In Genesim* I.i.8–15. For text and translation, see above, p. 67.

[33] Another example may be found in Exeter Book *Riddle 29*, where a creature, tentatively identified as the moon, travels *ofer wealles hrof* 'over the roof of the wall' (7b). This text could thus be a unique instance in which both the roof and wall of the 'cosmic hall' are mentioned. On the other hand, it is possible that the phrase may mean no more than 'over the mountain top' – see Anderson, 'Uncarpentered World', pp. 70–1.

[34] *The Christian Topography* II.17–20. For text and translation into French, see *Cosmas Indicopleustès: Topographie Chrétienne*, ed. W. Wolska-Conus, vol. 1, Sources Chrétiennes 141 (Paris, 1968), I, 320–4; for translation into Italian, see *Topografia christiana: libri I–V*, trans. A. Garzya, Radici 27 (Naples, 1992). For a summary of this image, see Dreyer, *History of Astronomy*, pp. 214–18. For discussion, see also Doig, *Concise History*

been available in Anglo-Saxon England,[35] and the commentaries derived from Theodore and Hadrian's teaching demonstrate that his ideas were known and disseminated by them.[36] The likelihood that a Greek cosmological work found followers among poets writing in Old English is probably not great, but what is important for this discussion is not so much the source of the cosmological image but rather its limited appearances. Wherever the *heofontimber* came from, it did not dominate or inspire the imaginations of Anglo-Saxon writers as the image of the sail/ tent did when the Old English *Exodus*-poet described the cloudy pillar leading the Israelites through the desert (71b–92).[37] The *heofontimber* is neither so elaborated nor much more prevalent. In itself it cannot be said to be the image through which the Anglo-Saxons understood the universe, nor can it be considered a poetic convention for representing such a scheme.

Although the 'cosmic hall' stands upon narrow foundations whose sources cannot be determined, it is important because it appears to be the only particularly Anglo-Saxon cosmological image that occurs in Old English poetry. Why this should be so is difficult to understand. One assumes that there was a native, pagan cosmology accompanying the pagan rituals and idols assiduously hunted down by Christian authorities,[38] especially since pagan practices apparently persisted throughout the Anglo-Saxon period, at least down to the reign of Cnut (1016–35),

of Astronomy, p. 44; Kimble, *Geography in the Middle Ages*, pp. 34–5; J. O. Thomson, *History of Ancient Geography* (Cambridge, 1948).

[35] See J. D. A. Ogilvy, *Books Known to the English, 597–1066*, Mediaeval Academy of America Publication 76 (Cambridge, MA, 1967), 123; no manuscript of Cosmas Indicopleustes is listed in Gneuss, 'Preliminary List', but it has been suggested that there may have been a manuscript in Canterbury in the seventh century. See Bischoff and Lapidge, *Biblical Commentaries*, p. 209.

[36] Bischoff and Lapidge, *Biblical Commentaries*, pp. 206 and 209–11.

[37] This *nette* 'net' (*Exodus* 74a), *segl* 'sail' (81b) or *feldhus* 'field-house' (85b) is bound with *mæstrapas* 'mast-ropes' (82a). For discussion of this image, see Lucas, 'The Cloud in the Interpretation of the Old English *Exodus*', ES 51 (1970), 297–311; *The Old English Exodus*, ed. E. B. Irving, Jr, Yale Studies in English 122 (New Haven, CT, 1953), pp. 31 and 74; H. D. Merritt, *Some of the Hardest Glosses in Old English* (Stanford, 1968), pp. 18–19.

[38] As instructed, for example, by Pope Gregory – see *Historia ecclesiastica* I.30 (pp. 106–8). See also Grendon, 'The Anglo-Saxon Charms', p. 143.

whose laws specify the kinds of practices that his loyal subjects were expected to avoid:

And we forbeodað eornostlice ælcne hæðenscipe. Hæðenscipe byð, þæt man deofolgyld weorðige, þæt is þæt man weorþige hæðene godas & sunnan oððe monan, fyr oððe flod, wæterwyllas oððe stanas oððe æniges cynnes wudutreowa, oððon wiccecræft lufige oððon morðweorc gefremme on ænige wisan, oððon on blote oððon fyrhte, oððon swylcra gedwimera ænig þingc dreoge.   (II Cnut 5)[39]

Such prohibitions suggest that the religion preceding Christianity in England paid considerable attention to the natural world.[40] If this religion partook of the characteristic features produced by the 'savage mind',[41] one would expect that this worship of sun, moon, water, stones, fire and trees played a part in an *imago mundi* by which its practitioners sought to understand their world and that these natural phenomena provided a means through which their myths sought to explain the facts of their existence in a logical way.[42] Yet one looks in vain to find more than hints of myths, much less pagan cosmology, in Old English poetry itself.[43]

AMALGAMATING TRADITIONS

The absence of pagan cosmology can be attributed to a particularly successful campaign of elimination by Christian writers,[44] with the result

---

[39] 'And we earnestly forbid all paganism. Paganism is when one honours idols, that is honours heathen gods, and the sun or the moon, fire or flood, springs or stones or any kind of tree, or when one loves witchcraft or performs murder in any way, whether in sacrifice or divination, or works any type of such illusion.' Text is taken from *Die Gesetze der Angelsächsen*, ed. F. Liebermann (Halle, 1903), I, 312.

[40] Cf. Jolly, *Popular Religion*, p. 27–8. Note also that this attention to the natural world was evidently not lost in the process of conversion to Christianity; it remained a part of popular religion throughout the Anglo-Saxon period. For a definition of popular religion, see *ibid.*, p. 9.

[41] See Lévi-Strauss, *The Savage Mind*, p. 263.   [42] *Ibid.*, p. 95.

[43] Hints of myths (but not cosmology) reside particularly in poems like *Deor* and *Widsith*, whose elliptical catalogues of events and names allow for much speculation and little certainty. Some critics have attempted to draw from the fuller mythological accounts in Norse literature to compensate for this, but it is impossible to know how much of this Norse material is relevant. For an argument for the value of such an approach, however, see B. Branston, *The Lost Gods of England*, 2nd ed. (London, 1993), pp. 1–9.

[44] These writers include Aldhelm, Bede and Alcuin, who refused to condone interaction

that the continuing worship of trees and stones made no impression on the texts eventually preserved. Yet one might also expect that, although any native cosmological system was eventually supplanted by Christian dogma, there would be evidence of a period of transition during which the old system influenced the new and the new system adapted itself to the expectations and understanding of its new converts,[45] adopting the kind of compromises advocated by Pope Gregory the Great to Abbot Mellitus.[46] This kind of integration of old and new systems of belief is well demonstrated in poems like the Old English poetic *Genesis*,[47] where the Old Testament God effortlessly assumes not only the attributes of the ideal Anglo-Saxon lord who protects and rewards his thegns,[48] but also the attributes of the Anglo-Saxon hero.[49] For example, when Satan begins to consider rebellion, God reacts with heroic fury:

> Cwædon þæt heo rice,   reðemode,
> agan woldan,   and swa eaðe meahtan.
> Him seo wen geleah,   siððan waldend his,
> heofona heahcining,   honda aærde,
> hehste wið þam herge.   Ne mihton hygelease,

between Christian and pagan ideas, as the more liberal humanists of the twelfth century did (R. Frank, 'The *Beowulf* Poet's Sense of History', in *The Wisdom of Poetry: Essays in Early English Literature in Honor of Morton W. Bloomfield*, ed. L. D. Benson and S. Wenzel (Kalamazoo, MI, 1982), pp. 53–65, at 56).

[45] W. A. Chaney, 'Paganism to Christianity in Anglo-Saxon England', *Harsard Theological Review* 53 (1960), 197–217, at 200; cf. Jolly, *Popular Religion*, pp. 25–7.

[46] *Historia Ecclesiastica* I.30 (106–8). See above, p. 66.

[47] See Evans, *Paradise Lost and the Genesis Tradition*, pp. 145–8; F. T. Utley, 'The Flood Narrative in the Junius Manuscript and in Baltic Literature', in *Studies in Old English Literature in Honor of Arthur G. Brodeur*, ed. S. B. Greenfield (Eugene, OR, 1963) pp. 207–26, at 213; Brockman, '"Heroic" and "Christian" in *Genesis A*: The Evidence of the Cain and Abel Episode', *MLQ* 35 (1974), 115–28; Skemp, 'Transformation of Scriptural Story'.

[48] See, for example, *Genesis* 1946b–9a. For discussion of this aspect of God's characterisation in relation to the state of humanity in the natural world, see above, p. 64.

[49] J. L. Greene, 'Indo-European Social Tripartism in Book I of the Cædmonian Paraphrase', *JIES* 6 (1978), 266–72. Cf. also W. Whallon, 'The Idea of God in *Beowulf*' *PMLA* 80 (1965), 19–23; P. Clemoes, 'Cynewulf's Image of the Ascension', in *England before the Conquest*, ed. Clemoes and Hughes, pp. 294–6. In the same way, once God had assumed the aspect of the hero, hell could become the site of an inversion of heroic ideals. A. Renoir, 'Self-Deception of Temptation: Boethian Psychology in *Genesis B*', in *Old English Poetry: Fifteen Essays*, ed. Creed, pp. 47–67, at 50–5.

> mæne wið metode,   mægyn bryttigan,
> ac him se mæra   mod getwæfde,
> bælc forbigde.   Þa he gebolgen wearð,
> besloh synsceaþan   sigore and gewealde,
> dome and dugeðe,   and dreame benam
> his feond, friðo   and gefean ealle,
> torhte tire,   and his torn gewræc
> on gesacum swiðe   selfes mihtum
> strengum stiepe.   Hæfde styrne mod,
> gegremed grymme,   grap on wraðe
> faum folmum,   and him on fæðm gebræc
> yrre on mode;   æðele bescyrede
> his wiðerbrecan   wuldorgestealdum.   (*Genesis* 47–64)[50]

Just how completely this description of God has been integrated into the tradition of heroic action can be seen when the passage is compared with Beowulf's exploits. Like God, Beowulf enters combat *gebolgen* 'swollen with rage' (1539b, 2220b, 2401b and 2550b) or *bolgenmod* 'enraged' (709a),[51] and his anger (*yrre*) features prominently (769b, 1532a, 1575a and 2092a).[52] Also like God, Beowulf fights by gripping his enemies in his grasp (*heardan clammum*, *mundgripe* (963b and 965a)), avenging any

---

[50] 'The fierce-minded [rebellious angels] said that they wanted to own the realm, and that they could just as easily do so. That expectation deceived them, after his [i.e. Satan's] ruler, the high king of heaven, the highest, raised his hand against the army. The rash ones could not rule over the host along with the creator, but rather the famous one put an end to their courage, bowed down their arrogance. When he became swollen with rage, he struck away victory and possession, glory and power, from the sinful enemies, and he deprived his foe of delight, peace and all joys, bright honours, and he avenged his anger mightily through his own strength, forcefully with a fall. He had a stern mind, was grimly enraged; in wrath he gripped the evil spirits with his hands and, angry in mind, broke them in his grasp; he sheared off his adversary from his native land, the realms of glory.'

[51] Grendel also approaches combat in this state (723b). For discussion of such heroic swollenness in Old English, Old Norse, Old Irish, Old Indic and Welsh, see P. L. Henry, 'Furor Heroicus', *Zeitschrift für celtische Philologie* 39 (1982), 235–42. Cf. also T. Pettitt, '*Beowulf*: The Mark of the Beast and the Balance of Frenzy', *Neophil* 77 (1976), 526–35. The attribution of this state to God, however, suggests that one should be cautious when linking Beowulf's anger to beast-like or berserk behaviour.

[52] Again, Beowulf's opponents share his mood. Grendel's mother approaches Heorot in anger (2073b), as does the dragon (2669b); an unspecified foe can be referred to as an 'angry one' (*yrre* (1447a) or *wraþ* (660a, 708b and 1619b)).

insult (2005b), depriving his foes of the ability to boast (2006–9a) and disappointing opposing expectations (2323b). However inappropriate the martial vocabulary of traditional poetry may appear to modern critics in other contexts,[53] in this case the triumphant power of the Old Testament God functions comfortably within poetic language and formulae apparently designed for secular heroes. The poem retains intact and uncontradicted both the Christian dogma of the fall of the angels and the conventions of Germanic heroism.[54]

The interaction between heroic, originally oral, poetics and Christian, written texts was not always so straightforward.[55] This can be demonstrated in *The Dream of the Rood*, in which the heroic ideology of unflinching advance into battle, especially battle against hopeless odds, is grafted upon the story of Christ's submission to crucifixion. Although the resulting poem is powerful,[56] and although the purpose of the poem, the glorification of God and the power of the Cross, is clear,[57] the transformation of a passive, suffering god into a heroic lord[58] remains incongruous.[59] The

---

[53] Most criticism in this vein has been levelled at *Andreas* – see Hill 'Soldier of Christ', pp. 71–2; Woolf, 'Saint's Lives', in *Continuations and Beginnings*, ed. Stanley, 37–66, at 53; E. G. Stanley, '*Beowulf*' in his *Continuations and Beginnings*, pp. 104–41, at 114. Cf., however, D. G. Calder, 'Figurative Language and its Contexts in *Andreas*: A Study in Medieval Expressionism', in *Modes of Interpretation*, ed. Brown, Crampton and Robinson, pp. 115–36 and C. Schneider, 'Cynewulf's Devaluation of Heroic Tradition in *Juliana*', *ASE* 7 (1978), 107–18.

[54] For another example of such a successful fusion, see Hill, 'Figures of Evil', p. 16; the Christian doctrine of envy coalesces with the ideals of the comitatus.

[55] Cf. O'Keeffe, *Visible Song*, p. 46; Lerer, *Literacy and Power*, pp. 42–60.

[56] For discussion of the poem's 'unique effectiveness', see N. D. Isaacs, 'Progressive Identifications: the Structural Principle of *The Dream of the Road*' in Isaacs, *Structural Principles*, pp. 3–18; cf. also Lee, 'Toward a Critique', pp. 163 and 166.

[57] Irvine, 'Anglo-Saxon Literary Theory', pp. 172–3.

[58] Woolf, 'Doctrinal Influences', pp. 144–5.

[59] Cf., however, Leiter, '*The Dream of the Rood*: Patterns of Transformation', p. 125, who says that the battle metaphor in the poem is 'consistent and cohesive'. For discussion of the heroic tradition behind Christ's apparently paradoxical disarming before the conflict, see A. Finlay, 'The Warrior Christ and the Unarmed Hero', in *Medieval English Religious and Ethical Literature: Essays in Honour of G. H. Russell*, ed. G. Katzmann and J. Simpson (Cambridge, 1986), pp. 19–29. For discussion of the patristic tradition behind this disarming, see Woolf, 'Doctrinal Influences', pp. 146–7. It is also interesting to note that when Christ makes a similarly heroic approach to battle in another Old English poem, *The Descent into Hell*, he is described as being without armour-bearing warriors (33–42a).

young hero[60] hastens (*efstan*) into battle *elne mycle* 'with great courage' (34a) and is accompanied by a loyal retainer who carries out his lord's command despite extreme circumstances as dictated by convention,[61] but when the Cross states that Christ *hine ðær hwile reste / meðe æfter ðam miclan gewinne* 'rested himself there for awhile, tired after the great conflict' (64b–5a), much of the account of the crucifixion has been omitted. Not only has the poet not told the audience anything it did not already know,[62] but he or she consistently diverts attention away from the crucial fact of Christ's death: Christ is not deprived of his life; he sends his spirit forth.[63] Thus when the Cross describes the act of crucifixion, it is the Cross and not Christ who is nailed (*Þurhdrifan hi me mid deorcan næglum* 'they drove dark nails through me' (46a)); when all creation laments the fall of the king, the Cross immediately shifts attention to those hastening towards it and their actions (55b–69a); when Christ's corpse begins to cool, the Cross tells of its own *egeslic wyrd* 'terrible fate' (74b).[64] Although it has been argued that the poem focuses on Christ defeated and then transformed,[65] the poem seems rather to elide Christ's defeat. As a result, while the Cross suffers the pain and sorrow normally ascribed to Christ[66] and performs his thegnly duties to perfection, Christ vaguely fights a battle and then returns in glory to his homeland, where he is able to reward his followers as any lord might do. The divine sacrifice for the sake of man's sin, the teachings of Christ regarding humility and non-violence and the church's calls to turn away from worldly lifestyles seem to have been forgotten.[67]

---

[60] See C. J. Wolf, who notes that the language and formulae used in this poem, including the 'Hero on the Beach' and 'Approach to Battle', mark Christ as a hero ('Christ as Hero in *The Dream of the Rood*', NM 72 (1970), 202–10, at 203–8).

[61] M. D. Cherniss, 'The Cross as Christ's Weapon: The Influence of Heroic Literary Tradition on *The Dream of the Rood*', ASE 2 (1973), 241–52, at 242.

[62] Cf. Irving, 'Crucifixion Witnessed', p. 108.

[63] Lee, 'Toward a Critique', p. 179.

[64] Cf. C. B. Pasternack, who argues that the poet uses grammar to subordinate the fact of the death to its effect ('Stylistic Disjunctions in *The Dream of the Rood*', ASE 13 (1984), 167–86, at 176–7).

[65] Leiter, 'Patterns of Transformation', pp. 94–6. Cf. also Macrae-Gibson, 'Christ as the Victor-Vanquished in *The Dream of the Rood*', NM 70 (1969), 667–72.

[66] Irving, 'Crucifixion Witnessed', p. 108.

[67] Nevertheless, it has been argued that the poem reveals the influence of the Christian doctrines of its time. See Shippey, *Old English Verse*, p. 163; H. R. Patch, 'Liturgical Influence in the *Dream of the Rood*', PMLA 34 (1919), 233–57; J. V. Fleming, 'The

THE FORGOTTEN UNIVERSE

These two poems, *Genesis* and *The Dream of the Rood*, provide two examples of Anglo-Saxon poets attempting (or perhaps unconsciously bringing about)[68] an amalgamation of old forms and ideas with Christian plots, characters and theological dogma,[69] but one can argue that the use of traditional poetic language in any Old English poem distorted Christian subjects to some extent, regardless of the poet's intentions.[70] Vernacular poetry thus provided a convenient medium for combining if not reconciling the disparate ideologies that contributed to the Anglo-Saxon literary tradition.[71] It is surprising, therefore, that no such amalgamation took place with respect to ideas of cosmology. While the absence may reflect a pious elimination of pagan cosmology, there is little evidence of this, either. No effort appears to have been made to replace or fill a gap left by a rejected cosmology, much less any argument for a present conception against any other; certainly there is nothing in Old English poetry like the apparently open-minded[72] listing of multiple truths in the Hiberno-Latin *Liber de ordine creaturarum*,[73] even

---

Dream of the Rood and Anglo-Saxon Monasticism', *Traditio* 22 (1966), 43–72; F. H. Patten, 'Structure and Meaning in *The Dream of the Rood*', *ES* 49 (1968), 385–401; R. B. Burlin, 'The Ruthwell Cross, *The Dream of the Rood*, and the Vita Contemplativa', *SP* 65 (1968), 23–43; N. A. Lee, 'The Unity of *The Dream of the Rood*', *Neophil* 56 (1972), 469–86; M. Schlauch, '*The Dream of the Rood* as Prosopopoeia', in *Essential Articles*, ed. Bessinger, Jr and Kahrl, pp. 428–41; Huppé, *Web of Words*, pp. 63–112; Woolf, 'Doctrinal Influences', pp. 137–53.

[68] Skemp, 'Transformation of Scriptural Story', p. 428.

[69] Cf. Wrenn, 'The Poetry of Cædmon', p. 418; Doane, *Genesis A*, p. 70; Opland, 'From Horseback to Monastic Cell'.

[70] Williams, 'Relation between Pagan Survivals and Diction'; cf. J. J. Campbell, 'Oral Poetry in *The Seafarer*', *Speculum* 35 (1960), 87–96, at 87.

[71] Another example of such reconciliation of ideologies may be found in *Andreas*; for discussion of how the poet rewrote his potentially unorthodox source to reconcile it with the doctrinal hermeneutic approved by the Church, see R. Boenig, *Saint and Hero: 'Andreas' and Medieval Doctrine* (Lewisburg, PA, 1991), p. 104.

[72] Smyth, 'Isidore of Seville and Early Irish Cosmography', p. 102.

[73] See, for example, section IV: *De firmamento caeli*, which provides multiple possibilities and concludes without choosing one over another. For the text, see *Liber de ordine creaturarum: un anónimo inlandés del siglo VII*, ed. M. Diaz y Diaz, Monografías dela Universidad de Santiago de Compostela 10 (Santiago, 1972), 106–10.

though this work was available and used by Anglo-Saxons from Bede onwards.[74]

One could argue that the speculation that abounds in the *Liber de ordine creaturarum* would be absurd in Old English poetry, which appears inclined rather to describe the natural world in series of maxims presented as unalterable facts.[75] That inclination, however, does not derive from a lack of sources. There were sources in Anglo-Saxon England that could have provided images and fully developed cosmological schemes, systems which they had inherited along with literacy and the Christian religion, both of which evidently had an important impact on their vernacular poetry, since the Old English poetry that remains is written and is dominated by Christian themes. For example, Bede[76] passed on information regarding the earth and the universe gathered from earlier writers, including not only the courses of the planets but also the zodiacal signs;[77] he seems to have an image of the earth beneath a busy sky, full of planets circling the earth regularly, 'fixed' stars moving in the opposite direction (but not far away since they are responsible for rain and hail),[78] comets and the spirits of the damned awaiting judgement.[79] Even more sophisticated accounts of classical Greek cosmology were available from Theodore and Hadrian;[80] Martianus Capella's *De nuptiis Philologiae et Mercurii*, with its simplified account of classical astronomy, eventually arrived in England as well.[81] Yet Anglo-Saxon writers fail to demonstrate

---

[74] Bede quotes from it (see, for example, *De natura rerum* iv and vii); the ninth century *Old English Martyrology* also draws on it. See J. E. Cross, '*De ordine creaturarum liber* in Old English Prose', *Anglia* 90 (1972), 132–40.

[75] For example, *Forst sceal freosan, fyr wudu meltan, / eorþe growan, is brycgian, / wæter helm wegan, wundrum lucan / eorþan ciþas* 'frost must freeze, fire melt wood, the earth grow, ice make a bridge, water bear a covering, [and] lock up the earth's seeds' (*Maxims I*, 71–4a). Yet, as will be discussed below, the apparently equally characteristic inclination toward riddles suggests that the Anglo-Saxons were not adverse to speculation, as does the delight in unusual facts displayed in *The 'Prose Solomon and Saturn'*, ed. Cross and Hill. See below, pp. 188–9 and 195.

[76] For a summary of Bede's views of the universe in the context of those of Plato and Aristotle, patristic writers like Basil and Augustine, as well as Boethius, Isidore and Hrabanus Maurus, see S. Viarre, 'Cosmologie Antique et Commentaire de la Création du Monde. Le Chaos et les Quatres Elements chez quelques Auteurs du Haut Moyen Age', *Settimane* 22 (1974), 543–73.

[77] *De natura rerum* xii–xvii.   [78] *Ibid.*, xi.   [79] *Ibid.*, xxv.

[80] Bischoff and Lapidge, *Biblical Commentaries*, p. 63.

[81] It was available as early as the end of the ninth century (Gneuss, 'Preliminary List',

154

much interest in or use of this material. Byrhtferth, for example, despite following Bede closely,[82] does not appear to grasp an image of the universe as Bede did. Instead, he delights in the mathematical relationships that constitute his diagram of the world (two solstices, two equinoxes, twelve months, twelve signs of the zodiac, four seasons, four ages of man, four letters in Adam's name, four elements and four virtues);[83] although he lists the lengths of the courses of the planets,[84] briefly mentions the dire events forecasted by comets[85] and states that the surrounding heavens are solid, spinning and painted with stars,[86] his interests did not lie in presenting an image of the physical cosmos but rather in the symbolism of numbers[87] and the science of computus.[88]

Byrhtferth's limited use of the material supplied by Bede may be considered typical in the sense that he was not concerned to grasp any image of the universe as a whole and instead picked up details that contributed to his particular interests. In the same way, the homilists who used 'The Devil's Account of the Next World'[89] were reporting a classical astronomical theory when they stated that the size of the world was insignificant in comparison with the immense expanse of the ocean surrounding it,[90] but their concern was not with astronomy, nor with understanding the shape of the universe, but with pointing out the world's moral insignificance; the cosmological image is completely

p. 8); Remigius of Auxerre's commentary on Martianus Capella was available at the beginning of the tenth (*ibid.*, p. 32).

[82] Other computistical sources used by Byrhtferth include Ælfric's *De temporibus anni*, Helperic's *De computo ecclesiastico* and Hrabanus Maurus's *De computo*. For these and other sources drawn upon by Byrhtferth, see *Byrhtferth's Enchiridion*, ed. and trans. Baker and Lapidge, pp. lxxiv–xciv.

[83] *Byrhtferth's Enchiridion*, ed. and trans. Baker and Lapidge, pp. 10–12.

[84] *Ibid.*, pp. 116–18.   [85] *Ibid.*, p. 120.   [86] *Ibid.*, p. 70.

[87] C. R. Hart, 'Byrhtferth and his Manual', *MÆ* 52 (1972), 95–107, at 100.

[88] Byrhtferth appears to have created his manual as a commentary on a computus like that preserved in Oxford, St. John's College 17, assembling material that he believed useful and arranging it in the same order. See P. S. Baker, 'Byrhtferth's *Enchiridion* and the Computus in Oxford, St John's College 17', *ASE* 10 (1982), 123–42; *Byrhtferth's Enchiridion*, ed. and trans. Baker and Lapidge, p. xxvi.

[89] For text and translation see Wright, *The Irish Tradition*, pp. 276–91; for commentary see *ibid.*, pp. 179–88.

[90] *Ibid.*, p. 182. For discussion of how this astronomical theory became a moral topos, see A.-J. Festugière, *La révélation d'Hermès Trismégiste, II: le dieu cosmique* (Paris, 1949), pp. 442–58.

divorced from its original context and no longer recalls it. In the same way, the *Genesis*-poet's description of the sky as a *hyrstedne hrof halgum tunglum* 'roof adorned with holy stars' (956) could be seen as reference to a belief in something like Byrhtferth's solid, 'painted' heaven rather than the possibly Germanic image of the roofed hall.[91] This passage may thus contain a hint of a fuller vision of the cosmos than that actually presented in the poem, a hint of a classical image divorced from its original context, but there is nothing else in the poem to make a connection more than tenuous.[92] If the *Genesis*-poet was knowledgeable about cosmology as a result of reading Bede or any other source, he or she took remarkably little away from it, despite the obvious place for such material in an account of the creation of the universe. This absence is not the failing of a single poet, but rather a reflection of a general disregard for cosmology.[93] Even Bede, in the end, was interested in planets and the motion of the moon primarily for reasons of computus.[94]

In the same way, the idea of the universe as a macrocosm, a mirror of the human body on a cosmic scale,[95] although supported by authorities like Augustine, Isidore and Gregory the Great, and although known and apparently well appreciated by the Anglo-Saxons,[96] was not used as a framework for an understanding of the structure of the universe. This originally Greek idea was transformed by Christian and Jewish writers so that the image of the celestial man was replaced with Adam, the

---

[91] Since Byrhtferth flourished late in the Anglo-Saxon period (late tenth to early eleventh century) and *Genesis A* is generally accepted to be early (if not earliest), there is no question of the poet adopting anything from Byrhtferth himself. For discussion of the date of *Genesis A*, see ASPR I, p. xxvi; Doane, *Genesis A*, pp. 36–7; R. J. Menner, 'The Date and Dialect of *Genesis A* 852–2936 (Part III)', *Anglia* 70 (1952), 285–94.

[92] One must also keep in mind that the firmament, described in the Bible (Gen. I.6–8 and 14–19) and explained by Bede in *In Genesim* I.vi–viii, could also underlie the idea of a solid roof.

[93] Gatch, *Loyalties and Traditions*, pp. 103–10.

[94] See, for example, *De temporibus liber*, pp. 13–14.

[95] This idea 'is basic for the understanding of medieval science' (Singer, *Short History of Scientific Ideas*, p. 59). See also D'Alverny, 'L'homme comme symbole', p. 124, and Cross, 'Aspects of Microcosm', pp. 1–2.

[96] D'Alverny, 'L'homme comme symbole', p. 168; Cross, 'Aspects of Microcosm', pp. 1–22. Aldhelm mentions it, for example, in his prose *De virginitate* III (MGH AA, 15, 230–1).

primordial man, in whom could be seen the image of God[97] and in whose name could be found the four points of the compass, the four elements and all the constituents of the created world.[98] Byrhtferth's *Enchiridion* and the prose and verse versions of *Solomon and Saturn*[99] indicate that the Anglo-Saxons were aware of and interested in Adam's extensive representative qualities. As the discussion of Byrhtferth has shown, and as the examination of other Old English poems will demonstrate, however, the interest in this aspect of Adam did not bring with it the cosmological structure that was originally implicit in it.

ALFRED'S POWER STRUGGLE

The exception to this general lack of interest in cosmology appears to be Alfred, who included Boethius's *De consolatione Philosophiae* among the works most necessary for his people to know (*niedbeðearfosta ... eallum monnum to wiotonne*).[100] This most necessary work, however, assumes a fairly comprehensive knowledge of astronomy in its readers, for Boethius[101] uses astronomical images freely and confidently,[102] especially to illustrate his theme of divine order. For example, to see the structure and laws underlying the universe, Lady Philosophy advises that one should observe the movements of particular heavenly bodies:

---

[97] D'Alverny, 'L'homme comme symbole', pp. 136–7.   [98] *Ibid.*, pp. 166–7.

[99] For Byrhtferth's diagram containing the correspondences between the letters in Adam's name and the elements, ages of man, seasons, zodiacal signs and months, see *Byrhtferth's Enchiridion*, ed. and trans. Baker and Lapidge, pp. 76 and 374. For commentary on the idea of the microcosm and macrocosm in *Solomon and Saturn*, see J. M. Evans, 'Microcosmic Adam', *MÆ* 35 (1966), 38–42, and L. G. Whitbread, 'Adam's Pound of Flesh: A Note on the Old English verse *Solomon and Saturn (II)*, 336–339', *Neophil* 59 (1975), 622–6.

[100] From Alfred's letter prefacing his translation of Gregory's *Pastoral Care*, in *King Alfred's West-Saxon Version of Gregory's Pastoral Care*, ed. H. Sweet, EETS os 45 (London, 1871), 6.

[101] For an introduction to Boethius and his learning, see H. Chadwick, *Boethius: The Consolations of Music, Logic, Theology and Philosophy* (1981; Oxford, 1990).

[102] According to Cassiodorus, Boethius translated Ptolemy's treatise on astronomy into Latin; unfortunately, this work is no longer extant. See D. Pingree, 'Boethius' Geometry and Astronomy', in *Boethius*, ed. Gibson, pp. 155–61, at 155 and 159; White, 'Boethius in the Medieval Quadrivium', in *Boethius*, ed. Gibson, pp. 162–205, at 163.

Si vis celsi iura tonantis
Pura sollers cernere mente,
Aspice summi culmina caeli.
Illic iusto foedere rerum
Veterem servant sidera pacem ...
Vesper seras nuntiat umbras
Revehitque diem Lucifer almum.
Sic aeternos reficit cursus
Alternus amor, sic astrigeris
Bellum discors exulat oris.

(*De consolatione Philosophiae* IV metre 6:1–5, 14–18)[103]

Such astronomical references are more than poetic images, however; the basis of Boethius's philosophical treatise is intimately entwined with his vision of the universe. In fact, his philosophy is based upon his cosmology. To explain how a good, omnipotent deity can see future events and yet not interfere with human free will, Lady Philosophy describes the position of God with respect to the universe:

est autem deo semper aeternus ac praesentarius status; scientia quoque eius omnem temporis supergressa motionem in suae manet simplicitate praesentiae infinitaque praeteriti ac futuri spatia complectens omnia quasi iam gerantur in sua simplici cognitione considerat ... unde non praevidentia sed providentia potius dicitur, quod porro ab rebus infimis constituta quasi ab excelso rerus cacumine cuncta prospiciat. Quid igitur postulas ut necessaria fiant quae divino lumine lustrentur, cum ne homines quidem necessaria faciant esse quae videant?

(*De consolatione Philosophiae* V prose 6:61–6, 69–75)[104]

---

[103] 'If you want to perceive the laws of the great thunderer with a pure, sharp mind, examine the heights of the highest heaven. There the stars serve the ancient peace of things by a just treaty ... Vesper announces the late shadows and Lucifer brings back the fruitful day. Thus reciprocal love restores their eternal courses; thus discordant war is exiled from star-bearing regions.' Cf. also *De consolatione Philosophiae* I metre 5:1–24 and IV metre 5:1–10 (see *Boethius*, trans. Tester).

[104] 'God, moreover, always has an eternal and present state; his knowledge also, having surpassed all motion of time, remains in the simplicity of its own present and, embracing all the infinite spaces of the past and future, he considers them in his own simple knowledge as if they were now happening ... As a result [God's knowledge] is called not foreseeing but rather providence, because, set far off from the lowest things, it views all things as if from the lofty peak of things. Why therefore do you claim that those things which are surveyed/illuminated by the divine light should be made necessary, when even men do not make necessary the things that they see?'

Boethius' philosophical turmoil over humanity's subjection to an arbitrary Fortune, a turmoil initially only augmented by Philosophy's assertion of God's foreknowledge of events, is thus resolved through the creation of a cosmological image that places God in a separate dimension, an eternal present, distant yet connected like a beam of light to the physical universe: 'The Boethian universe is a kind of brilliantly lighted, translucent pyramid projecting from the mind of God.'[105]

Alfred does not follow Boethius in postulating a separate existence for God in order to allow for both providence and free will.[106] Instead, God exists and acts in the same sequential reality inhabited by human beings; although untouched by time, his acts proceed chronologically from plan to completion.[107] Likewise, the natural world does not reflect order through its inherent form but through its subjection to the superior power of God.[108] Thus there is no cosmological image in Alfred's translation[109] but rather delight and awe over the immense power by which God forcefully imposes order on the natural world:

> Hæfð se alwealda   ealle gesceafta
> gebæt mid his bridle,   hafað butu gedon,
> ealle gemanode   and eac getogen,
> þæt hi ne moten   ofer metodes est
> æfre gestillan,   ne eft eallunga
> swiðor stirian,   þonne him sigora weard
> his gewealdleðer   wille onlæten.
> He hafað þe bridle   butu befangen
> heofon and eorðan   and eall holma begong.
> Swa hæfð geheaðærod   hefonrices weard
> mid his anwealde   ealle gesceafta
> þæt hiora æghwilc   wið oðer wind,
> and þeah winnende   wreðiað fæste,

---

[105] Payne, *King Alfred and Boethius*, pp. 34–5.   [106] *Ibid.*, pp. 18–20.

[107] *Ibid.*, p. 20.

[108] *Ibid.*, pp. 21–4. Cf. also the prose *Solomon and Saturn*: *Saga me hwæt ys god. Ic þe secge, þæt ys god þe ealle ðing on hys gewealdum hafað* 'Tell me what is God. I tell you, God is that which has all things in his power' (*Prose 'Solomon and Saturn'*, ed. and trans. Cross and Hill, p. 25).

[109] Note also that, although Alfred does retain Boethius's astronomical imagery, his translations of such images are less concise than the original and include fewer names. See, for example, *Meters of Boethius* 29 1–24, which parallels IV metre 6 cited above.

æghwilc oðer   utan ymbclyppeð,
þy læs hi toswifen.   (*Meters of Boethius 11*, 22–36a)[110]

Alfred's *Meters of Boethius* reflects the same image of God as ruler that appears at the beginning of *Christ and Satan* and in *Genesis*, and the representation of the natural world serves primarily to emphasise his physical power. To this end Alfred has expanded several passages where Boethius has briefly mentioned the concord of the four elements, focusing upon the strength and skill exercised by God in maintaining the opposing forces of the natural world in harmony.[111]

ORDER THROUGH POWER

In much the same way, *The Order of the World*[112] describes a superficially Boethian universe in which God unites opposing entities – *dæg wiþ nihte, deop wið hean, /lyft wið lagustream, lond wiþ wæge* 'day with night, low with high, sky with sea, land with wave' (83–4). Like *De consolatione Philosophiae*, the poem praises God for uniting all things, but, like Alfred's translation, it does not describe a cosmic plan or inherent form. Instead, God's power forcefully joins everything together:

Hwæt, on frymþe gescop   fæder ælmihtig,
heah hordes weard,   heofon ond eorðan,
sæs sidne grund,   sweotule gesceafte,
þa nu in þam þream   þurh þeodnes hond
heaþ ond hebbaþ   þone halgan blæd.
Forþon eal swa teofanade,   se þe teala cuþe,

---

[110] 'The all-ruler has bound all creation with his bridle, has done both, exhorted and also restrained all things, so that they can not ever rest against the behest of the creator, nor indeed again stir any more, when the guardian of victories wishes to relax the leather straps of power for them. He has grasped the bridle of both the heaven and earth and all the extent of the ocean. Thus the guardian of the heavenly kingdom has restrained all creation with his single power, so that each of them strives against the other, and though striving supports firmly, each embracing around the other, lest they separate.' See also *Meters of Boethius 13*, 1–13.

[111] For examples, see Payne, *King Alfred and Boethius*, p. 23.

[112] There has been little criticism of this poem, but for an edition and commentary see Huppé, *The Web of Words*, pp. 28–61. The poem is discussed at length by Isaacs, 'The Exercise of Art', and also mentioned by J. B. Trahern, 'Fatalism and the Millennium', in *The Cambridge Companion to Old English Literature*, ed. Godden and Lapidge, pp. 160–71, at 168–9, and Cross, 'Aspects of Microcosm', p. 20.

æghwylc wiþ oþrum;   sceoldon eal beran
stiþe stefnbyrd,   swa him se steora bibead
missenlice gemetu   þurh þa miclan gecynd.

(*The Order of the World* 38–46)[113]

This passage conforms to the pattern observed in other Anglo-Saxon references to the Creation[114] and serves the same purpose: the demonstration of the power of God. It is difficult to see a more complex philosophy or cosmology anywhere in the poem. It is possible that *miclan gecynd* refers to the Boethian or Platonic concept of 'form', but such meaning rests upon an emendation; while all editors follow Grein in emending manuscript *gemynd* to *gecynd*,[115] given the absence of any other indications of the philosophical concept of 'nature' or 'form', it might be preferable to retain the manuscript reading and translate, 'They all had to endure firm control, as the driver commanded them in various ways through his mighty purpose (*gemynd*)', rather than 'through that great nature'.

In fact, this apparently Boethian praise of God's might reveals a fundamentally different basis under closer examination. Boethius's argument relies upon the notion that all of creation is contained within and derives from the mind of God. The poet of *The Order of the World* proposes nothing so abstract. The mind or heart that he or she mentions[116] refers always to the inadequate human intellect; this mind is explicitly described as unable to contain the wonders of the natural world, which testify to the power of God:

Ic þe lungre sceal
meotudes mægensped   maran gesecgan,
þonne þu hygecræftig   in hreþre mæge
mode gegripan.   Is sin meaht forswiþ.
Nis þæt monnes gemet   moldhrerendra,

---

[113] 'Listen, in the beginning the father almighty, the high guardian of the host, created heaven and earth, the broad abyss of the sea – this manifest creation, which now under his constriction exalts and raises up holy prosperity through the hand of the prince. Therefore he who had power rightly joined all thus, each one with the other; they all had to endure that firm control, as the driver commanded them in various manners through that great nature.'

[114] For example, it includes the trio of heaven, earth and sea and refers to the spaciousness of creation (i.e. *sidne grund*). Cf. the discussion of *Christ and Satan* above, pp. 139–40.

[115] *The Exeter Anthology*, ed. Muir, II, 541.

[116] *hreþer* (10a, 25b and 28a), *mod* (26a), *ferhð* (35b) and *hyge* (37b).

þæt he mæge in hreþre   his heah geweorc
furþor aspyrgan   þonne him frea sylle
to ongietanne   godes agen bibod.

(The Order of the World 23b–30)[117]

That is, unlike Boethius, the *hygecræftig* man is *not* to seek to understand the patterns followed by heavenly bodies like the *heofoncondelle* 'heavenly candle' (54a), but rather to perceive the command and power that control them. Thus the order described in the poem derives from force, not 'nature' or an abstract plan in the mind of God. With this in mind it is worth looking again at the phrase, *in þam þream*, translated above as 'under his constriction' (41a). Many editors find that *þream* makes little sense in this context and translate it as *þreatum* 'in his multitudes', or *þrim* 'in these three (i.e. heaven, earth and sea)'.[118] However, given the initially hostile state of the universe posited in the Old English poetic *Genesis*[119] and the numerous references in this poem to God's restrictive power, described as his *miclum meahtlocum* 'great and mighty bonds' (88a), the meaning of 'oppression' or 'constriction' does not seem so out of place.

The Order of the World seems to share the understanding that underlies Alfred's re-imagining of Boethius' work. Although the focus on power is not inconsistent with Boethius's text, to a certain extent Alfred has missed the point of his original – perhaps because he did not grasp the subtlety of Boethius's argument, but more likely because he had a different message to convey. As with the Anglo-Saxon writers discussed above, establishing an image of the cosmos was not Alfred's primary intention, if he thought of it at all, and his translating of Boethius does not suggest a spark of interest in cosmology after all. Thus, although it would be tempting to attempt to fill in the gaps and reconstruct an overarching system that accounts for the little that remains,[120] one must keep in mind the likelihood that the survival of more texts would merely

---

[117] 'I shall quickly tell you about the famous power of the creator, greater than you, strong in thought, will be able to grasp in your mind. His might is very great. It is not in the capacity of a man, of any of those moving on the earth, that he might discover his high work further than that the lord grants him God's own command to perceive.'

[118] *Exeter Anthology*, ed. Muir, II, 541.   [119] See above, pp. 58–9.

[120] It can be argued that Tolkien's fiction was an attempt to do exactly this – to flesh out and make consistent the fragments of myth that can be extracted from stories and philological hints. See T. A. Shippey, *The Road to Middle Earth*, 2nd ed. (London, 1992), pp. 15 and 216.

provide more abundant evidence of lack of interest, or, at best, a greater abundance of inconsistency.[121] Based upon the manuscripts that do remain, there was no cosmological system within which Anglo-Saxon poets chose to place the deity, humanity and the natural world, nor any philosophical or physical structure within which they could define the relationships between them.

GOD'S AWKWARD POSITION

As a result, the contradiction between the natural world representing threats to humanity and the natural world representing the Saviour's power receives no comment in Old English poetry.[122] No poem attempts to offer an explanation for it, whether philosphical or cosmological. The poetry as a whole is thus ambiguous regarding the relationship between the deity and the natural world, and it leaves us – and, presumably, its original audience – with some difficult questions: Does God personally direct the hostility of a natural world that threatens the human race, society and individuals?[123] Or does he merely allow rather than command

---

[121] Thus the suggestions of critics like W. C. Johnson, Jr may be difficult to accommodate, for there does not appear to be a 'homogeneous world view' in Old English poetry upon which to base modern criticism. '"Deep Structure" and Old English Poetry: Notes Toward a Critical Model', *In Geardagum* 1 (1974), 12–18, at 16. A similar expectation of a single 'medieval world picture' is voiced in Gurevich, *Categories of Medieval Culture*, pp. 18–19.

[122] In *Solomon and Saturn II*, Saturn asks why snow binds the earth (301–5), but no answer is given. The text breaks off at this point, so we cannot tell if it contained a consideration of the relationship between the Saviour and the pernicious effects of snow. The next surviving lines in the poem refer to Doomsday.

[123] Regarding this issue there are inconsistencies and ambiguities even within individual poems. In *Beowulf*, for example, the relationship between God, who *onwindeð wælrapas* 'unwinds the water's chains' (1610a) and can easily save those loyal to him from a dragon (2291–3a), and *wyrd*, which swept many men away *on Grendles gryre* 'into Grendel's terror' (478a) but often saves those whose courage prevails (572b–3) remains a perennial topic for discussion, whether or not the argument centres on the pagan status of *wyrd*. For discussion of the latter issue, see E. G. Stanley, *Search for Anglo-Saxon Paganism* (Cambridge, 1975), pp. 92–121. The extent of the critical discussion of *wyrd* can only be suggested here, but see B. S. Phillpotts, 'Wyrd and Providence in Anglo-Saxon Thought', *Essays and Studies* 13 (1928), 7–27; A. H. Roper, 'Boethius and the Three Fates of Beowulf', *PQ* 41 (1962), 386–400; B. J. Timmer, 'Wyrd in Anglo-Saxon Prose and Poetry', *Neophil* 26 (1941), 24–33 and

or bless an autonomous force, the antagonism of the natural world that was evident from the beginning? Or does he thwart the natural world's otherwise inescapable might only enough to preserve chosen favourites? Such questions, of course, are most important because of the implications that the answers have for the question of God's proximity to humanity: if God is responsible for the onslaughts of the natural world, for example, his apparently unreasonable and unreasoning hostility has to be reconciled with doctrine describing his justice and mercy; on the other hand, the idea that God allows the depredations of the natural world raises the possibilities that he does not care – or is not able – to protect human beings.

Both previous and later writers sought to answer such questions by creating philosophical or scientific systems like Boethius's image of turning spheres, which explains the relationship between the divine mind (providence), fate and earthly events and also alludes to the courses of the stars.[124] As has been argued above, it is just this kind of system that is conspicuously absent from Old English poetry, and so individual poets had to choose how to use the representation of the natural world, had to choose whether to use it to define human issues or to define God, for, while either option possessed a clear tradition to follow, integrating the two created the awkward necessity of attempting to answer some very difficult questions.

That most poets avoided such awkward moments can be seen by comparing the representations of the natural world described in the previous three chapters with those outlined in this chapter. In previous chapters, the natural world was seen to batter against human beings and structures (both physical and abstract) and to define them as weak and fleeting in comparison with its strength. Especially in elegiac poems like *The Wanderer* and *The Seafarer*, the representation of the natural world conveyed a sense of insecurity and fatalism: as the *snottor* 'wise man' (*The Wanderer* 111a) considers a dismal scene of desolation, wind, and frost, he concludes, *Swa þes middangeard / ealra dogra gehwam dreoseð ond fealleþ* 'Thus this world weakens and fails every day' (62b–3). The only hope

213–28; Payne, *King Alfred and Boethius*, pp. 78–108 and 'Three Aspects of Wyrd'; K. Lochrie, '*Wyrd* and the Limits of Human Understanding: A Thematic Sequence in the *Exeter Book*', *JEGP* 85 (1986), 323–31.

[124] *De consolatione Philosophiae* IV prose 6:78–84.

offered by the poet is the security and *frofre* 'comfort' (115a) of God, which lies beyond the reality of worldly life indicated by the representation of the natural world.[125]

In this chapter, on the other hand, the natural world has been seen to define God through its absolute subjection to his power: everything is *clene* 'cleanly, completely' (*Christ and Satan* 7b) held, there is nothing outside of God's control (he *ymbhaldeð . . . alne middangeard* 'enfolds all the world' (7b–8b)), everything is counted (from the *daga enderim* 'limit of days' (12b) to *dropena gehwelcne* 'each drop of rain' (12a)), and contemplation of the world brings the conclusion that

> Ne waciað þas geweorc,   ac he hi wel healdeð;
> stondað stiðlice   bestryþed fæste
> miclum meahtlocum   in þam mægenþrymme
> mid þam sy ahefed   heofon ond eorþe.
>
> (*The Order of the World* 86–9)[126]

That is, the representation of the natural world conveys not insecurity but the powerful stability of God. The representations of the natural world described in the previous three chapters appear almost unthinkable in the context of this chapter.

Although one might accept or even expect contradictory associations with an entity as vast and varied as the natural world,[127] some Anglo-Saxon poets appear to have struggled with the incompatibility of Christian dogma with traditional representations of the natural world. The problem arises with the assertion of the intimate connection between God and his creation. According to many Christian thinkers, including the poet of *Christ and Satan*, God is very close to his creation, is intimately aware of each detail and directs every one of its actions. It is this proximity that allows Augustine of Hippo, for example, to see the natural world as a book that reveals God's will to humanity, the second of the two books in which God 'wrote' messages for mankind. Just like

---

[125] See above, pp. 48–51.

[126] 'This work [i.e. the world] does not weaken; instead he holds it well. It stands stoutly, covered firmly with great and mighty bonds in the powerful majesty with which he raised up heaven and earth.'

[127] S. Tucker, 'The Anglo-Saxon Poet Considers the Heavens', *Neophil* 41 (1957), 270–5, at 270–1.

the first book, the Bible, the natural world both requires and rewards scrutiny:

Est quidam magnus liber ipsa species creaturae: superiorem et inferiorem contuere, attende, lege. Non deus, unde eum cognosceres, de atramento litteras fecit: ante oculos tuos posuit haec ipsa quae fecit. Quid quaeris maiorem vocem? Clamat ad te caelum et terra: Deus me fecit. Legis quod scripsit Moyses. Quid legit, ut scriberet ipse Moyses, homo temporalis? Adtende pie caelum et terram.

(*Sermon on Matthew* XI.25–6)[128]

Although the Anglo-Saxons could have absorbed such an idea directly from Augustine,[129] they might equally have found it elsewhere, for the idea of nature as a book is not unique to Augustine; it occurs in literature both before and after him,[130] and is one of the most characteristic commonplaces of the Middle Ages.[131] In combination with the teaching of Anglo-Saxon authors like Alcuin, who advocates a pragmatic and opportunistic approach to interpretation that allows many symbols to mean the same thing and many referents to be denoted by the same symbol,[132] the idea of nature as a book could generate an expectation among the Anglo-Saxons that the details offered by the representation of the natural world in their texts should yield a plethora of symbolic or allegorical meanings.

This 'textuality' on the part of the natural world should remind us again that these ideas are part of a literary tradition, not necessarily part of an everyday relationship with the natural world. In a poem or other written text, an Anglo-Saxon audience could expect every aspect of the natural world to arise *þurh þeodnes hond* 'through the prince's hand' (*The*

---

[128] 'The appearance of Creation is itself a kind of great book: gaze upon, attend to, read its higher and lower [parts]. God did not make letters in ink from which you might know him: he placed before your eyes these things which he made. Why do you ask for a greater voice? Heaven and earth cry out to you: God made me. You read what Moses wrote. Why does mortal man read so that Moses should write? Attend devoutly to the heaven and earth.' Text is taken from *Sancti Augustini sermones post maurinos reperti*, ed. G. Morin, Miscellanea Agostiniana 1 (Rome, 1930), 360.

[129] The Anglo-Saxons possessed texts containing this teaching – for example, it appears in Augustine's *Confessiones*, which Bede cites in *In Genesim* I.xxvi.804–6. For discussion of Anglo-Saxon knowledge of Augustine, see above, 26, n. 26.

[130] For a summary of this idea in the Middle Ages, see Curtius, *European Literature*, pp. 319–26.

[131] Gellrich, *Idea of the Book*, p. 18.   [132] Bolton, *Alcuin and Beowulf*, p. 40.

Order of the World 41b) and to be consistent with his plan – a plan which, according to Bede, had designated the Anglo-Saxons as God's chosen people.[133] In a poem an Anglo-Saxon audience could expect every aspect of the natural world to convey a message from God.[134] Yet this literary tradition evidently did not exhaust the possibilities that the representation of the natural world offered, and as a result the expectations of an Augustinian natural world become problematic when, for example, a poem describes a wolf devouring a friendless man (*Maxims I* 146–51), or a shipload of men drowning at sea (Exeter Book *Riddle 3*, 17–33a). The poets in these instances do not attempt to interpret the potentially rich symbols of wolf, sea and storm, nor do they relate the slaughter to the will of God. Without such guidance from the poets, it is impossible to know how their audiences would have received these images, especially since we cannot know precisely what kind of audiences these poems had. Presumably, however, these audiences accepted the frequently exclaimed fact of humanity's inability to know God's mysterious ways,[135] and apparently some could stomach the thought of God himself relentlessly afflicting the human race, despite descriptions of him as merciful and just. For example, *Maxims I* presents disease as a specifically God-given scourge:

> Umbor yceð,   þa æradl nimeð;
> þy weorþeð on foldan swa fela   fira cynnes,
> ne sy þæs magutimbres   gemet ofer eorþan,
> gif hi ne wanige   se þas woruld teode.   (*Maxims I* 31–4)[136]

---

[133] The Christian Britons sinned by not attempting to turn the Anglo-Saxons from their heathen beliefs, Bede says, *Sed non tamen diuina pietas plebem suam, quam praesciuit, deseruit; quin multo digniores gentis memoratae praecones ueritatis, per quos crederet, destinauit* 'but nevertheless divine love did not forsake his own people, whom he foreknew; rather he assigned much worthier heralds of the truth for this renowned race, through whom they might believe' (*Historia ecclesiastica* I.22 (p. 68)).

[134] This expectation is reflected in the abundance of symbolic ornamentation in contemporary illuminated manuscripts; see Gellrich, *Idea of the Book*, p. 62.

[135] For example, *nænig fira þæs frod leofað / þæt his mæge æspringe þurh his ægne sped witan* 'no man so wise lives who can know [about the sun's] departure through his own strength' (*The Order of the World* 76–7); *God ana wat / hwæt him weaxendum winter bringað!* 'God alone knows what winter will bring to [a child] as he grows!' (*The Fortunes of Men* 8b–9).

[136] 'The newborn adds [to the population] where disease earlier took away; by this there are as many of the race of men on the earth [as before], nor would there be a limit to

167

The Anglo-Saxon apprehension of the horror of disease is amply demonstrated in Ælfric's description of God's vengeance on Herod: fever, swelling, insatiable hunger, coughing, difficulty with breathing, *wæterseocnyss* 'dropsy', worms, horrid smelling poison flowing from his feet, unbearable itching, internal inflammation, bad breath, sleeplessness, nightmares, shredded flesh and eyes like a dead man's.[137] Although the homily's intention to elicit an emotional response may have amplified the dread of the disease, it is worth noting that disease is depicted as punishment for a horrible crime. In *Maxims I*, this horrible punishment is applied generally and apparently indiscriminately to limit the population. The implication is that the limit on population serves humanity's best interests in the end, despite the horror of the means. The poet does not, however, go so far as to attribute the effects of, say, 'water-elf disease' to God's mercy.

Elsewhere even the unstated justification of population control is lacking. In Exeter Book *Riddle 3*, the poet describes God, rather than the usual malevolent elves,[138] as shooting human beings:

> Dol him ne ondrædeð   ða deaðsperu,
> swylteð hwæþre,   gif him soð meotud
> on geryhtu   þurh regn ufan
> of getsune læteð   stræle fleogan,
> farende flan.   (Exeter Book *Riddle 3* 53–7a)[139]

The poet does not suggest that the victim of this shooting deserves his fate,[140] nor that the end result will be of benefit; God simply attacks.

the offspring throughout the earth if he who established the world did not lessen them.'

[137] Ælfric's homily on the Nativity of the Innocents (*Natale innocentium infantum*), in *The Homilies of the Anglo-Saxon Church: The First Part, containing the Sermones Catholici or Homilies of Ælfric*, ed. B. Thorpe, 2 vols. (London, 1844), I, 86.

[138] For discussion of elves and elf-shot, see above, pp. 103 and 117–18; for the connection between elf-shot and lightning, see above, p. 133, n. 187.

[139] 'The foolish one does not dread the death-spear, but he will perish if the true creator rightly lets a missile, a travelling arrow, fly from above at him, out of the whirlwind through the rain.' For further discussion of this riddle, see above, pp. 129–30 and 133.

[140] Cf. the depiction of Christ armed with bow and arrows and accompanied by a variety of man-like creatures, some with spears and scourges, in the manuscript of the *Eadwine Psalter*; although the victim, whose body is covered with wounds, has been described as a 'diseased elf-ridden man' (Grattan and Singer, *Anglo-Saxon Magic and*

This is much different from the understanding of a storm's violence as described by Bishop Chad in Bede's *Historia ecclesiastica*. Chad declares that storms are raised by God in order to remind his people of Judgement Day:

'Propter quod' inquit 'oportet nos admonitioni eius caelesti debito cum timore et amore respondere ut, quoties aere commoto manum quasi ad feriendum minitans exerit nec adhuc tamen percutit, mox inploremus eius misericordiam et, discussis penetrabilibus cordis nostri atque expurgatis uitiorum ruderibus, solliciti ne umquam percuti mereamur agamus.'   (*Historia ecclesiastica* IV.iii (p. 344))[141]

Although both interpretations of the storm assume fear in the observer, Chad's storm does not strike down innocents at sea (as in Exeter Book *Riddle 3*, 24b–35a) or shoot human beings with death-spears; the emphasis is on God's mercy both in not striking and in reminding his people of their need to ask for forgiveness. Yet, while the image of God as the enemy of the human race seems odd in the context of both the Christian doctrine of a merciful redeemer and the characterisation of God as a generous heroic lord, it is not a unique case limited to the riddle-genre, for it appears again in *The Wanderer*:

> Yþde swa þisne eardgeard   ælda scyppend
> oþþæt burgwara   breahtma lease
> eald enta geweorc   idlu stodon.   (*The Wanderer* 85–7)[142]

Significantly, it is again in the context of the natural world that this surprising hostility of God appears: it is the means by which the creator has laid waste to the *eardgeard*. In fact, other than war, aspects of the natural world (frost, wind, birds and wolves) are the only means of death

Medicine, frontispiece), the text that accompanies it (Psalm 38) is unambiguous about the ultimate source of the arrows: the anger of God over sins. Cf. Thun, 'The Malignant Elves', pp. 386–7.

[141] '"For this reason", [Chad] said, "It is necessary that we respond to [God's] heavenly warnings with the proper fear and love so that, when the air is agitated, as often as he stretches out his hand as if to strike but as yet does not smite, immediately let us beg for his mercy, and, when the inner chambers of our heart have been shattered and the debris of our sins cleansed away, let us act so that we, thus troubled, do not ever deserve to be struck."'

[142] 'Thus the creator of men devastated this earth-dwelling until, devoid of the noise of inhabitants, the old works of giants stood empty'. For discussion of the *eald enta geweorc*, see P. J. Frankis, 'The Thematic Significance of *enta geweorc* and Related Imagery in *The Wanderer*', ASE 2 (1973), 253–69.

and destruction specified by the poet. These destructive elements apparently are the direct expression of God's will.

A PLACE OF ITS OWN

Normally, however, the Anglo-Saxons appear to have hesitated to tie the awful power of the natural world directly to God's will, and as a result there is an area of ambiguity in which some distance between God and the natural world arises. For example, although Bede apparently assumes that thunder always conveys messages in *De tonitruis*,[143] in *In Ezram* he suggests that diseases and weather can derive either from divine or natural causes[144] – he does not, however, provide a method for distinguishing between meaningful signs and unmeaningful phenomena. The same ambiguity underlies the description of Grendel as one who *Godes yrre bær* 'bore God's anger' (*Beowulf* 711b). If Grendel bears God's anger against the Danes, he is merely a tool or vessel whose ferocious rage derives from a God once again devastating an *eardgeard* 'earth-dwelling' and leaving it *burgwara breahtma lease* 'devoid of the noise of inhabitants' (*The Wanderer* 85–6). On the other hand, although *Genesis A*'s account of the fall of the angels reveals that swollen rage is not beyond the Anglo-Saxons' idea of God,[145] it is equally possible that Grendel endures God's anger himself, as punishment for his crimes.[146] In this case Grendel persecutes the Danes of his own will; God is thus absolved of responsibility for Grendel's senseless brutality. Yet, if God does not will Grendel's depredations, it is equally necessary that he does not forbid them, for it would be impossible for Grendel to act in opposition to the omnipotent anger of God. Grendel, therefore, like disease and weather, operates in a 'no-man's land' – a place outside God's will – where he can persecute human beings until opposed by a superior power.[147] Although such a 'place' or distance

---

[143] *De tonitruis libellus ad Herefridum*, ed. J.-P. Migne, PL 90 (Paris, 1850), cols. 609–14.

[144] McCready, *Miracles and the Venerable Bede*, pp. 27–8; see above, p. 120.

[145] See above, pp. 149–51.

[146] Cf. the interpretation of Berger and Leicester, who attempt to bridge the gap between these two interpretations: *godes yrre bær* is 'an odd phrase, suggesting that Grendel brought to others the divine wrath he felt (perhaps as his own) and under which he suffered'. 'Social Structure as Doom', p. 52.

[147] This 'place' is defined most often in temporal terms: Grendel ravages until *Ne wæs þæt wyrd þa gen, / þæt he ma moste manna cynnes / ðicgean ofer þa niht* 'it was by no means his

between God's will and the senseless, hostile actions of the natural world is, strictly speaking, heretical,[148] it appears generally to have been preferable to imagining the benign deity-king, modelled on the generous *winedryhten* 'friendly lord',[149] destroying his own chosen people without any explanation or justification. Just as the concept of the suffering Christ in *The Dream of the Rood* could not be completely assimilated into the reimagining of God as a heroic, Germanic lord, so the violent, destructive power of the natural world could not be completely integrated into the concept of a benign God who controlled every aspect of the natural world.

THE SELF-MOVING NATURAL WORLD

Into this space between God and the natural world there arose the concept of a semi-autonomous agent, a compromise between the two unacceptable ideas of God as mindlessly destructive and nature as beyond divine control. The detail afforded to this concept varies but is never extensive; Old English poets do not explicitly grant the natural world any semi-autonomous status, and they do not explicitly attribute any free will to it, perhaps because such a statement would be dangerously close to a declaration of belief in the pagan concept of animism. Yet, even in some prose texts the natural world can act of its own will. For example, the *Anonymous Life of St Cuthbert* describes how the sea willingly brought wood to the saint when he needed it.[150] Of course, the source of the saint's influence over the natural world is God, and one can see this episode as merely another example of the natural world reflecting God's will, like other episodes, in which God is explicitly named as the source for such events.[151] In this episode, however, God is not described as the instigator of the sea's action. Having established God's protection of and favour to the saint in other contexts, the writer here seeks to convey the saint's special status in a different way, by depicting an entity other than

---

fate that he might partake of any more of mankind after that night' (*Beowulf* 734b–6a).

[148] Cf. Job XXXVIII-XXXIX.   [149] See above, pp. 64–5.

[150] *Anonymous Life of Saint Cuthbert* III.iv, in *Two Lives of Saint Cuthbert*, ed. and trans. Colgrave, pp. 98–100.

[151] For example, when God sends dolphin flesh from the sea to nourish his saint. *Anonymous Life of Saint Cuthbert* II.iv, *ibid.* pp. 82–4.

God spontaneously recognising the saint's worth. That the sea normally maintains an impersonal to hostile disregard for human affairs renders the sea's helpful gesture a miracle; that the gesture was not compelled by God makes it notable even among the numerous accounts of the saint's recognition by God and mankind.

The story of the sea bringing wood is not the only example of this apparently self-willed, autonomous action by the natural world: Cuthbert also receives homage from foot-drying sea creatures and birds.[152] Normally, however, the natural world's autonomous action stands in opposition to saints; a saint demonstrates his or her power by prevailing against the natural world, just as he or she prevails against the devil.[153] Once again, of course, God is not absent from these interactions, but he is said to oppose not instigate the hostile action of the natural world. For example, Bede describes holy men, among them Germanus of Auxerre, Aidan and Oethelwald,[154] calming dangerous storms and thus saving the lives of hapless sailors in *wen / sliþre sæcce* 'expectation of savage strife', like those in Exeter Book *Riddle 3* (28b–9a). Germanus prevails against a storm roused by demons,[155] but the storms checked by Aidan and Oethelwald arise of their own accord, apparently without the consent of God, or, at least, without his express command. In this way Bede maintains that God and his saints have the ability to stop the destructive elements of the natural world, but he does not assert that God arouses these elements; the natural world acts independently until opposed by a superior power. That is, Bede like Alfred imagines God applying his irresistible force to a natural world that would otherwise move in opposition to his will.

The distance between God and the natural world is often more explicit in Old English poetry. In the metrical *Genesis* God leaves the stars for the recently fallen Adam and Eve *to frofre* 'as a comfort' (955a) and so appears to be directly responsible for the natural world's existence and actions. At the same time, however, Adam and Eve's future suffering from the elements (805–14a) is seen not as a punishment imposed directly by God, but rather as the result of God removing his protection: God does not

---

[152] *Anonymous Life of Saint Cuthbert* II.iii and III.v, *ibid.* pp. 80 and 100–2.

[153] See also above, pp. 44–7.

[154] *Historia ecclesiastica* I.17, pp. 54–6, III.15, p. 260 and V.1, pp. 454–6.

[155] This is in contrast with Old English poetry, which does not normally make a connection between the natural world and the devil. See above, pp. 43–5.

strike the first couple with his hand (as he had earlier struck Satan (50b)); he withdraws it.[156] The natural world is inherently and independently dangerous, and thus God does not have to transform it to create a punishment for the Fall. In fact, the *Genesis*-poet asserts that, from the very beginning, at its creation, the natural world was not only *idel and unnyt* 'empty and useless' (106a) but also *drihtne fremde* 'alien and hostile to the Lord' (105b). God's is not the only force animating the natural world.

In a similar way, in *Exodus* God actively protects the Israelites from the natural world: during the day he erects a sail or tent to protect them from the *færbryne* 'scorching heat' (72a), and at night his pillar of fire protects against shadows, ocean-storms and, strangely enough for a desert setting, the 'grey heath terror':

> Blace stodon
> ofer sceotendum   scire leoman;
> scinon scyldhreoðan,   sceado swiðredon,
> neowle nihtscuwan   neah ne mihton
> heolstor ahydan;   heofoncandel barn.
> Niwe nihtweard   nyde sceolde
> wician ofer weredum,   þy læs him westengryre,
> har hæðbroga,   holmegum wederum
> on ferclamme   ferhð getwæfde.   (*Exodus* 111b–19)[157]

Although the poet mentions human foes (Egyptians[158] and Ethiopians[159])

---

[156] Cf., however, the *Metrical Calendar* (or *Menologium*) where climactic extremes are described as deriving from God's will: winter *sigelbeorhte genimð / hærfest mid herige hrimes and snawes, / forste gefeterad, be frean hæse, / þæt us wunian ne moton wangas grene, / foldan frætuwe* 'seizes the sun-bright harvest with an army of rime and snow, binds it with frost by the command of the lord so that the green fields, the ornament of the earth, are not permitted to remain for us' (293b–7a). For discussion of this passage, see Larrington, *Store of Common Sense*, pp. 168–89.

[157] 'The gleaming radiance stood flashing over the archers; the shield shone [and] prevailed against shadow; the abysmal night-shadows could not conceal [any] hiding places nearby; the heavenly candle burned. By necessity the new night guardian had to camp among the troops, lest the terror of the desert, the grey heath-terror, should deprive them of life in the sudden grip of an ocean storm.' For a different reading of the last line, see J. R. Hall, '*Exodus* 119a: Ofer Clamme', *ELN* 22.3 (1985), 3–6.

[158] For discussion of the depiction of the Egyptians in the poem, see J. R. Hall, '*Exodus* 194–196', *The Explicator* 41 (1983), 2–3; J. F. Vickrey, 'Concerning *Exodus* 144–145', *ELN* 17 (1980), 241–9.

[159] Note that these *Sigelwara* also appear among the monsters and monstrous races in *The Wonders of the East* (§32, in Orchard, *Pride and Prodigies*, p. 202).

against whom God might have been required to provide defence, the martial imagery used to describe the Israelites implies that, as in *Judith*, the badly outnumbered underdogs might have miraculously overcome their human enemies in a conventional, human battle.[160] It is against the natural world, against the heat of the sun and the *har hæðbroga* (a wolf? a monster? a sandstorm?), that God's aid is needed. The natural world does not participate obediently in the plan of God; instead, God pits his superior strength against it so that his plan can be carried out.[161] Even the sea, which later becomes an obedient instrument of God's will, initially appears to the Israelites to be as much an enemy as the Egyptians: from the Israelites' point of view, *him on healfa gehwam hettend seomedon, / mægen oððe merestream* 'on both sides enemies lay in wait, the army or the sea' (209–10a).[162] Like the Israelites' human enemies, the natural world has a hostile, if impersonal, will of its own.

Later in *Exodus*, of course, the sea becomes a very personal instrument of God,[163] performing destruction like similar masses of water in *Genesis*

[160] J. F. Vickrey argues that the Israelites do in fact engage with the Egyptians in the sea; see '*Exodus* and the Battle in the Sea', *Traditio* 28 (1972), 119–40. For discussion of other martial aspects in the poem, see N. Speirs, 'The Two Armies of the Old English *Exodus*: *twa þusendo*, line 184b, and *ciesta*, lines 229b and 230a', *N&Q* 34 (1987), 145–6.

[161] Although the amount of criticism on this topic is vast, for some discussion of the Old English poet's use of typology and allegory to place his narrative in the larger context of God's plan, see S. R. Hauer, 'The Patriarchal Digression in the Old English *Exodus*, Lines 362–446', *SP* 78 (1981), 77–90; M. Luria, 'The Old English *Exodus* as a Christian Poem: Notes Toward a Reading', *Neophil* 65 (1981), 600–6; E. E. Martin, 'Allegory and the African Woman in the Old English *Exodus*', *JEGP* 81 (1982), 1–15; M. Allen, 'Name-Play and Structure in the Old English Exodus', *Literary Onomastics Studies* 10 (1983), 301–13; D. G. Calder, 'Two Notes on the Typology of the Old English *Exodus*', *NM* 74 (1973), 85–9; J. E. Cross and S. I. Tucker, 'Allegorical Tradition and the Old English *Exodus*', *Neophil* 44 (1960), 122–7; J. W. Earl, 'Christian Traditions in the Old English *Exodus*', *NM* 71 (1970), 541–70; P. F. Ferguson, 'Noah, Abraham, and the Crossing of the Red Sea', *Neophil* 65 (1981), 282–7; H. T. Keenan, '*Exodus* 312: "The Green Street of Paradise"', *NM* 71 (1970), 455–60; J. B. Trahern, 'More Scriptural Echoes'; R. M. Trask, 'Doomsday Imagery in the Old English *Exodus*', *Neophil* 57 (1973), 295–7; J. R. Hall, 'The Building of the Temple in *Exodus*: Design for Typology', *Neophil* 59 (1975), 616–21; T. D. Hill, 'The Virga of Moses and the Old English *Exodus*', in *Old English Literature in Context*, ed. Niles, pp. 57–65.

[162] For discussion of the Israelites' psychological state at this point, see E. B. Irving, '*Exodus* Retraced', in *Old English Studies*, ed. Burlin and Irving, pp. 203–23, at 214.

[163] Cf. J. R. Hall, 'Old English *Exodus* and the Sea of Contradiction', *Mediaevalia* 9 (1983), 25–44.

(1371b–406) and *Andreas* (1522–53). In all three cases the will behind the acts of these powerful elements of the natural world is explicitly God's (or God's saint in *Andreas*), but the point of such descriptions is that these events are miracles; as suggested by the much needed interference by saints in marine emergencies, God does not normally direct the sea's motions. These events are impressive demonstrations of God's power because the sea is normally undirected (or perhaps even self-directed) and apparently uncontrollable. The direct link established between God's will and the natural world in these cases makes the normal distance between them more evident. In fact, even in these miracles there is a suggestion of independence on the part of the sea, for the sea is at least partly anthropomorphised and seen as a creature in itself. For example, in the Old English metrical *Genesis* the sea is described as an *edmod flod* 'obedient flood' (*Genesis* 1405b) or *egorhere* 'sea-army' (*Genesis* 1402a), who acts according to the command of its lord. This anthropomorphisation is especially evident in *Exodus*, where the sea is described as a *nacud nydboda* 'naked messenger of evil' or *fah feðegast* 'hostile traveller' who *neosan come* 'came seeking' (*Exodus* 475–6a) its victims, rather as Grendel did (*Beowulf* 115a). Although God is also seen here acting with or through the sea,[164] the sea itself becomes a warrior with the human emotions of anger and pride. After *soð metod / þurh Moyses hand modge rymde* 'the true creator through Moses' hand made room for its anger' (479b–80),[165]

> Garsecg wedde,
> up ateah, on sleap.   Egesan stodon,
> weollon wælbenna.   Witrod gefeol
> heah of heofonum   handweorc godes,
> famigbosma   flodwearde sloh,
> unhleowan wæg,   alde mece,
> þæt ðy deaðdrepe   drihte swæfon,
> synfullra sweot.   Sawlum lunnon
> fæste befarene,   flodblac here,
> siððan hie on bugon   brun yppinge,
> modewæga mæst.   (*Exodus* 490b–500a)[166]

---

[164] For example, *se mihtiga sloh / mid halige hand, heofonrices weard* 'the mighty one, heaven's guardian, struck with his holy hand' (*Exodus* 485b–6).

[165] For discussion of these lines, see Lucas, '*Exodus* 480'.

[166] 'The sea became enraged, drew itself up, [and] slid upon [the Egyptians]. Horrors

This anthropomorphising of the natural world can be even more clearly seen in Exeter Book *Riddle 3*,[167] where the wind that rouses storms and makes the earth shake declares itself to be a *þrymful þeow* 'glorious slave' (67a) whose *frea* 'lord' (1a) either firmly restrains it or lets it rush out. Although the wind declares that it *onbugan ne mot / of þæs gewealde þe me wegas tæcneð* 'may not deviate from the control of him who shows me the ways' (15b–16), it has a force of its own that its lord must powerfully constrain (*fæste genearwað* (1b)). When it is released, it rampages through the world wreaking havoc without apparent direction. This violent, chaotic energy can be let loose or restrained by God, but does not originate in his will; left to its own devices and unhampered by the appeals of holy men, such energy slaughters sailors at sea, and, like a ravaging army (*atol eoredþreat* 'terrible troop' (49a)), strikes fear in those observing its advance. Although the degree of anthropomorphisation in this poem derives largely from its genre,[168] the description of the wind as a forceful entity that is released to roam freely and then repressed is not unique to this poem, for it appears in *Elene* as well. The wind

> for hæleðum   hlud astigeð,
> wæðeð be wolcnum,   wedende færeð
> ond eft semninga   swige gewyrðeð,
> in nedcleofan   nearwe geheaðrod,
> þream forþrycced.   (*Elene* 1272–6)[169]

stood [there]; wounds welled. High from the heavens the handwork of God fell on the army's path; the foamy-bosomed sea-guardian, the unfriendly wave, struck with an old sword so that the troops, the swarm of sinful ones, were put to sleep with a death-blow. Firmly surrounded, the army pale as water yielded up their souls after they bowed down under the glinting expanse, the greatest of proud waves.' For translation of *brun* as 'glinting', see Barley, 'Old English Colour Classification', p. 24. For a translation in which the *flodweard* is identified as God, not the ocean itself, see *Anglo-Saxon Poetry*, trans. Bradley, p. 63. Although God's role as defender of all creatures (*Genesis* 113a) suggests that he could be the guardian of the sea, one might also see the sea as the guardian of the Israelites. Cf. *The Whale*, in which it is a creature, the whale, which is identified as the *mereweard* 'sea-guardian' rather than the creator. Lucas also notes that there is ambiguity in the identity of the agent in this passage; see 'Exodus 480', p. 207.

167 For further discussion of this riddle, see above, pp. 40, n. 89, 129–30, 133 and 168–9.

168 Cf. *Old English Riddles of the Exeter Book*, ed. Williamson, pp. 26–7.

169 'rises up loudly before men, roams around the clouds, travels raging and then becomes completely silent again, narrowly restrained in its prison, forcefully crushed'.

Such descriptions of the natural world are not quite contradictions of God's control over the natural world, but they do allow for some ambiguity in the source of the will behind its violent actions.

In the end, then, it appears that Old English poets were more or less content to leave God's relation to the natural world as an unresolved paradox. Thus, the natural world is *sometimes* expected to be an ordered, harmonious reflection of God's design (and thus his power), and *sometimes* the hostile incursions of the natural world are ascribed to God, but more often the natural world is depicted as possessing a power and a will independent of God, and demonstrations of God's power take place either in opposition to or in conjunction with this semi-autonomous agent. Instead of a cosmological system ordained by a God who directs the natural world with a constant plan, the focus is on defining the power of a God who *can* make order out of chaos, who *can* wield, focus and transform the hostile power of the natural world into good as he did in Creation, but does not always do so. The representation of the natural world serves to demonstrate that ability; the natural world in Old English poetry is thus always potentially dangerous or rebellious so as to allow many opportunities for demonstration. This use of the natural world denies the Augustinian certainty that natural phenomena are always meaningful and always convey messages from God, but it nevertheless appears to have been a successful literary technique from both an aesthetic and religious point of view: it has produced not only beautiful poetry but also, as the *Christ and Satan*-poet says, cogent demonstrations of God's power for all earth-dwellers.

6

Enclosing the natural world:
knowledge and writing

The beginning of knowledge is the observation of how things are;
the beginning of law, the observation of how things ought to be.[1]

The power of the riddler is to describe the miraculous and to enclose
the limitless by signifying words.[2]

In previous chapters, I have described the power that the natural world
has to confine and define human beings, groups and concepts in Old
English poetry. In this chapter I take a different perspective and, to a
certain extent, reverse the argument. Where the previous chapters have
described the natural world as a force in opposition to human constructions ('humanity', 'society' etc.), this chapter focuses on the fact that the
representation of the natural world itself is a poetic construction. The
literature in which definitions of human beings, groups and concepts
take place thus enacts a process opposite to the one that it describes: as
Old English poets write about human beings who are encircled, confined
and defined by the hostile forces of the natural world, they enclose the
natural world in their representations of it and confine it to the roles
that they desire for it – roles like, for example, defining the ineffable
power of God. The posture of helplessness before the power of the
natural world, too, is a creation of Old English poets, for they
manipulate the representation of the natural world and make it what
they want it to be.

It is only in acts of representation, in writing, that humanity achieves
the ideal, biblically-enjoined relationship with the natural world which

---

[1] Larrington, *A Store of Common Sense*, p. 1.
[2] *Old English Riddles of the Exeter Book*, ed. Williamson, p. 370.

was lost in the Fall[3] – that is, absolute control and dominance over it.[4] There are some texts which suggest that the Anglo-Saxons actively appreciated the power of words,[5] especially the power of the written word, but they do not betray any self-conscious awareness of the ironic reversal of power that they effected in representing the natural world – there is no direct evidence that they were conscious of the power that they exercised as they used and manipulated the natural world in their writing. For example, Old English poets do not draw attention to the fact that they use descriptions of wolves or monsters in a literary way, to define their concept of society.[6] The Anglo-Saxons were, of course, familiar with literary methods which used the natural world to reflect on other topics; the Christian tradition of allegory is only the most important of the methods that their use of the natural world in their vernacular poetry does not follow.[7] That this poetry should not comment on allegorical methods of meaning is thus unsurprising; that it also makes no comment on the methods that it does use raises the question of whether or not Old English poets were consciously manipulating their representations of the natural world.

SELF-CONSCIOUSNESS AND POETIC TECHNIQUE

One might suppose that, since the texts discussed in previous chapters rarely focus on the natural world itself, the ideas expressed through the representation of the natural world about the state of humanity, for example, are betrayed unconsciously rather than deliberately achieved. A wider view of the attitudes held toward writing in Anglo-Saxon England, however, suggests that unconsciousness is unlikely. The Anglo-Saxons devoted a great deal of effort to the study of the techniques of writing; they were 'the undisputed schoolmasters of medieval Europe' in the

---

[3] See above, pp. 20–1.

[4] See Genesis I.28. Cf. also the Old English *Genesis* 196–205, which concludes with the statement, *Inc hyrað eall* 'all shall obey the two of you'.

[5] 'Bede copied Augustine [in *In Genesim* I.1771–5] in asserting that language is man's unique gift, which gives him the power to control nature rationally' (Jones, 'Some Introductory Remarks', p. 118). For discussion of the role of words in strengthening magical effects, see Storms, *Anglo-Saxon Magic*, pp. 32–3. For discussion of the power over the natural world claimed in Anglo-Saxon charms, see above, pp. 115–22.

[6] See above, p. 88.   [7] See above, pp. 16–17.

domains of grammar, orthography and metre,[8] evidenced, for example, in Aldhelm's composite manual of instruction on metre, the *Epistola ad Acircium*,[9] Alcuin's *Grammatica* and *Dialogus de rhetorica et virtutibus*,[10] Bede's *De arte metrica* and *De schematibus et tropis*[11] and Tatwine's *Ars grammatica*.[12] The characteristic ('hisperic' or 'hermeneutic')[13] language of some Anglo-Latin writers, including Aldhelm,[14] suggests that the Anglo-Saxons delighted in the display of rhetorical virtuousity. In the context of such deliberate artistry, it would be difficult to argue that Anglo-Saxon writers were unconscious of the effects that they achieved in their representations of the natural world.

One might still dismiss this evidence as irrelevant to the question of the representation of the natural world in the native language, since writing in Old English would not require an elaborate system of instruction

---

[8] P. Lendinara, 'The World of Anglo-Saxon Learning', in *The Cambridge Companion to Old English Literature*, ed. Godden and Lapidge, pp. 264–81, at 278. For discussion of the study of grammar in Anglo-Saxon England, see V. Law, *The Insular Latin Grammarians* (Woodbridge, 1982) and 'The Study of Latin Grammar in Eighth-century South-umbria', *ASE* 12 (1983), 43–71. Cf. also M. Lapidge, 'The Study of Latin Texts in Late Anglo-Saxon England (1), the Evidence of Latin Glosses', in *Latin and the Vernacular Languages in Early Medieval Britain*, ed. N. P. Brooks (Leicester, 1982), pp. 99–140, and Stork, *Through a Gloss Darkly*, pp. 70–8.

[9] For text, see MGH AA 15, 33–207; for translation of the letter accompanying the manual, see *Aldhelm: The Prose Works*, trans. Lapidge and Herren, pp. 34–46.

[10] *Alcuini grammatica*, ed. J.-P. Migne, PL 101 (Paris, 1851), cols. 849–902 and *Alcuni dialogus de rhetorica et virtutibus*, ed. J.-P. Migne, PL 101 (Paris, 1851), cols. 919–50.

[11] *Bedae arte metrica*, ed. C. B. Kendall, CCSL 123A, 82–141 and *Bedae De Schematibus et Tropis*, CCSL 123A, 142–71.

[12] *Bonifatii (Vynfreth) ars Grammatica*, ed. F. Glorie, CCSL 133, 3–93.

[13] For discussion of this style of writing, characterised by the use of unusual and difficult words, often of Greek origin, see A. Campbell, 'Some Linguistic Features of Early Anglo-Latin Verse and its Use of Classical Models', *Transactions of the Philological Society* (1953), 1–20, at 11; A. Campbell, ed. and trans., *Chronicon Æthelweardi: The Chronicle of Æthelweard* (London, 1962), p. xlv; D. Ware, 'Hisperic Latin and the Hermeneutic Tradition', in *Studies in Medieval Culture*, ed. J. R. Sommerfeldt, Western Michigan University Faculty Contributions 7th ser. 2 (Kalamazoo, MI, 1966), 43–8; M. Lapidge, 'The Hermeneutic Style in Tenth-Century Anglo-Latin Literature', *ASE* 4 (1975), 67–111 (repr. in his *Anglo-Latin Literature 900–1066*, pp. 105–49); K. R. Dungey, 'Faith in the Darkness: Allegorical Theory and Aldhelm's Obscurity', in *Allegoresis: The Craft of Allegory in Medieval Literature*, ed. J. S. Russell (New York, 1988), pp. 3–26.

[14] See M. Winterbottom, 'Aldhelm's Prose Style and its Origins', *ASE* 6 (1977), 39–76.

containing authoritative, even divine, models for imitation and would thus not necessarily be self-conscious about small matters, such as decorative flourishes describing the natural world. The corpus of Old English writing will not, however, support such an assumption. Translations from Latin to Old English, for example, reveal that the consciousness and attention to style that the Anglo-Saxons devoted to the study of Latin was transferred to – or perhaps always existed in – writing in Old English.[15] This is true even when the writer was not attempting exactly to mirror particular rhetorical effects in a Latin original: Old English poems, in addition to conforming to their own native style, have been found to contain classical rhetorical figures and techniques.[16] The reverse is also true: writers like Aldhelm betray not only classical Latin techniques but also traces of Old English style in their Latin poetry.[17]

Yet, although the existence and use of technical manuals for writing in Latin is well attested, there is no trace of a comparable tradition of manuals for writing in Old English.[18] Modern scholarship has reconstructed what such a manual for Old English poetry might have contained – rules about metre and alliteration,[19] constructions like the envelope

---

[15] M. C. Bodden, 'Anglo-Saxon Self-Consciousness in Language', *ES* 68 (1987), 24–39; Irvine, 'Anglo-Saxon Literary Theory'; J. J. Campbell, 'Learned Rhetoric in Old English Poetry', *MP* 63 (1966), 189–201.

[16] See above, p. 92, n. 14, but cf. J. Steen, 'The Anglo-Saxons and the Latin World', conference paper presented 15 July 1997 at the International Medieval Congress (Leeds).

[17] M. Lapidge, 'Aldhelm's Latin Poetry and Old English Verse', *Comparative Literature* 31 (1979), 209–31; A. Orchard, *The Poetic Art of Aldhelm*, CSASE 8 (Cambridge, 1994), 120–5.

[18] Howe, *Old English Catalogue Poems*, p. 13. Cf. also the statement by H. Gneuss that the Anglo-Saxons had no rules or guidebooks to offer guidance for linguistic borrowing; see *The Study of Language in Anglo-Saxon England*, Toller Lecture (Manchester, 1990; repr. from Bulletin of the John Rylands University Library of Manchester 72 (1990), 41–65), p. 32. It has been argued, however, that *The Husband's Message*, *The Wife's Lament* and *Wulf and Eadwacer* may be rhetorical copybook exercises, similar to those in the *Hisperica famina*. See A. Davis, '*Agon* and *Gnomon*: Forms and Functions of the Anglo-Saxon Riddles', in Foley, *De Gustibus*, pp. 110–50, at 114. Cf. also the suggestion that *Maxims II* and *Durham* are examples of literary exercises: see Williams, *Gnomic Poetry*, p. 109, and Schlauch, 'Old English *Encomium Urbis*', respectively.

[19] The most important development on the subject is Bliss's modification of Sievers's earlier work; see E. Sievers, *Altgermanische Metrik* (Halle, 1893), and A. J. Bliss, *The Metre of 'Beowulf'*, rev. ed. (Oxford, 1967). For the application of modern theories of

pattern and verse paragraph,[20] building blocks like the 'Beasts of Battle' and 'The Hero on the Beach'[21] and themes like exile and lord–thegn relationships[22] – but no written instruction from the period remains. Although one can argue that *The Order of the World* aims to teach young poets the proper topics and methods of poetry,[23] such instruction lacks the technical detail needed to determine the precision with which Anglo-Saxon poets employed representations of the natural world. The same is true of the description of the *scop* in *Beowulf*, the *guma gilphlæden* 'the man laden with songs' (868a), who *word oper fand / soðe gebunden* 'found other words truly bound together' (870b–1a) and began *on sped wrecan spel gerade, / wordum wrixlan* 'skilfully to create a story well, to vary [it] with words' (873–4a); from such accounts one can speculate profitably about attitudes toward poets and about the general methods of creating poetry[24] but not discern the details regarding metre and rhetorical figures which are amply provided in manuals for Latin poetry. This does not necessarily mean that there was no tradition of formal instruction for vernacular poetry, of course; the manuscripts containing written instruction may have been lost, or such instruction may have been transmitted orally.

Yet, however much deliberate craft can be identified in Old English poetry, the absence both of comments on representing the natural world

---

linguistics to the question, see G. Russom, *Old English Meter and Linguistic Theory* (Cambridge, 1987). For a more recent work, including a full bibliography and summary of past scholarship, see R. D. Fulk, *A History of Old English Meter* (Philadelphia, PA, 1992). See also M. J. Toswell, ed., *Prosody and Poetics in the Early Middle Ages: Essays in Honour of C. B. Hieatt* (Toronto and London, 1995).

[20] Seminal work on this topic was presented by A. C. Bartlett in *The Larger Rhetorical Patterns in Anglo-Saxon Poetry*, Columbia University Studies in English and Comparative Literature 122 (Morningside Heights, NY, 1935). See also the recent developments proposed by Pasternack in *Textuality of Old English Poetry*.

[21] See above, p. 94, n. 24 and p. 152, n. 60.

[22] See above, pp. 84 and 91–2.

[23] These are the *meotudes mægensped* 'the power of the creator' (24a), and to *ryht sprecan* 'to speak rightly' (13b) and *fæstnian ferðsefan* 'to make firm thought' (20a). See Isaacs, 'The Exercise of Art'. Isaacs sees the poem as divided into a 37-line introduction followed by a sample poem. Similar arguments have been made for *Deor* and *Widsith*; see E. I. Condren, 'Deor's Artistic Triumph', *SP* 78.5 (1981), 62–76, and D. A. Rollman, '*Widsith* as an Anglo-Saxon Defense of Poetry', *Neophil* 66 (1982), 431–9.

[24] For the speculations derived from this passage regarding the oral-formulaic nature of Old English poetry, see above, pp. 92–5.

within texts and of written instruction on the subject elsewhere means that answering the question of self-consciousness in representations of the natural world is necessarily subjective. Does the presence of standard poetic strategies, like the use of descriptions of the creation of the world and its wonders to establish the ineffable power of God,[25] prove that Old English poets were self-conscious about their representations of the natural world? One might think that such well-established strategies indicate that poets deliberately selected aspects of the natural world in order to achieve a particular effect, whether that effect was the glorification of God or the delineation of humanity's limits. One might equally argue, however, that such strategies reflect instead an unconscious following of tradition.

WISDOM LITERATURE

To achieve more certainty in this regard, it may prove useful to look at texts with representations of the natural world that do not fit neatly into the topics discussed in the previous chapters. Interestingly, until recently most of these texts have also been left out of the mainstream of criticism,[26] largely because they do not fit neatly into other modern constructions, namely the genres identified by critics. At the same time, however, these texts have been classed together and given a generic label, 'wisdom literature', which, although unfamiliar to modern readers, has apparently been very popular in the past.[27] Despite modern criticism's recognition of it, however, this genre (or supergenre or mode) is rarely well defined;[28] although the label is generally accepted and used, it appears most often to be an umbrella under which to collect miscellaneous texts – here and elsewhere.[29] One attempt to pin down its salient points proposes that it is

---

[25] See above, pp. 139–40.

[26] Bloomfield, 'Understanding Old English Poetry', pp. 16–17 and 25.

[27] Shippey, *Old English Verse*, pp. 53–79.

[28] Hansen, *Solomon Complex*, pp. 3–4. This is true of non-Anglo-Saxon texts as well; see summary, *ibid.*, pp. 29–30. Cf., however, Larrington's description of wisdom poetry in *Store of Common Sense*, pp. 1–9.

[29] See, for example, the chapter in C. L. Wrenn's *A Study of Old English Literature* (London, 1967), pp. 139–60, which is entitled 'Lyric, Elegy, and Miscellaneous Minor Poems'.

literature written in a non-realistic, non-narrative mode that hopes for and encodes the active involvement of its audience in both the self-conscious construction of meaning in the text and the application of that meaning outside of the text. It defines this double activity, which we might call both playful and serious, as essentially linguistic and quintessentially human. It often reminds its audience that such activity is necessary not because truth is absolute and context-free, but because all human understanding is contingent and context-bound. It celebrates human systems that organize experience while it recognizes their frailty. It sounds authoritarian, but in fact takes authority as its subject and hence may reflect on and question what it seems to take for granted. It often begins with last words, and rejects the possibility of ending; it may at points look closed in form, but often in fact relies on the impossibility of closure. It invokes and explores the power of past observation, recorded in certainly formally marked utterances, to control the present, and it thereby struggles with the fact that what we seem to need most desperately to fix is subject to infinite flux and endless rereading.[30]

The nature of this definition in itself reveals some of the problems with the genre. One cannot say that the definition is imprecise, yet it grants little help in determining which texts belong to the genre: one could argue that *Beowulf* sounds authoritarian yet also reflects on and questions what it takes for granted[31] and that it celebrates human systems even as it recognises their frailty,[32] but few critics would identify it as wisdom literature.

At the same time, however, this definition raises issues relevant to the present discussion, notably the question of the 'self-conscious construction of meaning'. As a result, I shall use 'wisdom literature' as a convenient term to designate the texts discussed in this chapter, even though these texts have not been chosen for their membership in the genre but rather collected as 'leftovers' and awkward exceptions. I shall not attempt to establish a precise definition of wisdom literature, but, since this list of exceptions coincides strikingly with the texts identified elsewhere as wisdom literature, I shall consider whether the different approaches to the natural world in these texts support the designation of this miscellaneous collection as a distinct genre in itself.

Wisdom literature is associated with some particular genres, including

---

[30] Hansen, *Solomon Complex*, pp. 10–11.

[31] See, for example, Duncan, 'Epitaphs for Æglæcan', p. 118.

[32] See, for example, Robinson, *'Beowulf' and the Appositive Style*, pp. 72–4; Berger and Leicester, 'Social Structure as Doom'.

proverbs, encyclopedic lists, riddles[33] and question-and-answer dialogues, but elements of wisdom literature appear throughout most Old English literature, and wisdom has been most often discussed in these broader contexts.[34] This diffusion through many genres complicates the identification of wisdom literature as a distinct entity, but one feature in this collection of disparate texts has been defined as characteristic: an adherence to creation theology,[35] 'the widespread belief, or hope, that the world shows to human understanding an order brought about and maintained by a just deity'.[36] In effect, wisdom literature has been defined to a great extent through its approach to the natural world. Creation theology is exemplified in the Old English *Metrical Calendar*, where the passing of the seasons is intertwined with God's will and the events of the church calendar.[37] As has been shown in the previous chapter, however, Old English poems present more ambivalence than certainty with regard to the natural world's ability to convey divine order to human understanding. This is as true of texts like *The Fortunes of Men*, texts which critics confidently label wisdom literature, as of other, more 'mainstream' texts like *The Wanderer*; the former poem's description of the *facen* 'treacherous' raven slicing into the helpless corpse, like the latter poem's description of the winter storm sending fierce hail *hæleþum on andan* 'in enmity against men' (105b), does not suggest an order created by a benevolent deity. Evidently a consistent assertion of creation theology is not required for an Old English poem to be considered as wisdom literature.

In fact, Old English wisdom literature, as represented by its

---

[33] The riddle genre in itself has been the subject of much debate, particularly with reference to the differences between literary and oral riddles. See R. A. Georges and A. Dundes, 'Towards a Structural Definition of the Riddle', *JAF* 76 (1963), 11–18; D. G. Blauner, 'The Early Literary Riddle', *Folk-Lore* 78 (1967), 49–58. For discussion of this issue with specific reference to the Old English riddles, see N. F. Barley, 'Structural Aspects of the Anglo-Saxon Riddle', *Semiotica* 10 (1974), 143–75; Tupper, 'Originals and Analogues', p. 97.

[34] See, for example, the discussion of the Old English elegies as wisdom literature in Shippey, *Old English Verse*, pp. 53–79; cf. also S. B. Greenfield, '*Sylf*, Seasons, Structure and Genre in *The Seafarer*', *ASE* 9 (1980), 199–211.

[35] This characteristic originally derives from criticism of Old Testament wisdom; see, for example, J. L. Crenshaw, 'Studies in Ancient Israelite Wisdom: Prolegomenon', in *Studies in Ancient Israelite Wisdom*, ed. J. L. Crenshaw (New York, 1976), pp. 26–7.

[36] Hansen, *Solomon Complex*, p. 82.   [37] See above, p. 173, n. 156.

riddles,[38] catalogue poems,[39] charms,[40] dialogues[41] and extracts from the *Physiologus*,[42] contains a wide variety of approaches to the natural world, some compatible with creation theology but some not. Similarly, sometimes these approaches echo the themes and uses of the natural world that have been discussed in previous chapters, but sometimes they contradict them. For example, it was asserted earlier that representations of the natural world never appear for their own sake or purely for decoration.[43] The description of an eel in *The Rune Poem*,[44] however, defies any

---

[38] For background to the riddle tradition, see A. Taylor, *English Riddles from Oral Tradition* (Berkeley, 1951); Williamson, *Old English Riddles*, pp. 3–28; Whitman, *Old English Riddles*, pp. 3–54; A. Hacikyan, *A Linguistic and Literary Analysis of Old English Riddles* (Montreal, 1966), pp. 1–5 and 26–41.

[39] Howe lists these as the *Metrical Calendar*, *Deor*, *The Fates of the Apostles*, *The Gifts of Men*, *The Fortunes of Men*, *Precepts*, *Maxims I*, *Maxims II* and *Widsith*. For definition of the term and discussion of these texts in the context of the encyclopedic tradition, see Howe, *Catalogue Poems*. I include the *Rune Poem* in this list.

[40] For background to the charms, see above, pp. 115–22; see also K. L. Jolly, 'Anglo-Saxon Charms in the Context of a Christian World View', *Journal of Medieval History* 11 (1985), 279–93; Skemp, 'Old English Charms'; H. Stuart, 'Utterance Instructions in the Anglo-Saxon Charms', *Parergon* ns 3 (1985), 31–7; L. M. C. Weston, 'The Language of Magic in Two Old English Metrical Charms', *NM* 86 (1985), 176–86.

[41] For a brief history of the tradition of debate and dialogue literature, see Lapidge, 'Three Latin Poems from Æthelwold's School', pp. 236–7. The dialogue style was popular in Anglo-Saxon England for the teaching of grammar (see *ibid.*, p. 237). I focus on dialogues indebted to the encyclopedic tradition. In Old English prose, these are *Solomon and Saturn* and *Adrian and Ritheus*; in Old English poetry, *Solomon and Saturn II*. Latin texts include pseudo-Bede's *Excerptiones patrum, collectanea, flores ex diversis, quaestiones, et parabolae*, ed. J.-P. Migne, PL 94 (Paris, 1850), cols. 539–60, which will be discussed below, pp. 188–9.

[42] For Latin texts corresponding to the three Old English chapters of the *Physiologus*, see *Old English Physiologus*, ed. Squires, pp. 102–11. For texts of the Latin *Physiologus* as a whole, see *Physiologus latinus: Editions préliminaires versio B*, ed. F. J. Carmody (Paris, 1939), and 'Physiologus Latinus Versio Y', ed. F. J. Carmody, *University of California Publications in Classical Philology* 12 (1941), 95–134. For translations of the Latin *Physiologus*, see *Physiologus*, ed. Curley, Clair, *Unnatural History*, and T. H. White, trans., *The Book of Beasts, Being a Translation from a Latin Bestiary of the Twelfth Century* (London, 1954). For background, see *Physiologus*, ed. Curley, pp. ix–xxxviii; *Old English Physiologus*, ed. Squires, pp. 14–22; F. N. M. Diekstra, 'The *Physiologus*, the Bestiaries and Medieval Animal Lore', *Neophil* 69 (1985), 142–55.

[43] See above, pp. 21–2.

[44] For an edition, translation and discussion of *The Rune Poem*, see *The Old English Rune Poem*, ed. Halsall.

attempt to wrestle a definition of humanity, society, individuals or God from it.

> (Iar, ior) byþ eafix,   and ðeah a bruceþ
> fodres on foldan,   hafaþ fægerne eard,
> wætre beworpen,   ðær he wynnum leofaþ.
>
> (*The Rune Poem* 87–9)[45]

One might have expected some description of the eel as a neighbour of *niceras*, inhabiting the same frightening, watery depths, or an account of God's creation of wondrous creatures, or perhaps a reference to the eel's edibility. If one of these had been the case, the eel would have been discussed in chapter 3, 4 or 5. Here, however, it appears that the Old English poet found the amphibious nature of the eel interesting in itself. Of course, the eel is not ultimately represented for its own sake but rather in explanation of the runic character that bears its name. Still, the descriptions applied to other members of the runic alphabet reveal that the poet could have directed his or her description of the eel to the usual ends: like the animal skin and tree in Exeter Book *Riddles* 26 and 53, the oak is transformed by man's skill and made into a ship (77–80); like Grendel, the aurochs is a *mære morstapa* 'notorious moor-stalker' (6a)[46] that impresses the poet with its dangerous qualities. One can go through *The Rune Poem* and multiply examples of nature's usual hostility to humanity and humanity's usual use of nature: the thorn is *reþe* 'fierce' against men (7–9); the yew is good for fire (35–7); elk-sedge *wundaþ grimme* 'grimly wounds' men (41–4); the sun guides seafarers (45–7); the sea terrifies seafarers (63–6). Yet there are also a few descriptions, like that of the eel, which do not seem to relate to the human condition: hail, ice and the birch tree (25–6, 29–31 and 51–4) appear merely interesting, not useful or dangerous, nor do they provide role models for human action, as the ash's heroic endurance against attack does (81–3).

This multiplicity of approaches to the natural world may be characteristic

---

[45] 'The eel is a river-fish, and although it always enjoys its food on land, it has a fair home, surrounded with water, where it lives joyfully.'

[46] Grendel is described as a *mære mearcstapa, se þe moras heold* 'notorious boundary-walker, who ruled the moors' (*Beowulf* 103). The aurochs is also a *felafrecne deor* 'very brave beast' (5a); note the verbal parallel with the wolf in *Maxims I*, a *felafæcne deor* 'very deceitful beast' (147a).

187

of wisdom literature in general;[47] it may also seem particularly important in Old English poetic wisdom literature, in which representations of the natural world can have a comparatively sizeable presence.[48] This increased presence is not, however, a consistent feature of all Anglo-Saxon wisdom literature, and so one must be cautious of asserting that attention to the natural world is characteristic of the genre. *Deor* devotes almost no attention to the natural world, for example, unless one counts its allusions to winter and the wolf: Weland's suffering is described as a *wintercealde wræce* 'winter-cold exile' (4a) and Eormanric's thoughts are *wylfenne* 'wolfish' (22a). These brief mentions are not irrelevant, of course. In the context of Adam's lament (*Genesis* 805–15)[49] and *The Battle of Maldon*'s vikings (96a),[50] mentioning 'winter' and 'wolf' can summon traditional ideas about the state of humanity and the vulnerability of human society in an extremely economical way – just as brief references to the Creation of the world can invoke traditional beliefs in the power of God.[51] One cannot say, however, that *Deor* concerns itself specifically with the natural world, even if it does use it in a deliberate way. In the same way, the prose *Solomon and Saturn*, although containing a great deal of information regarding the natural world, is not dominated by concerns with it; the same is true of *Adrian and Ritheus*. The authors or compilers base the majority of their questions on the bible and associated texts; many details regarding the natural world derive from commentaries on Genesis.[52] The similar list of questions and answers in pseudo-Bede's *Collectanea*[53] contains few references to the natural world, devoting itself primarily to questions like *Dic mihi quis primus sacerdos in Veteri Testamento fuit* 'tell me who was the first priest in the Old Testament', although it also includes

---

[47] See the definition of wisdom literature quoted above, which stresses that 'all human understanding is contingent and context-bound' (Hansen, *Solomon Complex*, p. 11). Cf. also Davis, '*Agon* and *Gnomon*', p. 147.

[48] Cf., for example, the attention paid to the natural world in *Beowulf*, one of the principal sources for descriptions of the natural world, to that in *Maxims II*. *Beowulf* boasts ten 'natural' animals (see Metcalf, 'Ten Natural Animals') in addition to its sea-monsters, Grendelkin and dragon; *Maxims II*, although just over one fiftieth of *Beowulf*'s length, contains almost as many animals (ten) and also devotes attention to trees and rivers.

[49] See above, pp. 19–21.   [50] See, above, pp. 55–6.   [51] See above, pp. 142–3.

[52] *Prose 'Solomon and Saturn'*, ed. Cross and Hill, p. 3.

[53] For discussion of this text, see F. Tupper, Jr, 'Riddles of the Bede Tradition: The "Flores" of pseudo-Bede', *MP* 2 (1904–5), 561–72.

some natural history. For example, the following question is placed shortly after the question quoted above: *Dic mihi qui sunt filii qui vindicaverunt patrem suum in utero matris suæ? Filii viperæ* 'tell me who are the sons who avenge their father in their mother's womb? The sons of the viper.'[54] This may arguably be considered interest in the natural world for its own sake, but such interest does not characterise the text as a whole.

As a result, although it is tempting to see the multiple approaches to the natural world in texts like *The Rune Poem* as characteristic of Anglo-Saxon wisdom literature,[55] it is important to remember that these representations of the natural world are part of a larger whole that does not necessarily require a representation of the natural world to achieve its intentions. As in the texts discussed in the previous chapters, the context of the whole determines the use of the natural world. In this case, however, the 'whole' often appears to be a more or less arbitrary list;[56] not only can no unifying approach to the natural world be found for the genre, but often no single approach can be found to dominate an individual text.[57] The miscellaneous nature of these texts might encourage one to accept their representations of the natural world simply as exceptions to the directed uses described above, but it is possible to find a

---

[54] The explanation behind this enigmatic statement can be found in Isidore, *Etymologiae* XII.iv.10: the female kills her mate, but her own young destroy her in the course of birth.

[55] Cf. Davis, who argues that 'multiformity' is the essential characteristic of the Old English riddles ('*Agon* and *Gnomon*', p. 147).

[56] The question of arbitrariness and form has been especially important in criticism of *Maxims I* and *II*. Thus Earl sees that the order described by the poet was not achieved in the poem ('*Maxims I*', p. 280); Greenfield and Evert describe *Maxims II* as a collection of commonplace ideas ('*Maxims II*', p. 354); T. A. Shippey is reluctant to assert that an explicit order exists (*Poems of Wisdom and Learning in Old English* (Cambridge and Totowa, NJ, 1976), pp. 13–19); Dobbie describes both poems as 'characterized by a lack of unity in content and arrangement' giving 'the impression of a purely mechanical juxtaposition of ideas gathered from a great diversity of sources' (ASPR 6, lxvi). On the other hand, R. M. Dawson argues for a structure based on association ('The Structures of the Old English Gnomic Poems', *JEGP* 61 (1962), 14–22). Similar arguments are made by P. B. Taylor, 'Heroic Ritual in the Old English Maxims', *NM* 70 (1969), 387–407; N. Barley, 'Structure in the Cotton Gnomes', *NM* 78 (1977), 244–9; N. Barley, 'A Structural Approach to the Proverb and Maxims, with Special Reference to the Anglo-Saxon Corpus', *Proverbium* 20 (1972), 737–50.

[57] For example, see discussion of *The Rune Poem* above, pp. 176–7.

framework for them in the concerns of wisdom literature, vaguely defined though they are. Thus the interest in knowledge both esoteric and mundane, which is evident in *Adrian and Ritheus*, for example, and constitutes the basis of the definition of wisdom literature quoted above, provides a key for the use of the natural world in these texts. In wisdom literature representations of the natural world, rather than contributing to a definition of humanity, society, an individual or God, participate in the question of how to know the world.[58]

LIMITING THE NATURAL WORLD

'The world' involves more than the natural world, and thus representations of the natural world are only one element of the question – and not the most important one.[59] Still, the interest in establishing knowledge, in uncovering and creating meaning, is arguably most acute with regard to the natural world, the 'Other' that remains outside human constructions[60] and is not always safely confined by God. As has been mentioned previously,[61] one method of limiting the natural world was suggested by Augustine, who declared that the natural world is a book that can and should be read, a reference work that can provide insights of interpretation for the other, more important book, the Bible. Although the representations of the natural world that have been discussed earlier did not use the natural world in this way, the concern in wisdom literature to establish knowledge shares a basic premise with Augustine's recommendation to 'read' the natural world, namely that natural phenomena, like written texts, contain hidden knowledge.[62] This basic premise is assumed in the *Physiologus*, a text whose 'scientific' content, at least until the

---

[58] Cf. Davis, '*Agon* and *Gnomon*', p. 147: the Exeter Book *Riddles* are 'concerned with the nature of knowledge and the knowable'.

[59] God and humanity are more important, as is evident from the beginning of *Maxims I*, which considers first God, then some human issues, before moving on to the natural world. A similar but more explicit arrangement appears in Eusebius's riddles, which begin with God and descend through Angel, Demon and Man before considering the Camel and other topics. For text see *Aenigmata Eusebii*, CCSL 133, ed. Glorie, pp. 209–71.

[60] Cf. above, pp. 70–4.   [61] See above, pp. 165–6.

[62] For discussion of the idea of the world as a book, see Curtius, *European Literature*, pp. 319–26.

twelfth and thirteenth centuries,[63] was subordinated to the moral interpretation that can be extracted from it.[64] The fragmentary Old English
translation of the *Physiologus*[65] is no exception. For example, the description of the whale's feeding habits does not contribute to a sense of
humanity's physical plight in the world; instead, when interpreted
correctly this description reveals the moral dangers that beset human
beings:

> Þonne hine on holme   hungor bysgað
> ond þone aglæcan   ætes lysteþ,
> ðonne se mereweard   muð ontyneð,
> wide weleras;   cymeð wynsum stenc
> of his innoþe,   þætte oþre þurh þone,
> sæfisca cynn,   beswicen weorðaþ,
> swimmað sundhwate   þær se sweta stenc
> ut gewiteð.   Hi in farað
> unware weorude,   oþþæt se wida ceafl
> gefylled bið;   þonne færinga
> ymbe þa herehuþe   hlemmeð togædre
> grimme goman.   Swa biþ gumena gehwam,
> se þe oftost his   unwærlice
> on þas lænan tid   lif bisceawað,
> læteð hine beswican   þurh swetne stenc,
> leasne willan,   þæt he biþ leahtrum fah
> wið wuldorcyning.   Him se awyrgda ongean
> æfter hinsiþe   helle ontyneð,
> þam þe leaslice   lices wynne
> ofer ferhtgereaht   fremedon on unræd.   (*The Whale* 51–70)[66]

---

[63] For the development and sources of the *Physiologus* from its Greek origins onward,
see G. Orlandi, 'La Tradizione del "Physiologus" e i Prodromi del Bestiario Latino',
Settimane 31 (1983), 1057–106; George and Yapp, *Naming of the Beasts*, pp. 1–6.

[64] The term 'physiologus' itself, although initially referring to a philosopher like
Aristotle, who based theories of natural phenomena on observation, came to mean 'one
who interpreted metaphysically, morally, and, finally, mystically the transcendent
significance of the natural world' (Curley, *Physiologus*, p. xv).

[65] The Old English translation includes only three chapters – the panther, whale and
partridge. For discussion of these poems, including an argument that they form a
discrete whole, see Squires, *Old English Physiologus*, pp. 22–30. Cf. also F. M. Biggs,
'The Eschatological Conclusion of the Old English *Physiologus*', *MÆ* 58 (1989),
286–97.

[66] 'When hunger afflicts [the whale] on the ocean and the combatant longs for food, then

191

Through this act of interpretation, the Old English translator renders the horrible power of the natural world acceptable. Elsewhere such a creature might have been called a *nicor* and considered one of the terrors that persecute helpless human beings, a fitting opponent for a hero.[67] Here, however, it is possible to contemplate the whale devouring human beings without fear, both metaphorically, as in the passage above, and literally, as when the poet describes the whale's annihilation of the sailors who foolishly dock on its back (*The Whale* 24–31a). The circumstances of destruction have been limited and made meaningful by the moral interpretation: it is only those fooled by the devil's tricks who perish.

One can observe a similarly mitigated natural world in Aldhelm's *Enigmata*.[68] Aldhelm pays considerable attention to the natural world, devoting forty-eight out of one hundred riddles to plants and animals; some of his observations are drawn from life rather than literary sources.[69]

> the sea-warden opens his mouth, his wide lips; a delightful smell comes from his inside, so that other races of sea-fish are deceived by it [and] swim briskly to where the sweet smell goes out. There they travel inside, an unwary troop, until the wide jaws are filled; then suddenly the grim jaws clash together around that war-booty. Thus it is for every man who too often considers his life unwarily in this loaned time, [who] lets himself be deceived through a sweet smell, a false joy, so that he is stained with crimes before the king of wonder. After their journey from here, the cursed one opens hell for those who in folly performed the joy of the body falsely instead of life's dues.'

[67] It has been argued that the *hranfisc* 'whale' is a familiar animal, separate from the *nicor*, an 'unknown devilish' sea-creature, 'the mythical counterpart of the whale' (Metcalf, 'Ten Natural Animals', pp. 387–8). However, both *Beowulf* and *The Whale* use a range of terms to describe the same creatures – in *Beowulf*, *hronfisc* 'whale' (540b), *merefisc* 'sea-fish' (549a), *feondscaða* 'harmful enemy' (554a), *aglæca* 'combatant' (556a), *mihtig meredeor* 'mighty sea-beast' (558a), *laðgeteona* 'hated harmer' (559b), *niceras* 'water-monster' (575a); in *The Whale*, *micel hwæl* 'mighty whale' (3b, 47b), *Fastitocalon* 'sea-turtle' (7b), *garsecges gæst* 'spirit of the ocean' (29a), *wæterþisa wlonc* 'proud water-rusher' (50a), *aglæca* 'combatant' (52a), *mereweard* 'sea-guardian' (53a). That is, Old English poets do not appear to have made a distinction between a 'natural' and 'devilish' whale; they mix epithets suitable for animals with those suitable for demons. The same lack of distinction between 'natural' and 'supernatural' is true of other animals – bears, for example, were considered revenants. See A. A. Wachsler, 'Grettir's Fight with a Bear; Another Neglected Analogue of *Beowulf* in the *Grettis Sag{a} Ásmundarsonar*', *ES* 66 (1985), 381–90, at 383, and Orchard, *Pride and Prodigies*, pp. 146–52.

[68] For translation see *Aldhelm: The Poetic Works*, trans. Lapidge and Rosier, pp. 183–211. Cf. also the text and translation in Stork, *Through a Gloss Darkly*.

[69] M. L. Cameron, 'Aldhelm as Naturalist: A Re-examination of Some of his *Enigmata*', *Peritia* 4 (1985), 117–33.

Even so, there is no fear for the elephant, though it is *trux* 'fierce' (*XCVI: Elefans*), only wonder over its inability to bend its knees, nor is there fear for the lion, since its bloody nature is directed solely at other animals (*XXXIX: Leo*). Rather than appearing as a limiting or defining force for human beings or constructions, the natural world is presented as fully subordinated to the intellectual activity of exploiting interesting connections, wordplay and literary skill. Often the physical characteristics of the creatures play only a small part in Aldhelm's scrutiny. Some, like the dove (*LXIV: Columba*), are defined primarily by their literary history (i.e. their actions in the Bible);[70] some, like the crow (*LXIII: Corbus*), are identified through manipulation of the letters in their name; some, like the crab (*XXXVII: Cancer*), refer to their place in the zodiac. Many, like the ram, use a combination of attributes:

> Sum namque armatus rugosis cornibus horrens,
> Herbas arvorum buccis decerpo virentes,
> Et tamen astrifero procedens agmine stipor,
> Culmina caelorum quae scandunt celsa catervis.
> Turritas urbes capitis certamine quasso
> Oppida murorum prosternens arcibus altis.
> Induo mortales retorto stamine pepli;
> Littera quindecima praestat, quod pars domus adsto.
>
> (*LXXXVI: Aries*)[71]

Although one can identify a physical sheep from the clues in this description, what is being defined by the riddle is not the animal but the word, *aries*, the only thing that can simultaneously be a horned herbivore, a constellation, a weapon of war, a source of clothing and a collection of letters that, when a letter is added, spells *paries* 'wall'.

Although Aldhelm's collection as a whole is too sophisticated and varied to be summarised by one quotation, this riddle can be considered

---

[70] For further discussion of Aldhelm's use of natural images borrowed from earlier writers, see P. D. Scott, 'Rhetorical and Symbolic Ambiguity: The Riddles of Symphosius and Aldhelm', in *Saints, Scholars and Heroes*, ed. King and Stevens, pp. 117–44, at 124–5.

[71] 'Inasmuch as I am rough and armed with wrinkled horns, I pluck the green plants of the fields with my cheeks, and nevertheless as I travel I am attended by a starry band, which ascend the lofty summits of the heavens in throngs. I shatter towered cities with my head's combat, overthrowing walled towns with their tall fortresses. I dress mortals in a robe of twisted thread; the fifteenth letter shows that I am part of a house.'

typical to the extent that it, like all the Latin riddles[72] but unlike the Old English ones,[73] demonstrates that it is concerned with 'classification and the intelligible ordering of experience'[74] rather than a powerplay of obfuscation and revelation between riddler and guesser.[75] That is, the 'answer' precedes each riddle;[76] one is invited to contemplate *rerum ... enigmata ... clandestina* 'the hidden mysteries of things' (Aldhelm's 'Verse Preface' to the *Enigmata*, 7–8),[77] or, better, the hidden mysteries of words, their etymologies and associations, rather than struggle to identify an object described in a purposefully misleading way. In this context the natural world, however it is described, retains no threatening force: in his *Enigmata* Aldhelm

ban[s] violence and danger from his surroundings by relegating them onto the page and into clearly designated compartments of verse, embedded moreover in a scholarly treatise that has little to do with problems of actual survival. He seldom makes any sort of danger the topic of a riddle, but menace lurks somewhere in the text, confined by it and held subordinate to the main subject, which is most often innocuous. A long invocation to God in the prologue and a

[72] In addition to Aldhelm's, there are Latin riddle collections from Symphosius, Aldhelm's model (*Aenigmata Symphosii*, ed. Glorie, CCSL 133A, pp. 611–723), Tatwine (*Aenigmata Tatvini*, ed. Glorie, CCSL 133, pp. 165–208), Eusebius (*Aenigmata Eusebii*, ed. Glorie, CCSL 133, pp. 209–71) and Boniface (*Aenigmata Bonifatii*, ed. Glorie, CCSL 133, pp. 273–343).

[73] For discussion of the relations between Latin and Old English riddles, see K. O'Brien O'Keeffe, 'The Text of Aldhelm's *Enigma* no. c in Oxford, Bodleian Library, Rawlinson C.697 and Exeter Riddle 40', *ASE* 14 (1985), 61–73; M. Nelson, 'Plus Animate: Two Possible Transformations of Riddles by Symphosius', *Germanic Notes* 18 (1987), 46–8; Williamson, *Old English Riddles*, p. 20; L. K. Shook, 'Riddles Relating to the Anglo-Saxon Scriptorium', in *Essays in Honour of Anton Charles Pegis*, ed. J. R. O'Donnell (Toronto, 1974), pp. 215–36 at 219; Whitman, *Old English Riddles*, pp. 108–33; F. H. Whitman, 'The Christian Background to Two Riddle Motifs', *SN* 41 (1969), 93–8; F. H. Whitman, 'Riddle 60 and its Source', *PQ* 50 (1971), 108–15; Tupper, 'Originals and Analogues'.

[74] *Aldhelm: The Poetic Works*, trans. Lapidge and Rosier, p. 61.

[75] For the theory that riddling is an act of competition, see J. Huizinga, *Homo Ludens: A Study of the Play Element in Culture*, trans. R. F. C. Hall (Boston, MA, 1955), pp. 105–18; cf. also Pavlovskis, 'Riddler's Microcosm', p. 227. For an application of this theory to Old English riddles, see Davis, 'Agon and Gnomon', p. 129.

[76] For a discussion of the reasons for Aldhelm's practice of 'giving away' the answers in his titles, see N. Howe, 'Aldhelm's *Enigmata* and Isidorian Etymology', *ASE* 41 (1985), 37–59.

[77] Cf. *Poetic Works*, trans. Lapidge and Rosier, pp. 65–6.

no less extensive praise of nature, His immediate creation, in the final riddle, establish further limits to keep in check a seething, tormented world.[78]

By locking the natural world in the shackles of dactyls and spondees,[79] enclosing it within rhetorical figures and literary allusions and limiting it to an inherited structure of one hundred riddles, all contained within the stated purpose of illustrating metre, Aldhelm achieves a victory similar to that of Beowulf over Grendel: he reduces the natural world to human scale and human terms.[80]

This literary enclosure of the natural world prevails throughout Old English wisdom literature. It can be seen, for example, in the list detailing the number of birds, snakes and fish in *Adrian and Ritheus*,[81] for these numbers come not from an actual count of nature's abundance but rather from Isidore's abundance or perhaps from vocabulary lists;[82] once contained in writing, transformed into letters and words, the natural world can be counted and limited. Similarly, the prose *Solomon and Saturn*'s proclamation of the best bird, plant, river and tree[83] establishes a ranking for literary not natural elements: the lily is best because it symbolises Christ, the dove is best because it symbolises the holy ghost, and the Jordan is best because Christ was baptised there.[84] Through such literary enclosure one can stand far from the natural world, safely abstracted from its dangers, and yet know it in what is proclaimed to be its entirety.[85] The comments on the natural world in *Maxims I* and *II* can be seen in the same way: although they may merely form a part of a miscellaneous collection, they appear to convey an understanding of the whole of the universe. Just as Old English poets accomplish the impossible task of expressing the ineffable power of God through the

---

[78] Pavolvskis, 'Riddler's Microcosm', p. 242.   [79] Cf. below, pp. 196–7.

[80] See above, p. 80.

[81] Such encyclopedic lists have been considered characteristic of the age; see Whitman, 'Medieval Riddling', p. 183.

[82] *Prose 'Solomon and Saturn'*, ed. Cross and Hill, pp. 152–3. Thus, although *Adrian and Ritheus* states that there are fifty-two kinds of birds, over a hundred are mentioned in Old English texts. See C. H. Whitman, 'The Birds of Old English Literature', *JEGP* 2 (1898), 149–98.

[83] *Prose 'Solomon and Saturn'*, ed. Cross and Hill, pp. 29–31.

[84] No justification for the superiority of the *wintreow* 'wine-tree' is given.

[85] Thus in *Maxims I* and *II* 'man and nature are displayed in a timeless universe, where everything is frozen at its most typical and in its proper place' (Larrington, *Store of Common Sense*, pp. 170–1).

literary convention of describing the creation of the universe, so these writers limit the expanse of the natural world through their apparently all-encompassing lists.[86] By creating these lists, they not only limit the extent of the natural world but also transform its overwhelming and chaotic abundance; that is, they can begin to represent, or, better, create in writing a natural world like the perfectly balanced harmony envisaged by Boethius.[87] Thus Aldhelm's last enigma (*C: Creatura*) contains the vastness of the universe in its paradoxical paired statements.[88]

POWER AND WORDS

This making sense out of the natural world parallels the making of things out of the natural world:[89] just as an anonymous craftsman applies his *ingeþonc* 'thought' and *swiþre hond* 'right hand' to natural materials in order to create a written *ærendspræce* 'message' (Exeter Book *Riddle 60*, 12–15), so Aldhelm labours to place his dactyls in order and remove stains and imperfections ('Verse Preface' to the *Enigmata*, 26–7). In both cases the imposition of human skill results in the creation of *wundres dæl* 'a thing of wonder' (Exeter Book *Riddle 60*, 10b), something beautiful and useful, whether art or artefact. As mentioned earlier, Old English poets do not comment on the difficulty of creating their art as Aldhelm does, but occasionally they refer to the exclusive knowledge and power they exercise in their descriptions of the natural world:

> Nænig oþrum mæg
> wlite ond wisan   wordum gecyþan,
> hu mislic biþ   mægen þara cynna,
> fyrn forðgesceaft.   (Exeter Book *Riddle 84*, 6b–9a)[90]

---

[86] Cf. Bloomfield, 'Understanding Old English Poetry', p. 17.

[87] For discussion of the differences between Boethius's conception of the universe and that presented in Alfred's translation of Boethius, see above, pp. 157–60.

[88] For example, *Altior en caelo rimor secreta tonantis / et tamen inferior terris tetra tartara cerno* 'higher than heaven I scrutinise the secrets of the thunderer, and nevertheless, lower than the earth, I perceive black Tartarus' (*C: Creatura* 21–2).

[89] See above, pp. 114–15.

[90] 'No one can make known with other words [this creature's] appearance and ways, how various the power of its race is, this ancient creature.' The riddle is solved as 'Water'. For discussion of the pagan associations remaining in this poem, see Williams, 'Relation between Pagan Survivals and Diction', pp. 667–70.

In proclaiming an ability to contain the natural world in words, the poet claims a power beyond that of ordinary people, like that of the saint and hero, but even more like that claimed in *The Journey Charm*. In both cases power is derived from knowledge but more specifically from the ability to convey that knowledge in words: poets can claim *worcsige* 'victory in deeds' (*The Journey Charm* 7a) as a result of their words, their *sygegealdor* 'victory song' (6a).[91]

The central place of words, especially written words, in establishing this power can be seen in *Solomon and Saturn*,[92] where opponents strive to prove their superiority on the basis of their knowledge:

> Hwæt! Ic flitan gefrægn   on fyrndagum
> modgleawe men,   middangeardes ræswan,
> gewesan ymbe hira wisdom;   wyrs deð se ðe liehð
> oððe ðæs soðes ansæceð.   Saloman was bremra,
> ðeah ðe S[atu]rnus   sumra hæfde,
> bald breosttoga,   boca c[æ]g[e],
> [le]ornenga locan.   (*Solomon and Saturn II* 179–85a)[93]

The knowledge under contention includes – but is not dominated by – the natural world; knowledge of strange birds (the *Vasa mortis* (281b)) is merely one of Solomon's weapons, equal to the ability to answer a riddle on old age (282–91) or to offer platitudes regarding life's unfairness (362–3). That is, the representation of the natural world is once again fully subjected to the concerns of wisdom literature. The issue is how to know the world, how to establish knowledge – an issue equally important to *The Order of the World*:

> Forþon scyle ascian,   se þe on elne leofað,
> deophydig mon,   dygelra gesceafta,
> bewritan in gewitte   wordhordes cræft,
> fæstnian ferðsefan.   (*The Order of the World* 17–20a)[94]

---

[91] For further discussion of this charm, see above, pp. 99–102.

[92] Cf. M. Nelson, 'King Solomon's Magic: The Power of a Written Text', *Oral Tradition* 5 (1990), 20–36.

[93] 'Listen! I have learned that long ago wise men struggled, that the rulers of the earth contended over their wisdom; worse does the one who lies or denies the truth. Solomon was more glorious, although Saturn, a bold chieftain, had some of the keys of books [and] locks of learning.'

[94] 'Therefore one who lives boldly, a deep-thinking man, must ask about the concealed

Once fixed in writing, knowledge, like an artefact created with skill and thought, can be useful and pleasing:

> Salomon cuæð:
> 'Bec sindon breme,   bodiað geneahhe
> weotodne willan   ðam ðe wiht hygeð.
> Gestrangað hie and gestaðeliað   staðolfæstne geðoht,
> amyrgað modsefan   manna gehwylces
> of ðreamedlan   ðisses lifes'.
>   Saturnus cwæð:
> 'Bald bið se ðe onbyregeð   boca cræftes;
> symle bið ðe wisra   ðe hira geweald hafað'.
>   Salomon cuæð:
> 'Sige hie onsendað   soðfæstra gehwam,
> hælo hyðe,   ðam ðe hie lufað'.   (*Solomon and Saturn II* 238–46)[95]

Other Old English poets can be even more enthusiastic about the power of books:

> Gif min bearn wera   brucan willað,
> hy beoð þy gesundran   ond þy sigefæstran,
> heortum þy hwætran   ond þy hygebliþran,
> ferþe þy frodran,   habbaþ freonda þy ma.
>
> (Exeter Book *Riddle 26*, 18–21)[96]

In this context, Solomon's power is similar to that claimed by the speaker in Exeter Book *Riddle 84* ('Water') and in the charm *For a Sudden Stitch*;[97] in all three cases a literary construction (a list of gnomic statements, a riddle about water, a charm) grants power over opponents and obstacles.

---

creation [and] write the power of the word-hoard into his understanding, establish his mind's thoughts.'

[95] 'Solomon said: "Books are glorious; they abundantly proclaim certain joy to those who think at all. They strengthen and fix firm-rooted thought [and] cheer the mind of each man from the woeful pride of this life." Saturn said: "Strong is he who tastes the power of books; he who has possession of them is always the wiser." Solomon said: "They yield victory to everyone firm in truth and healthful benefit to those who love them."'

[96] 'If the sons of men wish to use me, they will be more healthy because of it and more firm in victory, brighter in their hearts and happier in their thoughts, wiser in their lives; because of it they will have more friends.' The subject of the riddle is the parchment which is made into a book. For further discussion of this riddle, see above, pp. 113–14.

[97] See above, pp. 120–1.

MANIPULATING REPRESENTATION

Although these texts and issues are only partially concerned with the natural world, the prominence they give to writing's powers of containment leads back to the issue raised early in this chapter – the question of Anglo-Saxon self-consciousness in representations of the natural world. Are Anglo-Saxon representations of the natural world always enclosed in structures which, though less visible, are as deliberate as the *Rune Poem*'s alphabetic framework or Aldhelm's century of riddles? In wisdom literature this seems to be the case. Thus in the Exeter Book *Riddles* one can find poems employing the structures described in previous chapters, sometimes straightforwardly, sometimes not, but always deliberately, as part of their interrogation of human knowledge.[98] For example, in Exeter Book *Riddle 1* a poet presents the kind of storm that Adam fearfully anticipated,[99] a storm that *ræced reafige* 'ravages the hall' (6a) and terrifies with the prospect of *wælcwealm wera* 'the violent death of men' (8a), that defines human beings as helpless before its superior power. The representation of the storm is thus conventional enough, but its effect is different from that in Adam's Lament. The poet demands *Hwylc is hæleþa þæs horsc ond þæs hygecræftig / þæt þæt mæge asecgan* 'what man is so quick-witted and so strong of mind that he can declare' (1–2) the identity and origin of the storm – that is, the poet demands the audience to display its knowledge. Although the audience may still contemplate the helpless position of the human race, the poet invites the audience not to dwell on this position but rather to demonstrate its mastery over the information presented in the poem, to contain the description of the natural world's awesome power within an elusive literary reference to the story of Noah's Flood:

> hæbbe me on hrycge   þæt ær hadas wreah
> foldbuendra,   flæsc ond gæstas,
> somod on sunde.   (Exeter Book *Riddle 1*, 12–14a)[100]

The water borne by the storm, perhaps the water above the firmament,

---

[98] Cf. I. Hamnet, who argues that riddles serve to question and even threaten conceptual categories. See 'Ambiguity, Classification and Change: The Function of Riddles', *Man* 2 (1967), 379–92.

[99] See above, p. 19.

[100] 'I have on my back what previously covered the races of land-dwellers, their bodies and souls both in a sea.'

once covered the earth and drowned all its inhabitants.[101] Knowing this allows the audience to answer the riddle's real question, which is who controls the wind (i.e. God).

Exeter Book *Riddle 27*, on the other hand, begins with an account parallel to some of those in chapter 4, where elements of the natural world (*brungen of bearwum ond of burghleoþum* 'brought from the groves and mountain slopes' (2)) are subjected to human force and transformed into valued treasures (*Ic eom weorð werum* 'I am valuable to men' (1)).[102] Suddenly, however, roles are reversed:

> Nu ic eom bindere
> ond swingere, sona weorpe
> esne to eorþan, hwilum ealdne ceorl.
> Sona þæt onfindeð, se þe mec fehð ongean,
> ond wið mægenþisan minre genæsteð,
> þæt he hrycge sceal hrusan secan,
> gif he unrædes ær ne geswiceð,
> strengo bistolen, strong on spræce,
> mægene binumen; nah his modes geweald,
> fota ne folma. (Exeter Book *Riddle 27*, 6b–15a)[103]

This 'monster' appears similar to Grendel, who before encountering Beowulf had never lost a wrestling match and was known for depriving men of their feet and hands, among other things.[104] The subject of the riddle is not a monster, of course, but mead, which causes men to lose control of themselves. What is important for this discussion, however, is

---

[101] Foley interprets these lines very differently, seeing the subject of the poem as God the Father, Christ and the Cross. He translates: 'I have on my back / That which has heretofore protected the people, has shielded substance and spirit safely together.' See '"Riddle I" of the Exeter Book'.

[102] Mead is, in fact, intimately connected with scenes of treasure-giving; a powerful king deprives his enemies not only of warriors and weapons but also of *meadosetla* 'mead-benches' (*Beowulf* 5b). See E. W. Williams, 'Annals of the Poor: Folk Life in Old English Riddles', *Medieval Perspectives* 3 (1988), 67–82, at 77.

[103] 'Now I am a binder and scourger; I swiftly throw youths to the earth, sometimes old men. He who reaches out against me and contends against me with violence will swiftly discover that, if he does not first abandon his folly, he must seek the earth on his back, his strength stolen away. Strong in speech, [but] deprived of force, he will not have the power of his mind, [or] of his feet and hands.'

[104] *Sona hæfde / unlyfigendes eal gefeormod, / fet ond folma* 'swiftly he had completely consumed the dead man, feet and hands' (*Beowulf* 743b–5a).

the way in which the poet first describes the object in terms of the labour expended on it and its value to human beings. As a result, the audience expects some kind of artefact, a safely 'denatured' and passive object, like those in *Riddles 26, 53, 60* and *88*.[105] Having led the audience thus far, however, the poet then destabilises the supposedly safe area inside the human circle of light[106] by maintaining that the object still retains the dangerous power of the natural world.

Such examples could be multiplied, but the point is not to list how each particular riddle uses the natural world but rather to show how these uses of the natural world are manipulated, either to contribute to the identification of the object or to mislead the audience. Through such manipulation, the representations of the natural world in the Exeter Book *Riddles* contribute to the concerns that characterise wisdom literature in general: knowledge, certainty and uncertainty, power and limitations, and the ability of writing to contain and control.[107] In the end, this use of the natural world is not enough in itself to clarify what Anglo-Saxon wisdom literature is. However, the deliberateness evident in this use may have important implications, not only for the 'odd' exceptions and leftovers that have been called Anglo-Saxon wisdom literature, but also for the 'mainstream' texts analysed in previous chapters. One cannot be sure that self-consciousness in one kind of text guarantees a similar consciousness in another; the creators and solvers of the Exeter Book *Riddles* may not have been involved in the production of the Old English *Genesis* or *Beowulf*, or may not have seen the concerns of wisdom literature as appropriate in all compositions. Yet, in conjunction with the pedantic attention paid to writing in both Latin and Old English, such deliberateness suggests that the structures discussed in previous chapters, too, were elements of poetic art that Anglo-Saxon writers consciously employed.

[105] See above, pp. 113–15.
[106] See above, pp. 68, 78, 80 and 86.
[107] Hansen, *Solomon Complex*, p. 127.

7

Conclusion

Representations of the natural world in Old English poetry provide insights into a number of topics about which Anglo-Saxon writers failed – either through neglect or the disappearance of manuscripts – to leave much direct commentary. They can define the place and state ascribed to humanity. They can reflect the necessity as well as the fragility of human society. They can contribute to the depiction of extraordinary and exemplary individuals. They can declare the power of God even as they provide an arena for the interrogation of its application. They can furnish a body of information to be ordered by human knowledge and controlled in writing.

For all that they can do, however, the one thing that no representation of the natural world can do is supply a simple statement that summarises the functions of representations of the natural world throughout Old English poetry. Thus the problem associated with defining wisdom literature as a genre – its apparent lack of a consistent identity and unity – parallels the problem with representations of the natural world in Old English poetry generally: although one can identify some trends and structures within which representations of the natural world function, one cannot discern a unified concept that includes them all. For example, one cannot see in the natural world that defines human society as fragile and precious a connection with the natural world that reveals God's will. Even the apparently similar hostility with which the natural world faces humanity, human society and individuals reveals inconsistencies: having defined humanity as helpless before forces too powerful for it to oppose, the natural world is still available to define human society as a potent defence, necessary for survival in the face of such forces, and it is again possible to use it to define the power of individuals to act outside such

202

defences. Likewise, when used in defining God, the natural world is an entity powered directly by divine will, or an alien force held perpetually in check by divine power, or an autonomous agent which God occasionally uses to display his might but otherwise lets range – and rage – freely. The approach supplied by wisdom literature, adding the possibility of considering the natural world an 'interesting' body of facts contained and controlled in writing, provides a useful analogy to this collection of approaches, but cannot in itself serve as an over-arching or unifying principle: the siege of human society described by the *Beowulf*-poet cannot be made to celebrate the ability of writing to control knowledge.

Yet, although one cannot define a unified whole entitled 'the natural world' in Old English poetry, neither can one dismiss representations of the natural world as random or redundant. Although the eel in *The Rune Poem* appears on the surface to be described for its own sake, without relation to anything else in the poem or in Old English poetry as a whole, it participates in the imposed, alphabetic structure of the poem and thus to the theme, common to wisdom literature, of controlling the world; the apparently random details ascribed to the eel are shown to be part of a humanly comprehensible order.[1] In the same way, although I have not subjected every representation of the natural world in Old English poetry to scrutiny in the course of this study, it appears that even the briefest of allusions to the natural world, like the references to winter and the wolf in *Deor*,[2] can be shown to relate to themes which are recognised as central to Old English poetry.

Such an argument is not new; criticism of the Old English elegies, for example, has frequently noted the importance of the representation of the natural world in the development of the theme of exile.[3] Yet, although the argument is not new, it has not previously been extended to Old English representations of the natural world as a whole. As this study has shown, however, even when the representation of the natural world is demonstrably conventional, even when the elaboration lavished on a particular passage seems designed to provide an opportunity for a poet to demonstrate his or her skill, descriptions of the natural world are

---

[1] See above, pp. 186–7. [2] See above, p. 188.

[3] Greenfield does not mention it in his article ('Formulaic Expression'), but it is taken for granted by most commentators. See, for example, Clemoes, *Interactions of Thought and Language*, p. 267. For discussion of this idea with reference to *The Wife's Lament*, see above, pp. 86–8.

determined by their thematic, not decorative, function within a text. Thus the traditional depictions of Creation associated with the definition of God are comparable with the traditional descriptions of heroism in *The Battle of Maldon*;[4] in both cases, a traditional description is not merely a display of poetic mastery, nor even merely a device which allows the economical progression of the plot and provides opportunities for comparison with other texts. A desire to demonstrate rhetorical skill may determine the extent of the description in both cases, but the presence of the natural world, like the presence of the trappings of heroism in *The Battle of Maldon*, depends on more than ornamental concerns. However slight or conventional they may seem, representations of the natural world are never merely decorative descriptions.

The connection of representations of the natural world to thematic rather than descriptive concerns goes far to explain the lack of a single, consistent unity for them, since each one is determined by the function that it performs, and each text provides different contexts and themes to which it can be applied. As a result, the representation of the natural world can best be described not as a reflection of external reality, or even as a vast symbol of power – although that comes close to encapsulating the role it plays in many texts – but rather as a powerful cipher through which Old English poets developed their themes. That is, the natural world means nothing in itself, but can be used to mean almost anything.

The literary nature of this technique may be emphasised through comparison with representations of the natural world in a slightly later period. Starting in the twelfth century, some writers, like Alan of Lille, represent the natural world in the form of a goddess, *Natura*, the handmaiden of God.[5] Others, like Thomas Aquinas, turn back to Aristotle's idea of nature as an active principle of movement and source of innate characteristics.[6] Many stress the innate harmony and homogeneity

---

[4] For discussion of the relation of *The Battle of Maldon* to traditional ideas of heroism, see R. Woolf, 'The Ideal of Men Dying with their Lord in the *Germania* and in *The Battle of Maldon*', *ASE* 5 (1976), 63–81; Harris, 'Love and Death in the *Männerbund*'.

[5] For Alan of Lille's *De planctu naturae*, see PL 210, 431–82. For an English translation, see J. J. Sheridan, *Alan of Lille: The Plaint of Nature* (Toronto, 1980). For discussion of the figure of *Natura*, see G. D. Economou, *The Goddess Natura in Medieval Literature* (Cambridge, MA, 1972); Chenu, *Nature, Man, and Society*, pp. 18–22.

[6] For summary of the meanings of nature as understood by Aristotle and then interpreted by medieval thinkers, see Weisheipl, *Nature and Motion*, pp. 1–23 and J. A. Weisheipl,

of the universe (the 'chain of being' so important to later authors) and reject the idea, central to Alfred's translation of Boethius's *De consolatione Philosophiae*, that order is forcefully imposed upon the natural world by God.[7] Some see the order and harmony of the universe as a reflection of that in the human body and describe the one in terms of the other, the macrocosm in terms of the microcosm.[8] Although the idea of the microcosm and macrocosm was not unknown in Anglo-Saxon England,[9] it is apparent that the differences between representations of the natural world in the 'Dark' and 'High Middle Ages' are so great as to render finding a point of comparison difficult. This is not because later writers had no interest in defining humanity's place and state in the world or the other issues addressed by Old English representations of the natural world, of course. Nor is it because Old English poets were stifled by a conception of the natural world dominated by the sacred:[10] as the discussion above has demonstrated, they could conceive of the natural world as external to divine order without necessarily being evil or demonic. Yet they did not develop anything like the unifying theories of the later Middle Ages.

Although it is impossible to answer the question of why Old English poets failed to anticipate the approaches to the natural world undertaken as part of the renaissance of understanding in the twelfth century, one reason may be that none of these later schemes, despite their greater sophistication in approaching the natural world, would serve the purposes described in this study. For example, a natural world seen as a reflection of the human body, a macrocosm, would fail to provide contrasting or negative images against which to define humanity. A natural world

'Aristotle's Concept of Nature: Avicenna and Aquinas', in *Approaches to Nature*, ed. Roberts, pp. 137–60.

[7] See, for example, Arnold of Bonneval, *De operibus sex dierum*, prologue, ed. J.-P. Migne, PL 189 (Paris, 1850), cols. 1515–16. See Chenu, *Nature and Man*, pp. 6–9 for further examples.

[8] See Chenu, *Nature and Man*, pp. 24–31 for summary of the authors who contributed to the development of this idea.

[9] See above, pp. 156–7. It is worth noting, however, that in at least one case, the Anglo-Saxon transmission of this idea reveals that their sources were corrupt. See J. M. Evans, 'Microcosmic Adam', *MÆ* 35 (1966), 38–42.

[10] Pre-renaissance views of the natural world are often characterised by critics as 'sacramentalized' and blinded by mysticism. For example, see Chenu, *Nature and Man*, p. 5; see also above, pp. 13–16.

imagined as a golden chain of being, with each element naturally and inevitably striving for its proper place, would supply no images for human society's struggles for survival. A natural world reduced to an Aristotelian principle of movement and being would grant little help in depicting the victories of saints and heroes. A natural world allegorised as a goddess would render the ambivalent ascription of responsibility for the destructive power of the natural world impossible. Any totalising theory of the natural world would eliminate the need for the intellectual activity praised in wisdom literature.

In the end, it is possible (though unprovable) that the Anglo-Saxons did entertain philosophical ideas along the lines later developed by twelfth century writers. They did not, however, find use for them in their poetry. Instead, Old English poets found in the representation of the natural world multiple arenas in which they could define aspects of their experience. Neither a rhetorical flourish nor a distinct, philosophical whole, the representation of the natural world was a flexible literary technique through which the Anglo-Saxons produced a variety of literature. In some cases, the technique is still considered effective and powerful today. More important, through study of the representation of the natural world one can gain insight into the Anglo-Saxons' 'method of questioning'[11] – the ways in which they organised and made sense of their environment. We should thus not be disappointed because their representations of the natural world fail to be a cosmological or philosophical scheme, an allegorical system or a report of scientific observations. Old English representations of the natural world reveal something more complex and valuable: who and what the Anglo-Saxons thought they were.

[11] Heisenberg, *Physics and Philosophy*, p. 46; see also above, p. 1.

Bibliography

Abels, R. P., *Lordship and Military Obligation in Anglo-Saxon England* (London, 1988)

Abrams, J. W., 'The Development of Medieval Astronomy', in *By Things Seen*, ed. Jeffrey, pp. 187–209

Anderson, E. R., *Cynewulf: Structure, Style, and Theme in His Poetry* (Rutherford, NJ, London and Toronto, 1983)

'The Uncarpentered World of Old English Poetry', *ASE* 20 (1991), 65–80

Baker, P. S., and M. Lapidge, ed. and trans., *Byrhtferth's Enchiridion*, EETS ss 15 (Oxford, 1995)

Barley, N. F., 'Old English Colour Classification: Where do Matters Stand?', *ASE* 3 (1974), 15–28

Berger, H., Jr, and H. M. Leicester, Jr, 'Social Structure as Doom: The Limits of Heroism in *Beowulf*', in *Old English Studies*, ed. Burlin and Irving, pp. 37–79

Bessinger, J. B., Jr, 'Homage to Cædmon and Others: A Beowulfian Praise Song', in *Old English Studies*, ed. Burlin and Irving, pp. 91–106

Bessinger, J. B., Jr, and S. J. Kahrl, ed., *Essential Articles for the Study of Old English Poetry* (Hamden, CT, 1968)

Bischoff, B., and M. Lapidge, *Biblical Commentaries from the Canterbury School of Theodore and Hadrian*, CSASE 10 (Cambridge, 1994)

Bloomfield, M. W., 'Understanding Old English Poetry', *Annuale Mediaevale* 9 (1968), 5–25

Blum, P. Z., 'The Cryptic Creation Cycle in Ms. Junius xi', *Gesta* 15 (1976), 211–26

Bolton, W. F., *Alcuin and Beowulf: An Eighth-Century View* (London, 1979)

Bosworth, J., and T. N. Toller, *An Anglo-Saxon Dictionary* (Oxford, 1898)

Brehaut, E., *An Encyclopedist of the Dark Ages: Isidore of Seville*, Columbia University Studies in History, Economics, and Public Law 48 (New York, 1912)

Brennan, M. M., 'Hrothgar's Government', *JEGP* 84 (1985), 3–15

Brodeur, A. G., *The Art of Beowulf* (Berkeley and Los Angeles, CA, 1959)

Brown, P. R., G. R. Crampton and F. C. Robinson, eds., *Modes of Interpretation in Old English Literature: Essays in Honour of Stanley B. Greenfield* (Toronto, 1986)

Brynteson, W. E., '*Beowulf*, Monsters, and Manuscripts: Classical Associations', *Res Publica Litterarum: Studies in the Classical Tradition* 5 (1982), 41–57

Burlin, R. B., and E. B. Irving, Jr, ed., *Old English Studies in Honour of John C. Pope* (Toronto, 1974)

Calder, D. G., '*Guthlac A* and *Guthlac B*: Some Discriminations', in *Anglo-Saxon Poetry: Essays in Appreciation for John C. McGalliard*, ed. Nicholson and Frese, pp. 65–80

Cameron, M. L., *Anglo-Saxon Medicine*, CSASE 7 (Cambridge, 1993)

Campbell, J., 'Bede's *Reges* and *Principes*', in his *Essays in Anglo-Saxon History* (London, 1986), pp. 85–98

Chenu, M. P., *Nature, Man, and Society in the Twelfth Century: Essays on New Theological Perspectives in the Latin West*, ed. and trans. J. Taylor and L. K. Little (Chicago, 1968)

Chinery, M., ed., *The Kingfisher Natural History of Britain and Europe* (London, 1992)

Clair, C., *Unnatural History: An Illustrated Bestiary* (London, 1967)

Clanchy, M. T., *From Memory to Written Record: England 1066–1307*, 2nd ed. (Oxford, 1993)

Clark, G., 'The Traveller Recognises his Goal: A Theme in Anglo-Saxon Poetry', *JEGP* 64 (1965), 645–59

Clemoes, P., *Interactions of Thought and Language in Old English Poetry*, CSASE 12 (Cambridge, 1995)

Clemoes, P., and K. Hughes, ed., *England Before the Conquest: Studies in Primary Sources Presented to Dorothy Whitelock* (Cambridge, 1971)

Cockayne, T. O., ed., *Leechdoms, Wortcunning and Starcraft of Early England*, 3 vols., rev. ed. (London, 1961)

Colgrave, B., ed. and trans., *Two Lives of Saint Cuthbert: A Life by an Anonymous Monk of Lindisfarne and Bede's Prose Life* (Cambridge, 1949)

Colgrave, B., and R. A. B. Mynors, eds., *Bede's Ecclesiastical History of the English People* (Oxford, 1969)

Creed, R. P., ed., *Old English Poetry: Fifteen Essays* (Providence, RI, 1967)

Crombie, A. C., *Augustine to Galileo*, 2nd ed. (London, 1959)

Cross, J. E., 'Aspects of Microcosm and Macrocosm in Old English Literature', in *Studies in Honor of Arthur G. Brodeur*, ed. S. B. Greenfield (Oregon, 1963), pp. 1–22

Cross, J. E., and T. D. Hill, ed., *The Prose 'Solomon and Saturn' and 'Adrian and Ritheus'*, McMaster Old English Studies and Texts 1 (Toronto, 1982)

Curley, M. J., ed. and trans., *Physiologus* (Austin, 1979)

Curtius, E. R., *European Literature and the Latin Middle Ages*, trans. W. R. Trask (London, 1953)

D'Alverny, M.-T., 'L'homme comme symbole. Le microcosme', *Settimane* 23 (1975), 123–83

Damico, H., and J. Leyerle, ed., *Heroic Poetry in the Anglo-Saxon Period: Studies in Honor of Jess B. Bessinger, Jr*, SMC 32 (Kalamazoo, MI, 1993)

Desmond, M., 'The Voice of Exile: Feminist Literary History and the Anonymous Anglo-Saxon Elegy', *Critical Inquiry* 16 (1990), 572–90

Doane, A. N., *Genesis A: A New Edition* (Madison, WI, 1978)

The Saxon Genesis: An Edition of the West Saxon Genesis B and the Old Saxon Vatican Genesis (Madison, WI, 1991)

Doig, P., *A Concise History of Astronomy* (London, 1950)

Dreyer, J. L. E., *A History of Astronomy from Thales to Kepler*, 2nd ed. (New York, 1953)

Duncan, I., 'Epitaphs for Æglæcan: Narrative Strife in *Beowulf*', in *Modern Critical Interpretations: Beowulf*, ed. H. Bloom (New York, 1987), pp. 111–30

Ehwald, R., ed., *Aldhelmi Opera Omnia*, MGH AA 15 (Berlin, 1919)

Erzgräber, W., and S. Volk, ed., *Mündlichkeit und Schriftlichkeit im englischen Mittelalter*, ScriptOralia 5 (Tübingen, 1988)

Evans, J. M., *'Paradise Lost' and the Genesis Tradition* (Oxford, 1968)

'Microcosmic Adam', *MÆ* 35 (1966), 38–42

Fajardo-Acosta, F., 'Intemperance, Fratricide, and the Elusiveness of Grendel', *ES* 73 (1992), 205–10

Farrell, R. T., 'The Structure of the Old English *Daniel*', *NM* 69 (1968): 533–59

Flint, V. I. J., 'The Transmission of Astrology in the Early Middle Ages', *Viator* 21 (1990), 1–27

Flohn, H., and R. Fantechi, eds., *The Climate of Europe: Past, Present and Future, Natural and Man-Induced Climatic Changes: A European Perspective* (Dordrecht, 1984)

Foley, J. M., '"Riddle I" of the *Exeter Book*: The Apocalyptical Storm', *Neophil* 77 (1976), 347–57

Foley, J. M., ed., *De Gustibus: Essays for Alain Renoir* (New York, 1992)

Frank, R., '"Mere" and "Sund": Two Sea-Changes in *Beowulf*', in *Modes of Interpretation*, ed. Brown, Crampton and Robinson, pp. 153–72

'Some Uses of Paronomasia in Old English Scriptural Verse', *Speculum* 47 (1972), 207–26.

Freethy, R., *Man and Beast: The Natural and Unnatural History of British Mammals* (Poole, 1983)

Friedman, J. B., *The Monstrous Races in Medieval Art and Thought* (Cambridge, MA, 1981)

'The Marvels-of-the-East Tradition in Anglo-Saxon Art', in *Sources of Anglo-Saxon Culture*, ed. P. E. Szarmach and V. D. Oggins, SMC 20 (Kalamazoo, MI, 1986), pp. 319–41

Gatch, M. McC., *Loyalties and Traditions: Man and His World in Old English Literature* (New York, 1971)

Gellrich, J. M., *The Idea of the Book in the Middle Ages: Language Theory, Mythology, and Fiction* (Ithaca, NY, 1985)

George, W., and B. Yapp, *The Naming of the Beasts: Natural History in the Medieval Bestiary* (London, 1991)

Gibson, M., ed., *Boethius: His Life, Thought and Influence* (Oxford, 1981)

Glass, D., '*In Principio*: The Creation in the Middle Ages', in *Approaches to Nature*, ed. Roberts, pp. 67–104

Glosecki, S. O., *Shamanism and Old English Poetry*, Albert Bates Lord Studies in Oral Tradition 2 and Garland Reference Library of the Humanities 905 (London, 1989)

Gneuss, H., 'A Preliminary List of Manuscripts Written or Owned in England up to 1100', *ASE* 9 (1981), 1–60

Godden, M., and M. Lapidge, ed., *The Cambridge Companion to Old English Literature* (Cambridge, 1991)

Goldsmith, M. E., *The Mode and Meaning of 'Beowulf'* (London, 1970)

Grattan, J. H. G., and C. Singer, *Anglo-Saxon Magic and Medicine, Illustrated Specially from the Semi-Pagan Text 'Lacnunga'*, Wellcome Historical Medical Museum ns 3 (London, 1952)

Greene, D., and F. O'Connor, ed. and trans., *A Golden Treasury of Irish Poetry AD 600 to 1200* (London, Melbourne and Toronto, 1967)

Greenfield, S. B., 'The Formulaic Expression of the Theme of "Exile" in Anglo-Saxon Poetry', *Speculum* 30 (1955), 200–6 (reprinted in *Hero and Exile: The Art of Old English Poetry*, ed. G. H. Brown (London and Ronceverte, NC, 1989), pp. 125–31)

Grendon, F., 'The Anglo-Saxon Charms', *JAF* 22 (1909), 105–237

Griffith, M. S., 'Convention and Originality in the Old English "Beasts of Battle" Typescene', *ASE* 22 (1993), 179–99

Grimm, J., *Teutonic Mythology*, trans. J. S. Stallybrass, 4 vols. (London, 1880–8)

Gurevich, A. J., *Categories of Medieval Culture*, trans. G. L. Campbell (London, 1985)

Halsall, M., ed., *The Old English Rune Poem: A Critical Edition*, McMaster Old English Studies and Texts 2 (Toronto, 1981)

Halverson, J., 'The World of *Beowulf*', *ELH* 36 (1969), 593–608

Hanley, W., 'Grendel's Humanity Again', *In Geardagum* 11 (1990), 5–13

Hansen, E. T., *The Solomon Complex: Reading Wisdom in Old English Poetry* (Toronto, 1988)

Harris, J. L., 'Beowulf's Last Words', *Speculum* 67 (1992), 1–32

'Love and Death in the *Männerbund*: An Essay with Special Reference to the *Bjarkamál* and *The Battle of Maldon*', in *Heroic Poetry in the Anglo-Saxon Period*, ed. Damico and Leyerle, pp. 77–114

Heisenberg, W., *Physics and Philosophy: The Revolution in Modern Science* (London, 1958)

Henry, P. L., *The Early English and Celtic Lyric* (London, 1966)

Higley, S. L., '*Aldor on Ofre*, or the Reluctant Hart: A Study of Liminality in *Beowulf*', *NM* 87 (1986), 342–53

Hill, J., 'Figures of Evil in Old English Poetry', *LSE* 8 (1975), 5–19

'The Soldier of Christ in Old English Prose and Poetry', in *Essays in Honour of A. C. Cawley*, ed. P. Meredith, *LSE* ns 12 (1981), 57–80

Howe, N., *The Old English Catalogue Poems*, Anglistica 23 (Copenhagen, 1985)

Hume, K., 'The Concept of the Hall in Old English Poetry', *ASE* 3 (1974), 63–74

Huppé, B. F., *Doctrine and Poetry: Augustine's Influence on Old English Poetry* (Albany, NY, 1959)

The Web of Words; Structural Analyses of the Old English Poems 'Vainglory', the 'Wonder of Creation', the 'Dream of the Rood', and 'Judith', with Texts and Translations (Albany, NY, 1970)

Irvine, M., 'Anglo-Saxon Literary Theory Exemplified in Old English Poems: Interpreting the Cross in *The Dream of the Rood* and *Elene*', *Style* 20 (1986), 157–81

Irving, E. B., Jr, 'Image and Meaning in the Elegies', in *Old English Poetry: Fifteen Essays*, ed. Creed, pp. 153–66

A Reading of 'Beowulf' (New Haven, CT, and London, 1968)

'Crucifixion Witnessed, or Dramatic Interaction in *The Dream of the Rood*', in *Modes of Interpretation*, ed. Brown, Crampton and Robinson, pp. 101–13

Isaacs, N. D., 'The Exercise of Art, Part II: *The Order of the World*', in his *Structural Principles*, pp. 71–82

Structural Principles in Old English Poetry (Knoxville, TN, 1968)

Jackson, K., *Studies in Early Celtic Nature Poetry* (Cambridge, 1935).

Jamborn, L., 'An Edition of British Library MS. Harley 6258 B: *Peri Didaxeon*', (unpubl. PhD dissertation, Univ. of Ottawa, 1983)

Jeffrey, D. L., ed., *By Things Seen: Reference and Recognition in Medieval Thought* (Ottawa, 1979)

Jóhannesson, A., *Isländisches Etymologisches Wörterbuch* (Bern, 1956)

Jolliffe, J. E. A., *The Constitutional History of Medieval England from the English Settlement to 1485*, 2nd ed. (London, 1947)

Jolly, K. L., *Popular Religion in Late Saxon England: Elf Charms in Context* (Chapel Hill, NC, 1996)

Jones, C. W., 'Some Introductory Remarks on Bede's Commentary on Genesis', *Sacris Erudiri* 19 (1969–70), 115–98

Jones, C. W., ed., *In Genesim*, CCSL 118A

Jordan, R., *Die altenglischen Säugetiernamen* (Heidelberg, 1903)

Kelly, S., 'Anglo-Saxon Lay Society and the Written Word', in *Uses of Literacy in Early Mediaeval Europe*, ed. McKitterick, pp. 36–62

Kendall, C. B., ed., *Bedae De natura rerum*, CCSL 123A, 189–234

Kiessling, N., *The Incubus in English Literature: Provenance and Progeny* (Pullman, WA, 1977)

Kimble, G. H. T., *Geography in the Middle Ages* (London, 1938)

King, M. H., and W. M. Stevens, eds., *Saints, Scholars, and Heroes: Studies in Medieval Culture in Honour of Charles W. Jones*, vol. I (Collegeville, MN, 1979)

Klaeber, F., ed., *Beowulf and the Fight at Finnsburg*, 3rd ed. (Lexington, MA, 1922)

Koestler, A., *The Sleepwalkers: A History of Man's Changing Vision of the Universe* (London, 1968)

Krapp, G. P., and E. V. K. Dobbie, eds., *Anglo-Saxon Poetic Records*, 6 vols. (New York, 1931–53)

Lapidge, M., '*Beowulf*, Aldhelm, the *Liber monstrorum* and Wessex', *SM* 23 (1982), 151–92

   Anglo-Latin Literature 900–1066 (London and Rio Grande, OH, 1993)

   'Three Latin Poems from Æthelwold's School at Winchester', in his *Anglo-Latin Literature*, pp. 225–77

   '*Beowulf* and the Psychology of Terror', in *Heroic Poetry in the Anglo-Saxon Period*, ed. Damico and Leyerle, pp. 373–402

   'Stoic Cosmology and the Source of the First Old English Riddle', *Anglia* 112 (1994), 1–25

Lapidge, M., and M. Herren, trans., *Aldhelm: The Prose Works* (Cambridge, 1979)

Lapidge, M., and J. L. Rosier, trans., *Aldhelm: The Poetic Works* (Cambridge, 1985)

Larrington, C., *A Store of Common Sense: Gnomic Theme and Style in Old Icelandic and Old English Wisdom Poetry* (Oxford, 1993)

Leclercq, J., *The Love of Learning and the Desire for God: A Study of Monastic Culture*, trans. C. Misrahi, 2nd rev. ed. (London, 1961)

Lee, A. A., *The Guest-Hall of Eden* (New Haven, CT, and London, 1972)

   'Toward a Critique of *The Dream of the Rood*', in *Anglo-Saxon Poetry: Essays in Appreciation for John C. McGalliard*, ed. Nicholson and Frese, pp. 163–91

Leiter, L. H., '*The Dream of the Rood*: Patterns of Transformation', in *Old English Poetry: Fifteen Essays*, ed. Creed, pp. 93–127

Lerer, S., *Literacy and Power in Anglo-Saxon England* (Lincoln, NE, and London, 1991)

Lévi-Strauss, C., *The Savage Mind (La Pensée Sauvage)* (London, 1966)

Lindsay, W. M., ed., *Isidori Etymologiarum sive Originum Libri XX*, 2 vols. (Oxford, 1911)

Lucas, P. J., '*Exodus* 480: "mod gerymde"', *N&Q* 214 (1969), 206–7

Magennis, H., *Images of Community in Old English Poetry*, CSASE 18 (Cambridge, 1993)

Malone, K., 'Grendel and his Abode', in *Studia Philologica et Litteraria in Honorem L. Spitzer*, ed. A. G. Hatcher and K. L. Selig (Berne, 1958), pp. 297–308

Martin, B. K., 'Aspects of Winter in Latin and Old English Poetry', *JEGP* 68 (1969), 375–90

McCready, W. D., *Miracles and the Venerable Bede*, Studies and Texts 118 (Toronto, 1994)

McKitterick, R., ed., *The Uses of Literacy in Early Mediaeval Europe* (Cambridge, 1990)

Meaney, A., 'The Anglo-Saxon View of the Causes of Illness', in *Health, Disease and Healing in Medieval Culture*, ed. S. Campbell, B. Hall and D. Klausner (Toronto, 1992), pp. 12–33

Mellinkoff, R., 'Cain's Monstrous Progeny in *Beowulf*: Part II, Post-Diluvian Survival', *ASE* 9 (1980), 183–97

'Serpent Imagery in the Illustrated Old English Hexateuch', in *Modes of Interpretation*, ed. Brown, Crampton and Robinson, pp. 51–64

Metcalf, A., 'Ten Natural Animals in *Beowulf*', *NM* 64 (1963), 378–89

Migne, J.-P., ed., *Alani ab Insulis liber De planctu Naturae*, PL 210 (Paris, 1853), cols. 431–82

Muir, B. J., *The Exeter Anthology of OE Poems: An Edition of Exeter Dean and Chapter MS 3501*, 2 vols. (Exeter, 1994)

Nelson, M., 'An Old English Charm Against Nightmare', *Germanic Notes* 13 (1982), 17–18

Newton, S., *The Origins of Beowulf and the Pre-Viking Kingdom of East Anglia* (Cambridge, 1993)

Nicholson, L. E., and D. W. Frese, ed., *Anglo-Saxon Poetry: Essays in Appreciation for John C. McGalliard* (Notre Dame, IN, 1975)

Niles, J. D., '*Beowulf*': *The Poem and its Tradition* (Cambridge, MA, and London, 1983)

Niles, J. D., ed., *Old English Literature in Context: Ten Essays* (Cambridge, 1980)

Ohlgren, T., 'Five New Drawings in the *MS Junius 11*: Their Iconography and Thematic Significance', *Speculum* 47 (1972), 227–33

O'Keeffe, K. O'Brien, '*Beowulf*, lines 202b–836: Transformations and the Limits of the Human', *Texas Studies in Literature and Language* 23 (1981), 484–94

Visible Song: Transitional Literacy in Old English Verse, CSASE 4 (Cambridge, 1990)

Ong, W. J., *Orality and Literacy: The Technologizing of the Word* (London, 1982)

Opland, J., 'From Horseback to Monastic Cell: The Impact on English Literature of the Introduction of Writing', in *Old English Literature in Context*, ed. Niles, pp. 30–43 and 161–3

Orchard, A., *Pride and Prodigies: Studies in the Monsters of the 'Beowulf'-Manuscript* (Cambridge, 1995)

Pasternack, C. B., *The Textuality of Old English Poetry*, CSASE 13 (Cambridge, 1995)

Pavlovskis, Z., 'The Riddler's Microcosm: From Symphosius to St Boniface', *Classica et Mediaevalia* 39 (1988), 219–51

Payne, F. A., *King Alfred and Boethius: An Analysis of the Old English Version of the Consolation of Philosophy* (Madison, 1968)

'Three Aspects of Wyrd in *Beowulf* ', in *Old English Studies*, ed. Burlin and Irving, pp. 15–35

Pheifer, J. D., ed., *Old English Glosses in the Epinal-Erfurt Glossary* (Oxford, 1974)

Pons, E., *Le thème et le sentiment de la nature dans la poésie anglo-saxonne*, Publications de la Faculté des Lettres de l'Université de Strasbourg 25 (Strasbourg, 1925)

Pope, J. C., '*Beowulf* 505, "gehedde," and the Pretensions of Unferth', in *Modes of Interpretation*, ed. Brown, Crampton and Robinson, pp. 173–87

Radding, C. M., *A World Made by Men: Cognition and Society, 400–1200* (Chapel Hill, NC, 1985)

Remley, P. G., *Old English Biblical Verse*, CSASE 16 (Cambridge, 1996)

Roberts, J., 'A Preliminary "Heaven" Index for Old English', *LSE* 16 (1985), 208–19

Roberts, J., and C. Kay with L. Grundy, eds., *A Thesaurus of Old English*, vol. I, King's College London Medieval Studies 11 (London, 1995)

Roberts, L. D., ed., *Approaches to Nature in the Middle Ages*, Medieval and Renaissance Texts and Studies 16 (Binghamton, NY, 1982)

Robinson, F. C., *'Beowulf' and the Appositive Style* (Knoxville, TN, 1985)

Schlauch, M., 'An Old English *Encomium Urbis*', *JEGP* 40 (1941), 14–28

Schrader, R., 'Sacred Groves, Marvellous Waters, and Grendel's Abode', *Florilegium* 5 (1983), 76–84

Schuurmans, C. J. E. and H. Flohn, 'Climate Variability and its Time Changes in European Countries, Based on Instrumental Observations', in *The Climate of Europe*, ed. Flohn and Fantechi, pp. 65–117

Scragg, D. G., ed., *The Vercelli Homilies and Related Texts*, EETS os 300 (Oxford, 1992)

Shippey, T. A., *Old English Verse* (London, 1972)

Simpson, J. A., and E. S. C. Weiner, ed., *The Oxford English Dictionary*, 2nd ed., 20 vols. (Oxford, 1989)

Singer, C., *A Short History of Scientific Ideas to 1900* (Oxford, 1959)

Skemp, A. R., 'The Transformation of Scriptural Story, Motive, and Conception in Anglo-Saxon Poetry', *MP* 4 (1907), 423–70

'The Old English Charms', *MLR* 6 (1911), 289–301

Smyth, M., 'Isidore of Seville and Early Irish Cosmography', *Cambridge Medieval Celtic Studies* 14 (1987), 69–102

Spamer, J. B., 'The Old English Bee Charm: An Explication', *JIES* 6 (1978), 279–91

Squires, A., ed., *The Old English Physiologus*, Durham Medieval Texts 5 (Durham, 1988)

Stanley, E. G., ed., *Continuations and Beginnings: Studies in Old English Literature* (London, 1966)

Stork, N. P., *Through a Gloss Darkly: Aldhelm's Riddles in the British Library MS Royal 12.C.xxiii* (Toronto, 1990)

Storms, G., *Anglo-Saxon Magic* (The Hague, 1948)

Stuart, H., 'The Anglo-Saxon Elf', *SN* 48 (1976), 313–20

Taylor, P. B., 'Grendel's Monstrous Arts', *In Geardagum* 6 (1984), 1–12

Tester, S. J., trans., *Boethius: Tractates, De Consolatione*, Loeb Classical Library 74 (Cambridge, MA, 1973)

Thomas, K., *Man in the Natural World: Changing Attitudes in England 1500–1800* (London, 1983)

Thun, N., 'The Malignant Elves: Notes on Anglo-Saxon Magic and Germanic Myth', *SN* 41 (1969), 378–96

Tupper, F., Jr, 'Originals and Analogues of the *Exeter Book Riddles*', *MLN* 18 (1903), 97–106

Turville-Petre, E. O. G., *Scaldic Poetry* (Oxford, 1976)

Vaughan-Sterling, J. A., 'The Anglo-Saxon *Metrical Charms*: Poetry as Ritual', *JEGP* 82 (1983), 186–200

Walde, A., ed., *Vergleichendes Wörterbuch der indogermanischen Sprachen*, 3 vols. (Berlin, 1927–32)

Waterhouse, R., '*Beowulf* as "Palimpsest"', *In Geardagum* 13 (1992), 1–18

Watkins, C., ed., *The American Heritage Dictionary of Indo-European Roots* (Boston, 1985)

Weisheipl, J. A., *Nature and Motion in the Middle Ages*, ed. W. E. Carroll (Washington, DC, 1985)

Welldon, J. E. C., ed., *Sancti Aurelii Augustini De civitate Dei contra paganos libri XXII,* 2 vols. (London, 1924)

Whewell, W., *History of the Inductive Sciences*, 3 vols., 3rd ed., Cass Library of Science Classics 7 (London, 1857)

Whitman, F. H., 'Medieval Riddling: Factors Underlying Its Development', *NM* 71 (1970), 177–85

Old English Riddles, Canadian Federation for the Humanities Monograph Series 3 (Ottawa, 1982)

Williams, B. C., *Gnomic Poetry in Anglo-Saxon* (New York, 1914)

Williams, E. W., 'The Relation between Pagan Survivals and Diction in Two Old English Riddles', *PQ* 54 (1975), 664–70

Williamson, C., ed., *The Old English Riddles of the Exeter Book* (Chapel Hill, NC, 1977)

Woolf, R., 'Doctrinal Influences on "The Dream of the Rood"', *MÆ* 27 (1958), 137–53

Wormald, P., 'Bede, the *Bretwaldas* and the Origins of the *Gens Anglorum*', in *Ideal and Reality in Frankish and Anglo-Saxon Society: Studies Presented to J. M. Wallace-Hadrill*, ed. P. Wormald with D. Bullough and R. Collins (Oxford, 1983), pp. 99–129

Wrenn, C. L., 'The Poetry of Cædmon', in *Essential Articles*, ed. Bessinger and Kahrl, pp. 407–27

Wright, C. D., *The Irish Tradition in Old English Literature*, CSASE 6 (Cambridge, 1993)

Wright, J. K., *The Geographical Lore of the Time of the Crusades: A Study in the History of Medieval Science and Tradition in Western Europe* (New York, 1925)

Index

217

Index

bear, 6, 8, 71, 192 n.67

beast, 1, 8, 9 n.46, 12, 27–8, 32, 33 n.52, 36 n.73, 56 n.14, 85, 108 n.89, 136, 142, 144, 187 n.46

'Beasts of Battle', 8 n.41, 8 n.42, 10, 86, 94, 143, 182

Bede, 26 n.26, 39 n.85, 56 n.16, 128 n.170, 148 n.44, 154–6

De arte metrica, 180

De die iudicii, 111

In Ezram et Neemiam, 120

In Genesim, 67, 143 n.19, 146, 156 n.92, 166 n.129, 179 n.5

Historia ecclesiastica, 24–5, 27 n.30, 48, 66, 94 n.19, 147 n.38, 149, 167, 169, 172

De natura rerum, 29, 143 n.13, 154, 170

De schematibus et tropis, 180

De temporibus liber, 29

De temporum ratione, 29

De tonitruis, 170

bee, 6, 8 n.36, 11, 77 n.95

Bee Charm, The, 8 n. 36, 77 n.95

Beowulf, 1 n.2, 2 n.7, 8 n.37–40, 10, 30–32, 38, 40, 43 n.103, 44, 46 n.113, 47, 52 n.126, 60 n.27, 62–4, 67–88, 89–91, 93–4, 101, 102, 109, 114–15, 118, 119, 121, 122 n.148, 124, 125, 129–38, 141 n.6, 145, 150–51, 163 n.123, 170, 175, 182, 184, 187, 188 n.48, 192 n.67, 195, 200, 201, 203

bird, 1, 2, 6, 8, 21, 34 n.57, 36–7, 41, 43–4, 71, 128, 169, 172, 185, 193, 195, 197

Blickling homilies, 52 n.126, 60 n.27, 75 n.83

boar, 6, 8, 9 n.46, 34 n.57

Boethius, *De consolatione Philosophiae*, 154 n. 76, 157–62, 164 n.124, 196, 205

Boniface, *Aenigmata*, 194 n.72

boundary, 68, 70, 73–4, 81–5, 109, 116, 124 n.156, 130, 135–6, 187 n.46

Byrhtferth, *Enchiridion*, 155–7

Cædmon, 144–5

Cædmon's Hymn, 64–5, 94 n.19, 141 n.6, 146

Cain, 38, 73–4, 84 n.129, 86, 106, 109

camel, 34 n.57, 190 n.59

cannibalism, 34

cartography, 146 n.28

Cassiodorus, 11 n.57, 157 n.102

cat, 6 n.29

catalogue poem, 22, 148 n.43, 186

'circle of light', 68, 78, 80, 86, 108, 115, 201

chain of being, 205–6

charm, 5 n.23, 8 nn.35 and 36, 8 n.36, 77 n.95, 99–104, 107–10, 115–22, 125, 127, 179 n.5, 186, 197, 198

Chaucer, *The Nun's Priest's Tale*, 102 n.54

Christ, 25 nn.20 and 22, 56 n.14, 111

Christ and Satan, 43 n.102, 139–40, 141 n.6, 160, 161 n.114, 165, 177

clam, 7 n.34

cliff, 36–8, 40, 48, 49 n.122, 51, 138

climate, 3–5, 8

computus, 155–6

'cosmic hall', see world-hall

cosmology, 16–17, 22, 55, 97, 145–8, 153–63, 177, 206

Cosmos Indicopleustes, 146–7

crab, 7 n.34, 193

Creation, 2, 26, 30, 57–9, 62–74, 84, 96, 113, 139–40, 141 n.6, 142–6, 156, 161, 173, 177, 183, 188, 196, 204

creation theology, 185–6

crucifixion, 151–2

Cuthbert, Saint, 128 n.170, 171–2

Cynewulf, 144–5

Daniel, 56 n.14, 62 n.31, 83–4, 141–2, 144

'Dark Ages', 4, 13–15

deer, 2, 8 n.38, 9, 115

demon, see devil

Deor, 148 n.43, 182 n.23, 186 n.39, 188, 203

Descent into Hell, The, 151 n.59